Combating AIDS
in the developing world

Josh Ruxin, Coordinator
Agnes Binagwaho, Coordinator
Paul A. Wilson, Lead author

UN Millennium Project
Task Force on HIV/AIDS, Malaria, TB, and
Access to Essential Medicines
Working Group on HIV/AIDS
2005

EARTHSCAN

London • Sterling, Va.

First published by Earthscan in the UK and USA in 2005

ISBN: 1-84407-225-8 paperback

For a full list of publications please contact:

Earthscan
8–12 Camden High Street
London, NW1 0JH, UK
Tel: +44 (0)20 7387 8558
Fax: +44 (0)20 7387 8998
Email: earthinfo@earthscan.co.uk
Web: www.earthscan.co.uk
22883 Quicksilver Drive, Sterling, VA 20166-2012, USA

Earthscan is an imprint of James and James (Science Publishers) Ltd and publishes in association with the International Institute for Environment and Development

A catalogue record for this book is available from the British Library

Library of Congress Cataloging-in-Publication Data

A catalog record has been requested

This publication should be cited as: UN Millennium Project. 2005. *Combating AIDS in the Developing World*. Task Force on HIV/AIDS, Malaria, TB, and Access to Essential Medicines, Working Group on HIV/AIDS.

Photos: Front cover Jørgen Schytte/UNDP; back cover, top to bottom, Christopher Dowswell/UNDP, Pedro Cote/ UNDP, Giacomo Pirozzi/Panos Pictures, Liba Taylor/Panos Pictures, Jørgen Schytte/UNDP, UN Photo Library, Giacomo Pirozzi/UNICEF, Curt Carnemark/World Bank, Pedro Cote/UNDP, Franck Charton/UNICEF, Paul Chesley/Getty Images, Ray Witlin/World Bank, Pete Turner/Getty Images.

This book was edited, designed, and produced by Communications Development Inc., Washington, D.C., and its UK design partner, Grundy & Northedge.

The Millennium Projecct was commissioned by the UN Secretary-General and sponsored by the United Nations Development Group, which is chaired by the Administrator of the United Nations Development Programme. The report is an independent publication that reflects the views of the members of the Task Force on HIV/AIDS, Malaria, TB, and Access to Essential Medicines, who contributed in their personal capacity. This publication does not necessarily reflect the views of the United Nations, the United Nations Development Programme, or their Member States.

Printed on elemental chlorine-free paper

Foreword

The world has an unprecedented opportunity to improve the lives of billions of people by adopting practical approaches to meeting the Millennium Development Goals. At the request of the UN Secretary-General Kofi Annan, the UN Millennium Project has identified practical strategies to eradicate poverty by scaling up investments in infrastructure and human capital while promoting gender equality and environmental sustainability. These strategies are described in the UN Millennium Project's report *Investing in Development: A Practical Plan to Achieve the Millennium Development Goals,* which was coauthored by the coordinators of the UN Millennium Project task forces.

The task forces have identified the interventions and policy measures needed to achieve each of the Goals. In *Combating AIDS in the Developing World,* the Working Group on HIV/AIDS underscores the importance of scaling up both essential HIV prevention services and antiretroviral treatment. Only urgent expansion of treatment can prolong the lives of the nearly 40 million people who already carry HIV—and will limit the social and economic devastation their deaths would cause. Only reinvigorated and expanded prevention can ultimately bring the epidemic under control. In the hardest hit countries, much more must also be done to mitigate the impact of the epidemic, especially on orphans and other vulnerable children. The key to scaling up HIV/AIDS services, particularly antiretroviral treatment, will be sustained investment in health systems, especially the healthcare work force.

This report was prepared by a group of leading experts who contributed in their personal capacity and volunteered their time to this important task. I am very grateful for their thorough and skilled efforts. I am sure that the report, with its practical options for action, will make an extremely important contribution to bringing the AIDS epidemic under control and helping to achieve the Millennium Development Goals.

Jeffrey D. Sachs
New York
January 17, 2005

Contents

Boxes

Figures

Maps

Working group members

Coordinators

Agnes Binagwaho, National Commission to Fight AIDS, Kigali, Rwanda

Josh Ruxin, Columbia University, New York, N.Y., United States

Members

Bilali Camara, Caribbean Epidemiology Research Centre, Port of Spain, Trinidad and Tobago

Eka Esu-Williams, Population Council/Horizons Program, Johannesburg, South Africa

Paul Farmer, Partners in Health, Boston, Mass., United States

Helene Gayle, Bill and Melinda Gates Foundation, Seattle, Wash., United States

Catherine Hankins, Joint United Nations Programme on HIV/AIDS, Geneva, Switzerland

David Hoos, Columbia University, New York, N.Y., United States

Renate Koch, Latin American and Caribbean Council of AIDS Service Organizations, Caracas, Venezuela

Chewe Luo, United Nations Children's Fund, New York, N.Y., United States

Kasia Malinowska-Sempruch, Open Society Institute, New York, N.Y., United States

Martin Markowitz, Aaron Diamond AIDS Research Center, New York, N.Y., United States

Michael Merson, Yale University, New Haven, Conn., United States

Trevor Neilson, Global Business Coalition on HIV/AIDS, New York, N.Y., United States

Bernhard Schwartlander, The Global Fund to Fight AIDS, Tuberculosis, and Malaria, Geneva, Switzerland

Jeffrey L. Sturchio, Merck & Co., Inc., Whitehouse Station, N.J., United States

Paulo Roberto Teixeira, STD/AIDS Program, São Paulo, Brazil

Marco Antônio de Ávila Vitória, World Health Organization, Geneva, Switzerland

Diana Weil, World Health Organization, Geneva, Switzerland

Catherine M. Wilfert, Elizabeth Glaser Pediatric AIDS Foundation, Chapel Hill, N.C., United States

Debrework Zewdie, World Bank, Washington, D.C., United States

Preface

The Millennium Development Goals, derived from the Millennium Declaration adopted by world leaders at the 2000 Millennium Summit, have evolved into an organizing theme of UN development work as well as a common framework for both donor and developing nations. In 2002 the United Nations Secretary-General and the United Nations Development Programme launched the UN Millennium Project to recommend the best strategies for reaching the Millennium Development Goals. The Millennium Project's Task Force on HIV/AIDS, Malaria, TB, and Access to Essential Medicines, concerned with Millennium Development Goal 6 on combating HIV/AIDS, malaria, and other diseases, consists of four operationally independent working groups focusing on HIV/AIDS, malaria, tuberculosis, and access to essential medicines.

The mandate of the Working Group on HIV/AIDS is to recommend strategies for reaching the Millennium Development Goal for HIV/AIDS and its accompanying target: "Have halted by 2015, and begun to reverse, the spread of HIV/AIDS." Since the Goal and official target provide little guidance, we have as a first step proposed an interpretation of the Goal based on more specific targets of our own devising. In analyzing how these targets could be reached, we have focused on identifying successful approaches and on overcoming obstacles to their implementation and expansion, rather than on devising new approaches or technical means. While improved prevention and treatment methods are vitally important, there is a clear imperative to deploy more broadly and effectively those that we already have in hand.

The resolution of the 2001 UN General Assembly Special Session on HIV/AIDS lays out the general principles of a global response to AIDS and commits member states to a series of steps. The working group has sought to complete the work of identifying the most effective measures and to consider institutional and technical arrangements for implementing them. The framework of the Millennium Development Goals gives the UN Millennium Project a more ambitious and somewhat longer term perspective than many other initiatives. Accordingly, the working group has sought to emphasize the steps that will be required to reach ambitious goals for 2015, while recognizing the need for immediate progress.

The Millennium Project is an advisory body to the UN Secretary-General, and the United Nations system is clearly one audience for the working group's report. And, indeed, we offer some recommendations for how the UN system could more effectively assist countries to combat AIDS. But if our report is to contribute to achieving the Millennium Development Goals, it clearly must reach a broad spectrum of individuals and institutions concerned with the epidemic, from donor nations to developing country governments, nongovernmental organizations, and activists. We hope that the report will be useful to specialists and policymakers as well as intelligible to a broader audience.

Our AIDS report is best considered part of a broader body of analysis and recommendations; several topics important to the fight against AIDS are considered in greater depth in other reports of the UN Millennium Project. On questions of pharmaceutical pricing, access, and intellectual property rights, we have largely deferred to the Working Group on Access to Essential Medicines of our own working group. Our treatment of the links between HIV/AIDS and tuberculosis has been drafted in collaboration with the Working Group on Tuberculosis; broader consideration of the fight against tuberculosis is left to their report. Although we address the ways in which health systems will have to be strengthened to allow expansion of antiretroviral treatment, a more comprehensive analysis of health systems can be found in the report of the Task Force on Child Health and Maternal Health, which has made strengthening district-level health systems one of its central priorities. In addition, the health working groups are drafting a joint statement on health systems to reflect our shared conviction that strengthening these institutions will be the key to achieving all the health Millennium Development Goals. Finally, on general questions of development strategy, including poverty reduction strategies, the overall quantity and nature of development assistance, governance, and so on, we refer readers to the synthesis report of the UN Millennium Project as a whole: *Investing in Development: A Practical Plan to Achieve the Millennium Development Goals.*

In working to fulfill our broad mandate, we have relied in great part on the work of others. Our report draws from the vast body of existing research, as well as from our modest new analyses, some of which will be available as working group working papers, and the experience and judgment of working group members. We have sought to draw new attention to neglected issues, to redress what seem to us imbalances in current dogma, and to begin translating the high aspirations and idealism of the UN Millennium Project into practical action.

Acknowledgments

We wish to acknowledge Lara Stabinski's many contributions to the task force's work and to earlier versions of this report. We thank Jhoney Luiz Barcarolo, Margaret Kruk, and Joan Paluzzi for their indispensable assistance and support. We acknowledge the contributions of former task force members Eddie Greene, Maite Irurzun-Lopez, Ben Plumley, and Mark Stirling. We also thank Stan Bernstein, Ties Boerma, Ernest Darkoh, Helen de Pinho, Lynn Freedman, Caren Grown, Geeta Rao Gupta, Lisa Hirshhorn, Jim Kim, Roeland Monasch, John Stover, Neff Walker, John Williamson, and Daniel Wolfe for important contributions to our analysis and Etienne Karita, Doreen Mulenga, Luke Nkinsi, Renee Ridzon, Susan Stout, and David Wilson for participating in task force meetings.

Kevin De Cock, Daniele Dionisio, John McArthur, Ryan Manning, Ngashi Ngongo, Mary Robinson, David Serwadda, Sara Sievers, John Williamson, Yoshiko Zenda, and members of the UNAIDS Global Reference Group on HIV/AIDS and Human Rights provided valuable comments. Yanis Ben Amor and members of the Stop TB Partnership contributed to the section of the report on TB and HIV; Ruhella Hossain contributed to the chapter on orphans. Nima Tabloei prepared the figures and Maribel Avila and Lauren Margulies provided administrative support. We thank Chandrika Bahadur, Michael Faye, Michael Krouse, Guido Schmidt-Traub, and the rest of the Millennium Project secretariat for their assistance, and Dai Ellis, Ann Rosenberg, Ron Waldman, Karen Schmidt, Celina Schocken, and other colleagues at Columbia University for useful discussions. We thank the government of Rwanda for hosting the task force's meeting in Kigali in June 2003. The report was edited and produced by Meta de Coquereaumont, Patricia Leidl, Thomas Roncoli, Carol Rosen, Bruce Ross-Larson, Christopher Trott, Timothy Walker, and Elaine Wilson of Communications Development Incorporated.

Finally, Josh Ruxin and Paul Wilson acknowledge the support of the Center for Global Health and Economic Development at Columbia University, which provided a stimulating environment for carrying out this work..

Abbreviations

AIDS	acquired immunodeficiency syndrome
ART	antiretroviral therapy
CMH	Commission on Macroeconomics and Health
CCM	country coordinating mechanism
GDP	gross domestic product
HIV	human immunodeficiency virus
IMF	International Monetary Fund
INCB	International Narcotics Control Board
MAP	Multi-Country AIDS Program or Monitoring the AIDS Pandemic
MSF	Médecins Sans Frontières
NGO	nongovernmental organization
OECD	Organisation for Economic Co-operation and Development
PIH	Partners in Health
STI	sexually transmitted infection
TB	tuberculosis
UNAIDS	Joint United Nations Programme on HIV/AIDS
UNDP	United Nations Development Programme
UNGASS	United Nations General Assembly Special Session
USAID	United States Agency for International Development
UNICEF	United Nations Children's Fund
UNODC	United Nations Office on Drugs and Crime
WHO	World Health Organization

Millennium Development Goals

goals

Goal 1

Eradicate extreme poverty and hunger

Target 1.
Halve, between 1990 and 2015, the proportion of people whose income is less than $1 a day

Target 2.
Halve, between 1990 and 2015, the proportion of people who suffer from hunger

Goal 2

Achieve universal primary education

Target 3.
Ensure that, by 2015, children everywhere, boys and girls alike, will be able to complete a full course of primary schooling

Goal 3

Promote gender equality and empower women

Target 4.
Eliminate gender disparity in primary and secondary education, preferably by 2005, and in all levels of education no later than 2015

Goal 4

Reduce child mortality

Target 5.
Reduce by two-thirds, between 1990 and 2015, the under-five mortality rate

Goal 5

Improve maternal health

Target 6.
Reduce by three-quarters, between 1990 and 2015, the maternal mortality ratio

Goal 6

Combat HIV/AIDS, malaria, and other diseases

Target 7.
Have halted by 2015 and begun to reverse the spread of HIV/AIDS

Target 8.
Have halted by 2015 and begun to reverse the incidence of malaria and other major diseases

Goal 7	**Target 9.**
Ensure environmental sustainability	Integrate the principles of sustainable development into country policies and programs and reverse the loss of environmental resources

Target 10.

Halve, by 2015, the proportion of people without sustainable access to safe drinking water and basic sanitation

Target 11.

Have achieved by 2020 a significant improvement in the lives of at least 100 million slum dwellers

Goal 8	**Target 12.**
Develop a global partnership for development	Develop further an open, rule-based, predictable, nondiscriminatory trading and financial system (includes a commitment to good governance, development, and poverty reduction—both nationally and internationally)

Target 13.

Address the special needs of the Least Developed Countries (includes tariff- and quota-free access for Least Developed Countries' exports, enhanced program of debt relief for heavily indebted poor countries [HIPCs] and cancellation of official bilateral debt, and more generous official development assistance for countries committed to poverty reduction)

Target 14.

Address the special needs of landlocked developing countries and small island developing states (through the Program of Action for the Sustainable Development of Small Island Developing States and 22nd General Assembly provisions)

Target 15.

Deal comprehensively with the debt problems of developing countries through national and international measures in order to make debt sustainable in the long term

Some of the indicators are monitored separately for the least developed countries, Africa, landlocked developing countries, and small island developing states

Target 16.

In cooperation with developing countries, develop and implement strategies for decent and productive work for youth

Target 17.

In cooperation with pharmaceutical companies, provide access to affordable essential drugs in developing countries

Target 18.

In cooperation with the private sector, make available the benefits of new technologies, especially information and communications technologies

Executive summary

AIDS is a global catastrophe, threatening social and economic stability in the most affected areas, while spreading relentlessly into new regions. In the past year, 3 million people died of AIDS, more than ever before and more than from any other infectious disease. Meanwhile, about 5 million more became infected with HIV. More than 39 million people carry the virus worldwide, 25 million of them in Sub-Saharan Africa. More than 2 million children are living with HIV, 15 million have been orphaned by the epidemic, and millions more have been made vulnerable by the illness of parents and family members. The suffering caused by AIDS has been compounded by the deadly synergy between HIV and tuberculosis. The spread of HIV has contributed to as much as a fourfold increase in the number of tuberculosis cases in parts of Africa. More than 10 million people worldwide are infected with both tuberculosis and HIV.

Despite local successes, national and international responses to the epidemic remain inadequate, whether judged by the limited reach of prevention and treatment programs or by their negligible impact on the course of the epidemic. For example, only 8 percent of those who need antiretroviral therapy in the developing world are receiving it (and only 4 percent in Sub-Saharan Africa); only 8 percent of pregnant women are offered services for preventing transmission to their infants; and even in the hardest-hit regions, most young people do not have reliable information on protecting themselves from infection. Moreover, the distribution of treatment and prevention services remains profoundly inequitable.

Yet the past few years have seen important breakthroughs. First, the epidemic is now firmly on the agenda of the United Nations system, development agencies, the World Bank, and many world leaders. The most significant manifestation of this increased visibility was the 2001 UN General Assembly

National HIV prevalence among adults ranges from a fraction of a percent to well over 30 percent

Special Session on HIV/AIDS (UNGASS). Second, resources for AIDS programs in the developing world have increased more than sixfold since 1996, with substantial new resources becoming available through the Global Fund to Fight AIDS, Tuberculosis and Malaria; the World Bank; and bilateral channels, including the U.S. government's large new initiative. There has been particularly strong commitment to funding expanded access to antiretroviral treatment. More resources will be necessary, but the central challenge is now to overcome the obstacles to scaling up prevention, treatment, and support for affected households, and thus to translate money and commitment into results on the ground.

Epidemic diversity

Global statistics cannot convey the growing diversity of the epidemic, which takes radically different forms in different communities, countries, and regions. National HIV prevalence among adults ranges from a fraction of a percent to well over 30 percent; the virus spreads through different populations by different means; and national capacity and willingness to respond vary enormously. Africa remains by far the most affected region, but there is no uniform "African epidemic." While Southern Africa faces stubbornly high prevalence and growing mortality, the epidemic may be waning in parts of East Africa, and in some other countries prevalence has remained low. Rates of infection are growing alarmingly in Russia and other parts of the former Soviet Union and in parts of India, China, and Southeast Asia. While the epidemic in these regions remains largely restricted to particularly vulnerable populations, there are some indications of spread into the general population. The older epidemics of Latin America and the Caribbean continue to evolve, but seem relatively stable. Some governments are increasingly confronting the challenge of AIDS head on, but others continue to deny its significance or even its existence within their borders.

These increasing differences among countries and regions need to be more broadly appreciated and taken into account at the international level by donors, advocates, and journalists. At the local level, policymakers must be guided by the best possible information on local conditions, while at the same time incorporating the lessons learned from neighboring countries and other regions.

For the purposes of this report, we will often make use of a simple dichotomy that captures several important features of many national epidemics. On one hand are the most affected countries, almost all in Sub-Saharan Africa and almost all very poor. There, prevalence is high, transmission is primarily by heterosexual intercourse, and the epidemic is well established in the general population. In this context the fundamental challenges to reversing the epidemic are lack of resources, weak health systems, and the barriers to widespread behavior change posed by poverty and gender inequality. On the other hand are many countries of Eastern Europe, Asia, and Latin America, with

The outcome goals and the coverage targets provide clear benchmarks

lower prevalence epidemics concentrated in key populations, such as injecting drug users, sex workers, and men who have sex with men. In these countries, the greatest obstacles to containing AIDS are denial, lack of political will, and misguided, punitive policies toward those most affected by the epidemic.

This basic distinction is a recurring theme of our report. Perhaps inevitably, our report focuses in large part on the high-prevalence African epidemics, but several of our most important recommendations apply with particular force to those countries with concentrated epidemics.

The Millennium Development Goals and the UN Millennium Project

The Millennium Development Goals represent an unprecedented global commitment to combating poverty, hunger, disease, and inequality. Goal 6, "to combat HIV/AIDS, malaria, and other diseases," elevates the fight against AIDS to a place among the world's highest development priorities, recognizing the enormous suffering the epidemic causes, as well as the threat it poses to achievement of the other goals.

The Working Group on HIV/AIDS of the UN Millennium Project Task Force on HIV/AIDS, Malaria, TB, and Access to Essential Medicines has been asked to outline how this goal and the accompanying target, "to have halted and begun to reverse the spread of HIV/AIDS by 2015," can be met. In working to fulfill this broad mandate while avoiding unnecessary duplication, we have relied in great part on the work of others. Our report is drawn from the vast body of existing research, as well as from our modest new analyses and the experience and judgment of working group members. We have sought to draw new attention to neglected issues, to redress what seem to us imbalances in current dogma, and to begin translating the high aspirations and idealism embodied in the Millennium Development Goals into recommendations for practical action.

Interpreting the AIDS Goal

The Millennium Development Goal for AIDS and its target lack the quantitative benchmarks that make some of the other goals verifiable commitments. To give the AIDS goal a rigorous interpretation, the working group proposes two demanding but attainable targets for 2015:

- Reduce prevalence among young people to 5 percent in the most affected countries and by 50 percent elsewhere by 2015.
- Ensure equitable and sustainable access to antiretroviral therapy to at least 75 percent of those in need by 2015.

To motivate specific action, we supplement the overall goals with coverage targets for key prevention and treatment interventions. Together, the outcome goals and the coverage targets provide clear benchmarks for measuring both overall progress and concrete action.

Treatment can assist prevention in important ways, but treatment alone will not bring the epidemic under control

The working group recognizes that it might be possible to reduce HIV prevalence and bring treatment to many without reaching the poorest and most vulnerable populations, or by sacrificing progress in other areas, such as maternal and child health. This would not be acceptable. Our report stresses two basic requirements for ensuring equitable access to AIDS services, especially antiretroviral treatment. First, the poor will be left out—and other health priorities jeopardized—unless the health systems that serve them are strengthened. Second, women, children, and marginalized populations, such as injecting drug users, may be excluded if their right to prevention and care services is not vigorously defended.

Ten imperatives

We have organized our most important findings into 10 basic imperatives that, if followed, should ensure that the world meets the Millennium Development Goal for AIDS.

Reinvigorate prevention

As the UNGASS Declaration of Commitment stated, prevention must be the mainstay of the response to the epidemic, as only by preventing new infections can the epidemic eventually be brought under control. The long-overdue drive to expand treatment—energized by the WHO/UNAIDS initiative to provide antiretroviral therapy to 3 million people by 2005 ("3 by 5") and large influxes of funds—has mobilized activists, national governments, and the United Nations system, and now dominates the AIDS agenda at all levels. Every effort must now be made to bring the same sense of urgency and excitement to meeting ambitious prevention goals. Unless prevention remains a fundamental priority of leaders, donors, and those who battle the epidemic on the ground, tens of millions more will become infected and the need for treatment will grow inexorably. As is now widely recognized, treatment can assist prevention in important ways (see below), but treatment alone will not bring the epidemic under control.

Effective prevention requires a combination of interventions, providing tools to block the various routes of infection as well as enabling those at risk to make use of these tools. Much has been learned about what works in prevention, and the working group endorses a standard list of interventions. These include:

- Education and behavior change campaigns for youth and the general population.
- Harm reduction, behavior change, and condom promotion programs focused on vulnerable populations.
- Voluntary testing and counseling.
- Control of sexually transmitted infections.
- Prenatal testing and antiretroviral drugs to prevent mother-to-child transmission.

Where epidemics are highly concentrated, programs for the general population must not substitute for services for those most in need

- Health system precautions and blood safety.

Although the effectiveness of each of these interventions has been demonstrated, most reach only a fraction of those who could benefit from them. These proven measures must be scaled up rapidly; this will require increased resources and renewed commitment to comprehensive prevention. But reaping the benefits of these prevention measures will also require overcoming the structural barriers to their widespread adoption, in particular profound gender inequities and the political and legal obstacles to reaching critical high-risk populations with effective services (see below).

As HIV prevention programs are scaled up, links should be strengthened to the broader set of reproductive health services, including family planning and safe motherhood. Although reproductive health and HIV programs share many goals and have much to teach one another, these ties have generally been weak.

Although the technologies we have in hand can avert millions of infections, prevention efforts would be greatly strengthened by new and improved tools. Research on microbicides and other female-controlled methods must be a particularly high priority. Although an effective vaccine is unlikely to be available in time to help in meeting the Millennium Development Goals, the potential impact of a vaccine justifies a sustained, long-term commitment to research and development even in the face of setbacks. Social science and operational research leading to more effective use of existing prevention tools is just as important. Improved monitoring and evaluation is also essential: without better information on the epidemic and on the effectiveness of programs, decisions will continue to be made in the dark.

Focus on vulnerable populations

Although all of these elements of prevention are important, clear priorities reflecting local circumstances are essential, even when resources are not immediately limiting. Failure to set appropriate prevention priorities can be a political choice: the most important programs are sometimes willfully neglected in the name of the rest. In particular, the working group reiterates the fundamental importance of focusing prevention efforts on populations most at risk, especially in concentrated epidemics. Few elements of HIV prevention doctrine rest on as solid an empirical and theoretical foundation. We believe that the single highest priority in Russia, Ukraine, much of China and Southeast Asia, as well as in large parts of India and Latin America, should be needle exchange and opiate substitution services for injecting drug users, who bear the greatest burden of new infections in these areas. Similarly, information, condoms, and health services for sex workers and men who have sex with men must be a central priority where these groups are at particularly high risk. We stress that governments have a responsibility to ensure that all people, even those at low risk, receive basic information about HIV and how to protect themselves. But

Treatment and care must stand alongside prevention as essential elements of a comprehensive response to the epidemic

where epidemics are highly concentrated, programs for the general population must not be allowed to substitute for services for those most in need.

Bringing effective prevention to drug users is not primarily a matter of resources and technical capacity, although these are of course important, but a question of policy and political will. Success requires adopting evidence-based public health approaches to drug use and its consequences instead of the failed criminal enforcement strategies employed today by almost all governments where injecting drug use is fueling the spread of HIV. The working group urges national governments to stop exacerbating the epidemic by criminalizing and imprisoning drug users and to provide instead proven harm-reduction services, including needle and syringe exchange and drug-substitution treatment. To help achieve this end, moreover, the UN system must speak with a single voice against punitive approaches, affirming clearly that harm reduction is both good policy and fully consistent with international drug control treaties. The UN and some national governments have taken promising steps in the past year, but it remains to be seen whether official statements will translate into changes on the ground.

Other vulnerable populations also suffer from discriminatory laws and ill-conceived punitive approaches: policies that drive sex workers and men who have sex with men underground and away from prevention and care services are counterproductive and should be abandoned.

In high-prevalence, generalized epidemics, the greatest prevention priority must be to bring about widespread behavior change by promoting open discussion of HIV, gender, and sexuality; stimulating and supporting community mobilization; and combating stigma and gender inequality. Programs must be designed to reach young people and accommodate their distinct needs. Even where prevalence in the general population is high, however, prevention campaigns must focus special attention on those whose circumstances or behavior puts them at higher risk of contracting or transmitting HIV.

Ensure equitable access to treatment

The working group believes that treatment and care must stand alongside prevention as essential elements of a comprehensive response to the epidemic. Only treatment can prolong the lives of the 39 million people who already carry HIV and, in the highest prevalence countries, forestall continued catastrophic rates of illness and death and the attendant social and economic devastation. Moreover, the current situation, in which access to life-saving treatment is primarily determined by ability to pay or country of residence, is fundamentally unjust.

After years of delay, a growing number of governments, donors, and international organizations are at last committed to rapidly scaling up antiretroviral therapy. We endorse the WHO/UNAIDS 3 by 5 initiative, which aims to provide antiretroviral therapy to 3 million people by the end of 2005, and

The greatest barrier to widespread access to treatment is the deplorable state of health systems

propose a target of reaching 75 percent of those in need by 2015. Our report focuses less on making the case for expanding treatment—we consider this battle to be largely won—and more on how to overcome the considerable challenges to bringing treatment to those who need it in the poorest countries.

The working group believes that the greatest barrier to meeting the goal of widespread access to treatment is the deplorable state of health systems in most of the hardest-hit countries. Poverty, misplaced priorities, and years of externally imposed restrictions on social spending have left health services for over 2 billion people dysfunctional, inaccessible, or priced beyond the reach of the poor. The greatest challenge in the most affected countries is an acute shortage of skilled healthcare workers.

As remedying this situation will take time, treatment programs must be designed to make optimal use of existing staff. Nurses, clinical officers, and other personnel must assume roles assigned to doctors in the rich countries. Appropriately trained lay people must help provide counseling, adherence support, and other vital services now handled by healthcare personnel. Clinical protocols and drug regimens must be simplified to the greatest extent possible. Communities, and especially people living with HIV, must be involved in decisionmaking and must contribute to treatment delivery itself. In fact, if treatment programs are to succeed, they must build strong ties to communities and to community AIDS initiatives in prevention, home-based care, and orphan support.

In some countries, notably those that have received large grants from the Global Fund, the U.S. government, or other sources, the cost of antiretroviral drugs is no longer the primary obstacle to expansion of treatment programs. In the longer run, however, the sustainability of antiretroviral therapy in the developing world will require bringing prices down further. Cheaper and more convenient second-line regimens, drug formulations for infants and children, and diagnostics are particularly urgent priorities. More research is also needed into the most efficient and effective ways to deliver treatment and ensure adherence where clinical staff are scarce and health infrastructure is weak.

Invest in health systems as AIDS services are expanded

Even with the most creative delivery strategies, it will be impossible to bring antiretroviral treatment to all who need it in the poorest countries without strengthening health systems and recruiting and training many new health workers. Critical prevention measures, including the treatment of sexually transmitted infections and services to prevent mother-to-child transmission, also depend on functioning health systems. Moreover, the health Millennium Development Goals as a whole, and more generally the elusive goal of bringing basic health services to all, will never be met without vigorous financial and political commitment to health systems. Since it will take years to expand

Investing in health systems is essential to ensuring equity in AIDS treatment

the pool of skilled health-care workers, investments in training capacity, along with other critical elements of health systems, must begin now. Thus countries must build for the future as they urgently expand access to treatment and other services in the short run.

The working group recommends that a significant share of new treatment resources be devoted to investments that benefit health systems generally. Moreover, treatment should be integrated whenever possible into existing structures of care rather than delivered through stand-alone systems. These measures will ensure that progress toward the goal of universal treatment access is sustainable and that gains against AIDS are not achieved at the expense of other health priorities, including combating malaria and tuberculosis and improving maternal and child health.

The deadly interactions between HIV and tuberculosis make strong links between HIV and tuberculosis programs particularly important. In addition to joint planning and greater communication at all levels, several specific steps should be taken, including offering HIV testing and counselling to tuberculosis patients and providing treatment to coinfected individuals.

Investing in health systems is also essential to ensuring equity in AIDS treatment in the most affected countries. Where many do not have access to even basic healthcare, antiretroviral therapy will benefit the better off first. While expansion of treatment cannot wait for health systems to be fully built, access will remain inequitable if scaling up is not accompanied by steps to strengthen basic services for the poor.

In many of the countries facing concentrated HIV epidemics, by contrast, the key to treatment equity is guaranteeing access to vulnerable populations: injecting drug users, sex workers, men who have sex with men, and ethnic minorities. In Russia, China, Viet Nam, and many other places, it will be very important to ensure that access to treatment is not denied to the very groups who need it most. The working group urges countries to develop systems for monitoring access to antiretroviral therapy among these critical populations, as well as among women and among children under age 15.

Integrate prevention and treatment

The working group shares the current enthusiasm for integrating prevention and treatment. We call for the incorporation of concrete prevention elements into treatment plans now being developed in many countries. Much will have to be learned by experience, but the essential elements of integration should include:

- Rapidly expanding HIV testing, including traditional voluntary counseling and testing as well as routine offer of testing in appropriate clinical settings, with strong links to prevention services, treatment, and care.
- Incorporating prevention counseling, referral to reproductive health services, and other prevention measures into clinical settings.

Prevention and care programs will fail if they ignore the underlying determinants of the epidemic

- Ensuring that diagnosis and treatment of sexually transmitted infections are available wherever HIV care is provided.
- Harmonizing prevention and treatment messages, both in the community and through other channels, to ensure that treatment reinforces prevention rather than undermining it. It will also be important to carefully monitor attitudes and behavior as treatment is scaled up to allow prevention messages to be modified quickly if behavior changes.

The advent of treatment in the developing world represents an enormous opportunity for prevention, but fulfilling this promise will require influencing the design of treatment programs and devoting real resources to incorporating vigorous prevention elements. As the experience of the developed world shows, access to treatment will not bring down the rate of new infections by itself.

Address root causes: empower women and girls

Prevention and care programs will fail if they ignore the underlying determinants of the epidemic: poverty, gender inequality, and social dislocation. At a minimum AIDS programs must take these sources of social vulnerability into account; in the longer run they must be tied to efforts to reduce them. The relative powerlessness of women and girls, together with pervasive gender attitudes and practices, contribute particularly strongly to the spread of HIV. Much can be done now to ensure that AIDS programs recognize the special vulnerability of women and girls. But the most powerful answers to the problem of women's vulnerability will be those that transcend AIDS: promoting girls' primary and secondary education, guaranteeing equal property rights and economic opportunity, and combating violence against women.

Plan for orphans and vulnerable children

UNICEF estimates that more than 12 million children in Sub-Saharan Africa have lost one or both parents to AIDS; this number is projected to grow to 18 million by 2010. An equal or greater number of children have been made vulnerable by the epidemic in other ways—by the illness of parents or other family members or by living in a household struggling to care for many orphans. This enormous tragedy has received far too little attention. Countries must develop national strategies for assisting families and communities to care for orphans, ensuring that they are able to attend school, protecting them from exploitation, and enforcing their rights to property. Donor nations and international organizations must provide greatly expanded resources and technical assistance.

It is important to recognize that even in Sub-Saharan Africa the majority of orphans have lost their parents to causes other than AIDS, although in the hardest-hit countries of Southern Africa the epidemic is greatly increasing the burden on families and communities. In most circumstances it is neither just nor practical to target services specifically to children affected by AIDS.

The poorest countries cannot defeat AIDS without much greater help from the international community

Instead, communities should be involved in determining which children and which households are in greatest need. At the national and international levels, the attention and resources that the AIDS crisis is finally bringing to the needs of orphans should be used to spur progress toward the goal of supporting *all* vulnerable children.

Require more from the United Nations

The United Nations, with its established presence in almost every country and its broad legitimacy, is uniquely placed to play a central role in the fight against the global epidemic. Through UNAIDS and its cosponsors, the UN system has made important contributions at the global level, placing AIDS at the top of the international agenda and building international consensus around basic elements of a comprehensive response. The working group believes the UN could do more, particularly in two areas. First, it should be far bolder in holding accountable member nations that have failed to honor their commitments to fighting AIDS. The UN should draw attention to the failures in leadership, misguided policies, and gaps in financing that continue to stymie an effective response.

Second, the UN is not doing enough to help countries meet their objectives. It must focus on providing more useful and appropriate technical and management assistance; in many countries, its record in these areas has been poor. The fundamental problem has been insufficient, and in some cases inadequate, personnel on the ground. In many of the hardest-hit countries, UN staffing falls far short of what would be required to help governments do what is necessary. Remedying this shortcoming will require substantial new resources.

More broadly, the UN Millennium Project as a whole is calling for UN country teams to assume a greater role in assisting countries to plan for achieving the Millennium Development Goals. The project recognizes the constraints and institutional deficiencies that will make this a daunting challenge for the UN. But there simply is no other institution, or set of institutions, that can play this role.

Expand international and domestic financing and remove barriers to its use

International financing for AIDS and, more broadly, for building the health systems needed to combat the epidemic remains insufficient. Although there is wide consensus that a comprehensive response to the epidemic would require at least $10 billion per year, UNAIDS estimates that only $6 billion was spent in 2004. The Global Fund to Fight AIDS, Tuberculosis, and Malaria was created in 2001 to begin filling the gap between country needs and funds available from traditional bilateral and multilateral sources. Despite significant successes and widespread enthusiasm among its recipients, the Global Fund lacks the resources to fulfill its commitments. At least $2.3 billion in additional funds will be needed in 2005 alone. Moreover,

Scaling up established interventions could save millions of lives and bring the epidemic under control

donor aid in general must be more predictable and free of conditions that reduce efficiency and distort policy.

While the poorest countries cannot defeat AIDS without much greater help from the international community, they can demonstrate commitment by increasing national spending on AIDS and health systems, creating a true partnership with donors.

In many developing countries, restrictions on public sector spending and hiring are a major obstacle to making use of new resources in the fight against AIDS. The International Monetary Fund and other international financial institutions should work with national governments and donors to find creative ways to reconcile substantial increases in spending on health and other social services with macroeconomic stability.

Empower governments and hold them accountable

An increasing number of national and international organizations—bilateral donors and their contractors, UN agencies, international and local nongovernmental organizations, foundations, the private sector, government ministries, national AIDS coordinating bodies—are involved in delivering, funding, or overseeing AIDS services. Better coordination at all levels will be essential to a more effective response and will depend on establishing clear roles and responsibilities.

It is particularly important that ministries of health and national AIDS councils or commissions end confusion over the division of responsibilities between them. National ownership and control should be an overriding principle: donors and international organizations must ensure that their work contributes to national priorities and national plans as defined by governments, working with other stakeholders. Furthermore, where well-developed government strategies are in place, donors should move toward broad and flexible financing of government programs, including capacity-building and salary support. As a first step, the working group endorses UNAIDS' call for "three ones" at the country level: one AIDS action framework, one national AIDS coordinating body, and one monitoring and evaluation system.

In many of the hardest-hit countries, as well as those threatened by growing epidemics—India, China, Russia—AIDS still does not receive sufficient attention and resources from national leaders and governments. The UN, as well as the Bretton Woods institutions and donors, must demand that these countries take the threat of AIDS seriously and back words with budgetary commitments. National governments should be required to demonstrate how they plan to combat the epidemic, who will be responsible, and how progress will be measured.

Conclusion

We now have in hand a range of proven, effective ways to control the spread of HIV and to prolong the lives of those who are already infected. The working group believes that scaling up these established interventions could save millions of lives and bring the epidemic under control. But success will depend critically on how this is done. First, prevention and treatment must be scaled up together: just as for years life-saving treatment was considered too difficult or too expensive for the developing world, there is now a danger that prevention will be overlooked. Second, expansion of AIDS services must be accompanied by sustained investment in health systems, especially in human resources, and programs must be structured to minimize destructive competition for skilled staff and other scarce resources. Third, programs must be designed and policies put in place to ensure that prevention and treatment services reach the poor and the vulnerable populations who need them most. Success will require greatly increased resources from donor nations, as well as stronger commitment from many governments in affected countries.

Chapter 1

Epidemic and response

In the little more than two decades since it was recognized as a distinct disease, HIV/AIDS has grown into one of the greatest epidemics in human history, spreading to every corner of the globe and wreaking enormous devastation. The overwhelming suffering already caused by AIDS and the threat it now poses to prospects for human and economic development were recognized by hundreds of national leaders at the Millennium Summit in 2000 in New York City, when they included "combating HIV/AIDS, malaria, and other diseases" among the Millennium Development Goals (UN General Assembly 2000; UN Statistics Division 2003). The Working Group on HIV/AIDS of the UN Millennium Project on HIV/AIDS, Malaria, TB, and Access to Essential Medicines has been asked to outline how this Goal and the accompanying target, "to have halted and begun to reverse the spread of HIV/AIDS by 2015," can be met.

The epidemic

A comprehensive overview of the state of the epidemic can be found in recent reports from the Joint United Nations Program on HIV/AIDS (UNAIDS) and the World Health Organization (WHO)—no detailed survey will be attempted here (UNAIDS 2002d, 2004a; UNAIDS/WHO 2002, 2003, 2004b). AIDS took about 3 million lives in 2004, surpassing malaria and tuberculosis as the greatest killer among communicable diseases, while roughly 5 million more people became infected with HIV, the virus that causes AIDS (UNAIDS/WHO 2004b). The number of people living with HIV is now estimated at 39 million. Incidence—the rate of new infections—may have leveled off in a few countries already devastated by the epidemic, but is rising in Russia and the former Soviet states and appears to be growing in India

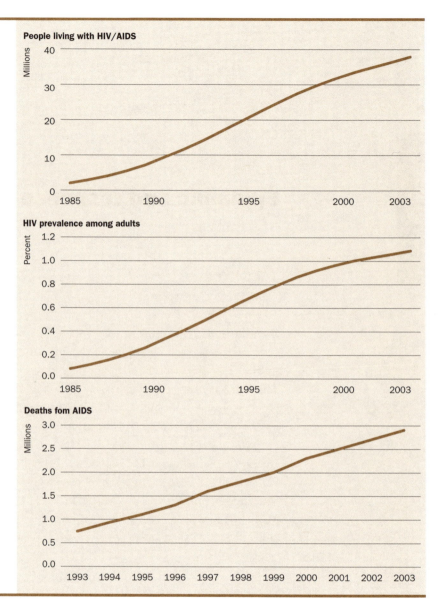

Figure 1.1

Deaths from AIDS and total population carrying the virus continue to grow

Source: UNAIDS 2004.

People living with HIV/AIDS

HIV prevalence among adults

Deaths fom AIDS

and China. Mortality from AIDS and the total population carrying the virus continue to grow (figure 1.1).

Regional variation

The notion of a global AIDS epidemic conceals enormous diversity in prevalence rates, modes of transmission, and affected populations, as well as in the underlying cultural and economic context that influences the spread of the disease and constrains efforts to control it.

The geographic distribution of infection and death remains highly uneven (map 1.1). Sub-Saharan Africa, where 70 percent of deaths have occurred, continues to bear the greatest burden (UNAIDS 2002d; UNAIDS/WHO

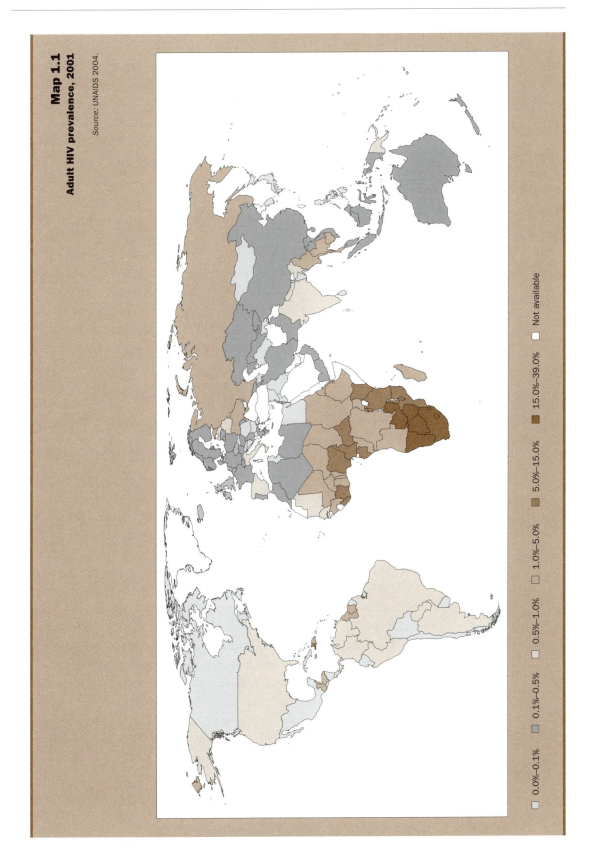

Map 1.1
Adult HIV prevalence, 2001

Source: UNAIDS 2004.

0.0%–0.1%   0.1%–0.5%   0.5%–1.0%   1.0%–5.0%   5.0%–15.0%   15.0%–39.0%   Not available

**The future
course
of these
epidemics
remains very
uncertain**

2004b). Although the continent's overall adult prevalence rate of 7–8 percent is far higher than those of other regions, national and local differences are considerable and growing (map 1.2). Southern Africa, despite being struck by the epidemic later than other parts of the continent, is now by far the hardest-hit region, with prevalence above 35 percent in Botswana and Swaziland and above 20 percent in four other countries (UNAIDS 2004a). Moreover, although prevalence has probably peaked in much of the region, there are no clear signs that it has begun to decline.

In East Africa, where the epidemic first exploded, rates of infection remain high but are falling in some places. Although an early and broad-based prevention response deserves much credit for Uganda's particularly striking success (see box 2.3), the causes of the broader decline are not well understood. Elsewhere on the continent, prevalence varies considerably, from below 1 percent and apparently stable in Senegal to more than 13 percent in the Central African Republic. Nigeria and Ethiopia, with large populations and prevalence rates around 5 percent, are facing very large epidemics. Response to the epidemic has been just as varied. A few nations, benefiting from visionary leadership and involved communities, have mounted effective prevention campaigns (Global HIV Prevention Working Group 2002; UNAIDS 2001a; UNAIDS/WHO 2002). But many others remain mired in denial and disorganization. This diversity has important implications for every aspect of the response to AIDS and for the weight it should be accorded relative to other priorities—few generalizations about "AIDS in Africa" are likely to be very useful. Throughout Sub-Saharan Africa, however, poverty and crippled health systems pose enormous challenges to the battle against AIDS.

Outside Africa, parts of Southeast Asia, the Caribbean, and Latin America are next hardest hit, while rates of infection in Western Europe and North America are below 1 percent and relatively stable. China, India, and the countries of the former Soviet Union, together home to a large share of the world's population, are currently the focus of increasing concern (National Intelligence Council 2002). Although in these regions prevalence in the general population is thought to be relatively low, rates are increasing rapidly in vulnerable populations, prevention efforts and political leadership have been inadequate, and the stage is set for far more serious epidemics. Here as well, however, local conditions are too varied to be well captured by national averages, especially in India and China. Moreover, the future course of these epidemics remains very uncertain, and predictions of high prevalence in the general population risk distracting leaders from what needs to be done now (MAP 2004).

Types of epidemic

National epidemics vary greatly not only in their scale but in their nature (Global HIV Prevention Working Group 2003; UNAIDS 2004a; UNAIDS/WHO 2003, 2004b). In much of Sub-Saharan Africa and parts of the Caribbean,

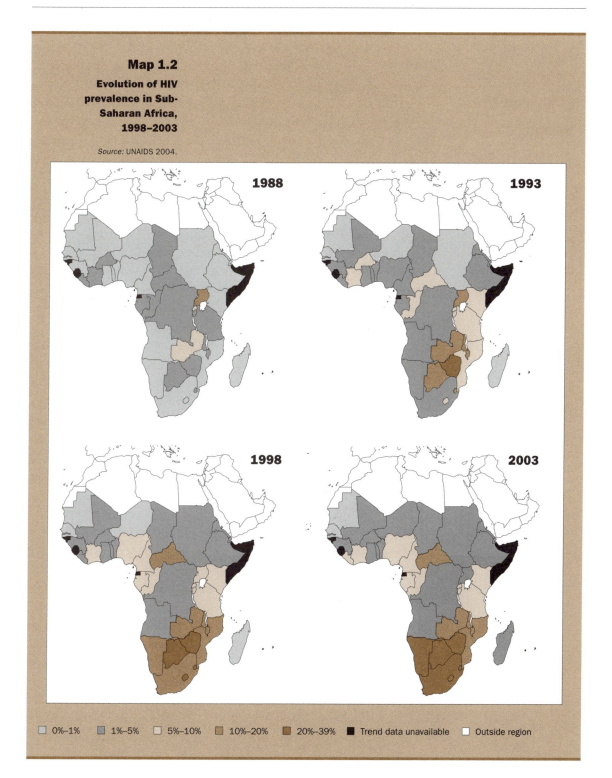

Map 1.2

Evolution of HIV prevalence in Sub-Saharan Africa, 1998–2003

Source: UNAIDS 2004.

1988 — 1993 — 1998 — 2003

☐ 0%–1%   ☐ 1%–5%   ☐ 5%–10%   ☐ 10%–20%   ☐ 20%–39%   ■ Trend data unavailable   ☐ Outside region

the epidemic is widely established in the general population and heterosexual transmission predominates. Elsewhere most epidemics are so far largely concentrated in vulnerable populations, with important consequences for prevention

Nations differ enormously in the financial and institutional resources they can bring to combating the epidemic

strategy, human rights, and political context. In Russia, Eastern Europe, and parts of Asia, for example, most infections have occurred among injecting drug users, while men who have sex with men and commercial sex workers are most affected in some other regions. Concentrated epidemics of this kind can be a stage on the path to a broader epidemic involving the general population, although the conditions that determine whether this transition will occur are not well understood. Finally, nations differ enormously in the financial and institutional resources they can bring to combating the epidemic.

These differences, which imply differing priorities for action and differing constraints, must inform any discussion of the AIDS crisis. This report will not attempt a comprehensive taxonomy of local conditions. But our discussion will often rely on two very basic distinctions:

- *Between countries with concentrated epidemics (high prevalence in vulnerable populations, low in the general population) and those with generalized epidemics (general population prevalence above 1 percent).* This distinction is particularly pertinent to prevention, where the two types of epidemics call for quite different approaches.
- *Between the poorest countries and those with greater resources and capacity.* This separation, which does not always correspond precisely to per capita income, is perhaps most relevant to treatment, since increasing access in the most impoverished settings will require not only much external assistance, but also creative new approaches. This distinction is compounded by the fact that most of the countries where the need for treatment is the greatest are also among the poorest.

Since almost all of the hardest-hit countries are very poor, while many of those with concentrated epidemics are somewhat better off, one can distinguish two critical classes of countries. On one hand are the high-prevalence and very low-income countries, including much of Sub-Saharan Africa, Haiti, and perhaps a few others. There the fundamental barriers to controlling the epidemic are lack of resources and capacity, making AIDS in important respects a *development* issue. Moreover, the devastation is already so great that mitigating the social and economic consequences of the epidemic must be as great a priority as controlling it. On the other hand is a class of countries with higher average incomes (or substantially more developed institutional capacity) and epidemics concentrated in marginalized populations. This category includes China, Russia, Viet Nam, and much of Latin America. Here the greatest obstacle to success is often discrimination and an unwillingness of governments to provide services to despised populations. Thus, in these countries HIV/AIDS must be seen as fundamentally a *human rights* issue.

We recognize that many countries do not fit easily into either category. South Africa and Botswana, where prevalence is very high, are middle-income

The epidemic has grown explosively in some places while remaining relatively stable in others

countries with stronger health systems than their neighbors. Many countries with largely concentrated epidemics, including some in West Africa, are very poor. Moreover, the response to HIV/AIDS in poor, high-prevalence countries involves important human rights issues as well, including stigma, gender discrimination, and the obligation of governments to do what they can despite limited means. We believe that this simple dichotomy is useful nonetheless, and we will return to it often in this report.

In countries with concentrated epidemics, the growing importance of HIV spread among injecting drug users is worth particular attention (Deany 2000; Wolfe and Malinowska-Sempruch 2003). While this mode of transmission is responsible for about 10 percent of new cases worldwide, it is driving some of the world's fastest growing epidemics and may account for as many as a third of new infections outside Africa (Wolfe and Malinowska-Sempruch 2003). The majority of cases in the well-established epidemics in Russia, Ukraine, Malaysia, Viet Nam, and China derive from injection; this route of transmission also plays an important or dominant role in parts of India, Central Asia, Indonesia, Eastern Europe, South America, and much of the developed world. Injecting drug use—and HIV infection among users—is spreading rapidly, fueled by the growing international movement of goods and workers, as well as by economic dislocation. Epidemics among injecting drug users are characterized by explosive growth once the virus is introduced and by the extreme social marginalization, even demonization, of those at risk. The urgent need to overcome the political and institutional barriers to bringing effective HIV prevention and treatment to this most vulnerable population will be a major theme of this report (see chapter 2).

Causes of epidemic diversity

Why has the impact of HIV/AIDS varied so dramatically? History offers a partial explanation, since the virus reached some regions before others. Yet other factors are clearly at work. Even within the African continent, where the virus first appeared, the epidemic has grown explosively in some places while remaining relatively stable in others. Many explanations, ranging from the biological to the cultural and the socioeconomic, have been offered for these striking differences in rate of spread. Epidemiological studies have added to our understanding of these issues without so far offering a persuasive explanation for variations in prevalence (Boerma and others 2002; Buve 2002; Buve and others 2001).

This report is primarily concerned with what must be done to control the epidemic, not with its history. Yet understanding the causes of its strikingly disparate impact can inform action by focusing attention on key underlying factors. Moreover, better understanding of the conditions for rapid growth of the epidemic might allow us to target prevention efforts to those areas and populations most at risk.

The correlation between HIV/AIDS and poverty is by no means perfect

HIV/AIDS and poverty

At a more fundamental level, any attempt to understand the root causes of HIV/AIDS must consider its striking association with poverty and social vulnerability, a central theme that transcends regional variation and differences in mode of transmission (Barnett and Whiteside 2002a; Cohen n.d.; Farmer 1999; Parker 2002; Stillwagon 2000; World Bank 1999). This relationship is perhaps most obvious when one looks across countries: almost all the hardest-hit countries are poor. Africa, the poorest of the continents, is the epicenter of the epidemic. Haiti, the poorest place in the Western Hemisphere, also suffers from the highest HIV prevalence, with other struggling Caribbean and Central American nations not far behind. In Asia, too, HIV/AIDS now strikes hardest amidst poverty and social disruption. The same association holds within countries as well. The epidemic is often concentrated in marginalized populations and among people driven by economic need and despair to behaviors and professions that increase their risk of infection (Hallman 2004; Poundstone and others 2004).

The correlation between HIV/AIDS and poverty is by no means perfect. Botswana and South Africa, Africa's wealthiest nations, are among the hardest hit. In countries with generalized epidemics, the virus has struck at rich and poor alike. Being better off can create its own risks, such as the wherewithal to purchase sex. Moreover, the causal links between poverty and HIV risk are complex. Lack of education and poor access to healthcare surely play an important role. Poor nutrition and exposure to other diseases may increase susceptibility to HIV infection and speed progression to AIDS. Lack of economic opportunity fuels migrant labor, thereby disrupting families, while economic need may drive women to take up sex work and to enter or remain in risky relationships. Barnett and Whiteside have argued that the notion of underlying socioeconomic risk should be broadened to include what they call "low social cohesion"—economic inequality and social disruption—as well as poverty itself (Barnett and Whiteside 2002a; Barnett and others 2000). In fact, both low average income and high income inequality correlate with higher HIV prevalence (World Bank 1999).

One way that poverty increases vulnerability to AIDS is obvious: access to lifesaving treatment for those who already carry the virus remains overwhelmingly inequitable. Most of those who need antiretroviral therapy in affluent countries are receiving it, compared with only 8 percent of those in the developing world (WHO 2004a). In most poor countries, only the few who can afford to pay for it have benefited so far from treatment (see chapter 3).

Just as poverty fuels HIV/AIDS, the epidemic is deepening poverty and threatening economic development in the most affected countries, creating enormous financial hardship for families and communities and robbing nations of people in their most productive years (Barnett and Whiteside 2002b; Cohen n.d.). A recent World Bank study predicted that South Africa faces economic collapse unless it takes vigorous action against the epidemic (Bell and others 2003). Although such

The global response has been far too small and has come far too late

apocalyptic scenarios are speculative—and not so far borne out by the experience of countries further along the epidemic curve—they cannot be dismissed. (This issue is discussed briefly in chapter 4.) It is clear, however, that the impact of AIDS on individuals and households is enormous and that this devastation will get worse before it gets better, even where prevalence is falling. Moreover, much of this burden of suffering falls on the poor, and this disproportionate impact must inform all aspects of the response to the epidemic.

The response

A comprehensive response to HIV/AIDS must include *prevention* of new infections, *treatment and care* for those who are already infected, and *mitigation* of the impact of the disease on families, communities, and societies. By any standard the global response has been far too small and has come far too late. Most of the world's population has no access to reliable information or prevention services, let alone treatment; in much of the world political commitment is still lacking; and resources in the developing world are woefully inadequate. Yet, there has been important progress on several fronts.

First, we have learned a great deal about what works in fighting the epidemic. On the prevention side, we can now draw on a substantial list of proven interventions to combat the major modes of transmission, ranging from harm reduction for injecting drug users, to condom promotion among sex worker and their clients, to drugs for prevention of mother-to-child transmission (Global HIV Prevention Working Group 2002). These measures are imperfect, and critical gaps in the arsenal remain, notably vaccines and microbicides. Moreover, we understand the technical means of prevention far better than we understand how to bring their benefits to all who need them and to overcome the barriers to access posed by poverty, gender inequality, and stigma. But there is little doubt that much more widespread access to the interventions we have in hand would bring substantial gains (Stover and others 2002).

In treatment, the great breakthrough was the development of effective combinations of antiretroviral drugs, which have brought almost miraculous benefits in the developed world and in Brazil, cutting AIDS deaths dramatically and allowing many people with HIV to resume normal lives. Moreover, steady progress is being made in simplifying regimens, in managing patients without sophisticated infrastructure and specialized personnel, and in bringing down drug prices. There is every reason to believe these drugs could bring the same relief to the developing world, but access to antiretroviral therapy remains scandalously inequitable. Although at present these drugs reach only a tiny fraction of those who could benefit from them, there is now broad commitment on the part of affected countries, donors, and international organizations to the urgent expansion of treatment in the developing world. The WHO/UNAIDS initiative to provide antiretroviral therapy to 3 million people by the end of 2005 ("3 by 5") has provided a great boost to these efforts.

The last few years have seen encouraging signs of greater political engagement in the fight against AIDS

Second, we can now learn from a number of successes on a local and even national level. Some countries—Brazil and Senegal among them—appear to have succeeded in arresting the epidemic at an early stage, while others—Uganda, Thailand, and perhaps now Cambodia—have managed to reverse its growth after it has taken stronger hold (UNAIDS 2002d). These examples demonstrate the importance of coherent strategy and committed leadership, the viability of specific approaches, and the possibility of progress on a far greater scale. The feasibility of antiretroviral treatment in developing countries has been demonstrated by pilot projects, such as those undertaken by Partners in Health in Haiti and by Médecins Sans Frontières in South Africa, Malawi, and elsewhere, as well as by Brazil's remarkably successful nationwide program and Botswana's growing national initiative (Coetzee, Hildebrand, and others 2004; Levi and Vitoria 2002; MSF Malawi 2004; Mukherjee and others 2003; Onyango and others 2004).

Third, the last few years have seen a number of encouraging signs of greater political engagement in the fight against AIDS at the national, regional, and international level. In Sub-Saharan Africa, there is now widespread recognition that HIV/AIDS threatens development and social stability, and a growing number of national leaders have spoken out forcefully. Meeting in Abuja, Nigeria, in April 2001, African leaders declared that "containing and reversing the HIV/AIDS epidemic, tuberculosis, and other infectious diseases should constitute our top priority for the first quarter of the twenty-first century" (Organization for African Unity 2001). International institutions ranging from the World Bank to UNICEF now list AIDS among their top priorities. A particularly important development is the growing commitment to scaling up treatment.

The most important international manifestation of this growing commitment was the 2001 United Nations General Assembly Special Session on HIV/AIDS (UNGASS). The resolution adopted by this assembly, the Declaration of Commitment on HIV/AIDS, unambiguously acknowledged the importance of decisive action against the epidemic, affirmed a set of fundamental principles that should govern the response, and committed member states and the UN system to a number of concrete measures. The declaration recognized the role of poverty, illiteracy, and conflict in exacerbating the spread of HIV and warned of the impact of AIDS on development and stability (UN General Assembly 2001). It asserted that while prevention must be the "mainstay" of the response, access to treatment must be expanded and integrated with prevention efforts. It acknowledged the importance of empowering women and girls; combating stigma and discrimination; promoting effective collaboration between the international community, national governments, nongovernmental organizations, and the private sector; and involving people living with HIV. It committed governments to developing comprehensive national HIV/AIDS strategies and to establishing

In 2003 only 8 percent of pregnant women were offered services for preventing mother-to-child transmission

specific kinds of programs by specific dates. In addition, the declaration contains a small number of specific, quantitative targets (box 1.1).

Although the Declaration of Commitment is not itself a plan, it is a coherent declaration of goals and principles and continues to serve as the guiding framework for international action on HIV/AIDS, including that of the UN Millennium Project Working Group on HIV/AIDS. Unfortunately, progress in implementing the UNGASS resolutions has been disappointing (see below).

Despite these important and encouraging advances, the world's response to the epidemic remains profoundly inadequate. The epidemic continues to rage out of control in much of the world, dooming new generations in already devastated regions and spreading to new populations elsewhere. The great majority of those who are infected face illness and death without help from modern medicine; fragile societies confront the economic and social impact of the epidemic without a clear plan or large-scale assistance. Richard Feachem, the executive director of the Global Fund, asserted in 2003: "If in 1982, when we became aware of the virus, we had decided to do nothing in order to observe its course without intervention, the world would be roughly where it is today" (KaiserNetwork.org 2003a). While such a sweeping statement neglects the areas where we have made a difference, it may be distressingly close to the truth.

Another measure of how far our efforts have fallen short is how few people they reach. Beyond the handful of national success stories, most effective prevention and treatment initiatives remain at the project stage, rarely achieving national scale. Although data on coverage levels are poor, it is clear that only a small fraction of those in need have access to vital prevention and treatment services. For example, it is estimated that in 2003 only 8 percent of pregnant women were offered services for preventing mother-to-child transmission, 16 percent of sex workers were reached by targeted prevention programs, and only 8 percent of those in need are receiving antiretroviral treatment (Policy Project 2004; UNAIDS 2003b).

Progress toward the specific UNGASS targets, monitored by UNAIDS using a set of agreed indicators, is similarly disappointing (UNAIDS 2003b).

Box 1.1

Selected targets set at the UN General Assembly Special Session on HIV/AIDS

Source: UN General Assembly 2001.

47. Reduce prevalence among young people (15- to 24-year-olds) by 25 percent in the most affected countries by 2005, globally by 2010.

52. Ensure that, by 2005, 90 percent of young people have access to information, education, and services necessary to avoid infection.

53. Reduce HIV infection among infants by 20 percent by 2005, by 50 percent by 2010.

80. Bring spending on combating the epidemic in low- and middle-income countries to $7 billion–$10 billion.

Capacity constraints can make it difficult to spend large amounts of new money effectively

While some measures of political leadership and government policy show improvement—most countries in Sub-Saharan Africa have adopted national HIV/AIDS strategies—indicators of basic knowledge, behavior, and access to services remain very low, even in countries that have voiced a strong commitment to addressing the epidemic. Perhaps most revealing is that most countries have failed to report at all on most indicators, reflecting the pervasive lack of capacity that continues to plague national responses.

At the heart of these failings—still—is lack of funds. Although total spending on HIV/AIDS in the developing world has risen in recent years, reaching an estimated $6 billion in 2004, it is still only half of what will required in 2005, and less than a third of need in 2007, according to UNAIDS (UNAIDS 2004b). But there are other obstacles as well, including in many places lack of political leadership and inadequate governance. Weak health systems, especially lack of trained staff, stand in the way of expanded access to treatment and to the more clinical prevention measures. In the short run these capacity constraints can make it difficult to spend large amounts of new money effectively; in the long run resolving them will itself require considerable investment.

The Millennium Development Goal on HIV/AIDS

The Millennium Development Goal on HIV/AIDS and the corresponding target, "Have halted by 2015 and begun to reverse the spread of HIV/AIDS," on which the task force's mandate rests, are vague and set no specific benchmarks for success. What does "halting the spread of HIV/AIDS" mean, and how will we know when it has been achieved?

The most straightforward interpretations of the HIV/AIDS target are plainly unsatisfactory. A very literal reading of the target suggests bringing the number of new infections to zero—this is plainly not possible by 2015. A more realistic and natural interpretation, halting and beginning to reverse the growth in new infections or incidence, is also unsatisfactory for several reasons. First, it sets too low a standard, especially when understood at the national level. Stabilizing incidence at anywhere near current levels in the hardest-hit countries cannot be considered success. The second major problem with defining the target in this way is that it would require us to do nothing for those who are already infected.

The official indicators (box 1.2) are useful, but incomplete in that none address access to treatment. But in the absence of quantitative targets they do not solve the problem of defining the goal in a way that informs action and allows progress to be monitored. Thus there is no completely satisfactory interpretation of the HIV/AIDS target, considered in isolation. To give the goal specificity—and to motivate our analysis of what will be required to meet it—we have chosen to supplement its wording with quantitative benchmarks derived from the Millennium Development Goal indicators and the other

major internationally endorsed statements on HIV/AIDS, most importantly
the UNGASS declaration. These targets take the form of benchmarks for the
Millennium Development Goal indicators, extensions to 2015 of UNGASS

Box 1.2

**HIV/AIDS indicators
for the Millennium
Development Goals**

Source: UN Statistics Division
2003.

Indicator 18.   HIV prevalence among 15- to 24-year-old pregnant women.
Indicator 19.   Condom use rate of the contraceptive prevalence rate.
19a.   Condom use at last high-risk sex.
19b.   Percentage of population ages 15–24 with comprehensive correct
knowledge of HIV/AIDS.
Indicator 20.   Ratio of school attendance of orphans to school attendance of nonorphans ages 10–14.

Box 1.3

**Proposed
prevention and
treatment targets**

Prevention: outcome targets
- Reduce prevalence among young people to 5 percent in the most affected coun-
tries and by 50 percent elsewhere by 2015.
- Reduce prevalence within key vulnerable populations by 50 percent by 2015.

Prevention: intervention coverage targets
- Ensure that by 2015 affordable HIV testing and appropriate counseling are offered
at all clinics for sexually transmitted diseases, tuberculosis, and antenatal care
globally, and at all medical facilities in high prevalence countries.
- Ensure that 100 percent of patients receiving HIV treatment and care have access
to effective "prevention for positives" by 2015.
- Ensure that 80 percent of injecting drug users have access to harm reduction services by 2015.
- Ensure that 80 percent of pregnant women have access to services to prevent
mother-to-child transmission by 2015.
- Ensure that 100 percent of young people have access to reliable information about
the epidemic and how to protect themselves by 2015.

Treatment: overall target for antiretroviral therapy
- Ensure equitable and sustainable access to antiretroviral therapy to at least 75
percent of those in need by 2015.

Treatment: additional targets
- Ensure that by 2015 women, children under age 15, and members of key vulnerable populations are receiving antiretroviral therapy in numbers proportional to
their representation in the population in need. Ensure that by 2005 countries have
in place a system for monitoring access to treatment among these populations in
both the public and private sectors.
- Ensure that by 2005 all graduating—and by 2010 all practicing—doctors, nurses,
and medical officers in high-prevalence countries are trained and certified to initiate and follow patients on antiretroviral therapy.
- Ensure that, by 2015, 75 percent of patients with sexually transmitted infections
are appropriately diagnosed, counseled, and treated.

targets for 2005, and coverage targets for key prevention or treatment interventions endorsed by UNGASS as essential elements of a comprehensive response. The proposed targets are listed in box 1.3 and discussed in detail in the appropriate sections of the report.

Organization of the report

This report does not attempt a general overview of the current status of the epidemic and its impact. Instead, it concentrates on the issues that must be resolved if the goal of bringing the global HIV/AIDS epidemic under control by 2015 is to be met. Chapters 2 and 3 consider prevention and treatment and the critical links between them. These chapters review the essential interventions in each area and discuss some of the key issues involved in implementing them on a larger scale. The targets listed in the previous section are discussed in greater detail.

Chapter 4 addresses the growing crisis of orphaned and vulnerable children and touches on some other aspects of the epidemic's impact. Our treatment of impact is far from comprehensive, however, and we treat only in passing critical issues like the effect of AIDS on food security, on education and other sectors, and on political and economic stability. In chapter 5 we turn to financial and institutional aspects of the response to the epidemic, including cost estimates, channels for international funding, donor coordination, capacity constraints, and the role of the United Nations. Our broadest recommendations are outlined in the executive summary. Additional recommendations are listed at the end of each chapter.

Chapter 2

Prevention

Global HIV prevention efforts have reached a decisive stage. On one hand, we now have available a set of prevention interventions whose effectiveness has been proved by numerous successful programs (Global HIV Prevention Working Group 2002). On the other hand, success on a larger scale remains elusive: in only two repeatedly invoked cases, Thailand and Uganda, have well-established national epidemics been reversed (UNAIDS 2002d).[1] While the rate of new infections is stabilizing in some of the hardest-hit countries of Sub-Saharan Africa, it remains far too high, and the extent to which prevention efforts have contributed to the leveling off is not clear (UNAIDS 2004a). Moreover, incidence continues to rise in the newer epidemics in the countries of the former Soviet Union and Asia, despite the experience gained in Africa and elsewhere (UNAIDS 2004a). Even in the rich world, once vigorous efforts to control the epidemic seem to have lost momentum, and risky behavior is on the rise in some populations (Stolte and Coutinho 2002). Thus, on the global scale, prevention cannot be said to be working, despite scattered signs of progress.

Conventional wisdom argues that the problem is one of scale—of bringing a set of proven interventions to those who need them, of moving from projects to national programs—and that the primary obstacle is lack of resources. Indeed, most people in the developing world still do not have access to basic prevention services, and rapid scale-up of coverage remains a central priority (Global HIV Prevention Working Group 2003; Policy Project 2004). There is no doubt, moreover, that the gap between what comprehensive coverage would cost and the resources currently available to developing countries remains large (Commission on Macroeconomics and Health 2001; Global HIV Prevention Working Group 2003; UNAIDS 2004b). For some prevention services, notably prevention of mother-to-child transmission and treatment of sexually transmitted infections, the challenge is indeed primarily that of scaling up, and

The impetus for lasting change must come from communities

of strengthening health systems to make this possible. Health systems, which are even more important to treatment, are discussed in chapter 4.

But for other critical aspects of prevention other challenges are at least as important. In the high-prevalence, generalized epidemics of eastern and southern Africa, successful prevention will require broad-based changes in behavior. At an individual level, we know that using condoms consistently and having fewer sexual partners can prevent most new infections. But at a population level patterns of sexual behavior have often proved resistant to change. Part of the answer is greater coverage of standard prevention services and provision of basic information and motivation for change through the media, schools, and other channels. This will require more resources. But the experience of 20 years has taught that success will require greater attention to two additional factors.

First, we now understand that the capacity of individuals to change their behavior and to protect themselves is often very constrained by economic circumstances, by gender inequities, and by cultural norms. Thus, greater efforts should be focused on addressing these broader obstacles to behavior change, especially the rigid gender roles and inequalities that put both women and men at greater risk. Second, the working group believes that one of the greatest lessons of the few relatively large-scale HIV prevention success stories is that the impetus for lasting change—and much of the difficult work of addressing deeply rooted cultural norms—must come from communities themselves. Donors and national governments can do much to stimulate, support, and expand this local response, but must do so in ways that respect and enhance the leading role of communities and local civil society. Community involvement will be essential to other aspects of the response to the AIDS epidemic as well—this is a recurring theme of our report.

Where epidemics are largely concentrated in marginalized populations, the greatest obstacles to successful prevention are often stigma, disregard for human rights, and counterproductive government policies. The social scorn and even violence that afflict sex workers, men who have sex with men, and injecting drug users in many settings, now often exacerbated by HIV stigma, can be an almost insuperable barrier to reaching these vulnerable populations with prevention services even when resources are available. Many governments refuse to acknowledge the existence of these populations or their right to prevention services, setting inappropriate prevention priorities that endanger those at risk and squander the opportunity to bring the epidemic under control at an early stage. Moreover, many governments continue to pursue failed punitive policies toward sex work and drug use, driving those at risk of HIV infection further underground and enhancing the spread of the virus through incarceration or forced (and ineffective) drug treatment. Although effective prevention interventions for sex workers, injecting drug users, and men who have sex with men are well known, scaling them up will depend fundamentally on protecting

The prospect of greatly expanded access to treatment offers great opportunities, as well as some risks, for prevention

the rights of these vulnerable populations, reversing harmful government policies, and setting appropriate priorities.

Over the last two years, funders, international organizations, and the general public in both affected and donor nations have focused much of their attention on the great challenge of bringing effective treatment to the millions who urgently need it. The prospect of greatly expanded access to treatment offers great opportunities, as well as some risks, for prevention. There is widespread expectation—and some evidence—that the availability of treatment will benefit prevention by encouraging testing, reducing stigma, offering opportunities for counseling and other prevention services, and lowering viral load. More broadly, the movement to expand treatment has brought enormous new energy and substantial new resources to the fight against AIDS in many countries and at the international level.

The working group strongly endorses the new emphasis on integrating treatment and prevention and shares the sense of excitement that it has already brought to discussions of prevention. We caution, however, that treatment access is not a panacea, and that bringing antiretroviral drugs to those who need them will not by itself bring the epidemic under control. Many of the anticipated prevention benefits will not materialize on their own, even if the most ambitious treatment targets are met. They must be earned through deliberate planning and effort. It is worth acknowledging that nearly universal treatment access in the developed world has not eliminated new infections. The next few years will be critical in this regard, since it is now, when ambitious treatment programs are being designed, that effective prevention elements must be built in if the opportunity for better integration is not to be lost.

Moreover, prevention must remain a priority in its own right. While prevention and treatment can support each other in important ways, they often compete for scarce resources, including the time and attention of advocates, leaders, program managers, and staff. If politicians and managers in affected countries focus primarily on treatment, prevention programs will languish even if funds are available. Nonetheless, if the new energy and resources that the effort to scale up treatment has brought are turned to building a truly integrated response, one that incorporates prevention and treatment as well as care for children and affected people—and strengthens the links among them—great progress can be made on all fronts.

For prevention to keep the attention of communities, governments, and donors, it must be infused with a new urgency and focus to match the current drive to scale up treatment. One way to bring this about would be to define clear, compelling, and ambitious goals for global HIV prevention to set alongside the "3 by 5" target that has energized treatment efforts. Such a target already exists: the UNGASS Declaration of Commitment affirmed the goal of reducing prevalence in young people by 25 percent in the most-affected countries by 2005 and globally by 2010 (UN General Assembly 2001).

**The general
principles of
a successful
response
apply broadly**

This goal has received relatively little attention, however, and neither the starting point nor the class of "most-affected" countries has been defined. In the section below on targets, we make specific suggestions on these points. We extend the UNGASS goal to 2015, moreover, proposing the target of reducing prevalence among young people by 50 percent, or to 5 percent in the most affected countries, by 2015. Finally, as a way of linking these outcome targets to concrete action, we propose a set of coverage targets for specific prevention interventions.

This chapter begins by outlining a set of essential prevention interventions, reviewing the current state of access to each, and proposing targets for 2015. We then turn to a series of critical issues that must be addressed if expanded access to the basic interventions is to bring decisive success. These considerations include establishing appropriate priorities, integrating prevention and treatment, recognizing the importance of gender, and increasing community involvement. In closing, we discuss briefly several important controversies in HIV prevention and some promising new ideas and technologies.

Essential prevention interventions

There is now substantial if incomplete agreement on a set of prevention measures that can stem the spread of HIV infection when carried out as part of a comprehensive plan backed by committed leadership (Global HIV Prevention Working Group 2002; UNAIDS 2002d). Some national programs based on these approaches have achieved considerable success, and it has been estimated that making these basic prevention measures available worldwide by 2005 would prevent 29 million new infections by 2010 (Stover and others 2002). Although cultural, epidemiological, and economic differences among regions and countries must be taken into account, the general principles of a successful response apply broadly. This widely accepted approach was endorsed in some detail by UNGASS (UN General Assembly 2001). The necessary measures include:

- Education and communication campaigns conveying basic facts about HIV/AIDS and its transmission, promoting behavior change, and combating harmful myths and stigma.
- Programs focused on vulnerable groups.
- Access to the technical means of prevention: male and female condoms; sterile needles and syringes.
- Voluntary testing and counseling.
- Control of sexually transmitted infections.
- Prevention of mother-to-child transmission.
- Precautions to prevent transmission in healthcare settings.

Each of these measures has proved effective in some settings, at least on a small scale. Although it is difficult to rigorously evaluate prevention interventions,

The evidence is strong enough to justify a concerted effort to scale up known prevention approaches

especially those aimed at behavior change and especially in the developing world, we believe that the evidence is strong enough—and the need urgent enough—to justify a concerted effort to scale up these known prevention approaches, while at the same time continuing to experiment and to gather rigorous data on effectiveness. (See Global HIV Prevention Working Group 2002, and Jha and others 2001, for reviews.)

At the same time, we stress that scaling up these interventions may not be sufficient to bring the full benefit they promise or to reverse the epidemic. As we argue above, a comprehensive prevention strategy must also create conditions that allow people to respond to prevention messages and to make use of technical means of protection. The necessary additional steps include:

- Legal and other measures to fight discrimination against people living with AIDS.
- Legal and policy changes to protect the rights of vulnerable populations at high risk of HIV and remove barriers to effective prevention services.
- Broad campaigns and specific measures aimed at reducing the special vulnerability of girls and women to HIV, changing harmful gender norms, and reducing broader gender inequities.
- Community mobilization to combat HIV/AIDS and mitigate its impact.

These complementary or facilitating policies and programs, sometimes called "structural interventions," may be more important than the prevention measures themselves in some circumstances; we list them separately to preserve a distinction between the technical interventions and what must be done to make them effective. Some of these issues are discussed in greater detail later in this chapter. This section will define the seven interventions and highlight a few key issues. As this is not a technical manual, we will not discuss in detail how best to implement each one.

Information, education, and behavior change campaigns

Awareness and education programs conveying basic information about HIV and its transmission, along with campaigns intended to change behavior, are both a powerful prevention tool and an essential foundation for other interventions. Information and prevention messages can reach people through many channels, from the mass media to conversations with friends and neighbors, and in many settings, including schools, workplaces, and communities.

The mass media—radio, television, print—can be powerful tools for imparting information about HIV and its transmission, combating stigma and discrimination, and improving the milieu for more targeted efforts. Awareness programs must be designed to reach all sectors of society, since basic information is a right and many studies have shown great disparities in knowledge about HIV between men and women, between rural and urban areas, and across education level47s.[2]

The Stop AIDS–Love Life campaign in Ghana employs mass media and community-level interventions

But experience shows clearly that information alone is not enough: campaigns must also provide emotional and social motivation for change (FHI 2002). This requires going beyond imparting basic facts to promoting greater discussion of sexuality, gender, and relationships: silence on these matters has proved a powerful impediment to changing established norms. Although the mass media can have a role here too, in many circumstances community-based campaigns may be more effective in turning awareness into action (Low-Beer and Stoneburner 2003). Ideally, behavior change campaigns should operate on several levels at once and involve a broad range of government institutions, community groups, and the private sector.

What kind of behavior change should mass media and other campaigns promote? The answer depends on the mode of transmission that prevails in the target population, as well as on cultural and sometimes political considerations. Where transmission is primarily sexual, prevention campaigns can focus on making sex safer by promoting the use of condoms or on reducing the number of sexual contacts and delaying sexual debut, or both. (The debate between condom promotion and approaches stressing abstinence and fidelity, which has grown more heated in recent years, is reviewed later in this chapter.) It is clear, however, that these messages will have little effect if circumstances greatly constrain behavior change. In particular, if women are unable to require the use of condoms or to refuse sex, the key to effective prevention may not be increasing knowledge or motivation but strengthening women's capacity to protect themselves (see the section on gender below).

The evidence that broad-based prevention campaigns can impart information is stronger than the evidence that they can change behavior, let alone reduce new infections. But this is not surprising, given the difficulty of attributing changes in behavior to particular influences. An example of apparent success is the Stop AIDS–Love Life campaign in Ghana, which employs both mass media and community-level interventions, including the involvement of people living with HIV/AIDS, traditional chiefs, and religious leaders, to promote safer behavior and reduce HIV stigma. It is too early to know if the program has reduced new infections, but awareness of the program is widespread, and it has coincided with a substantial increase in condom use that correlates strongly with exposure to the campaign (Center for Communications Programs 2003).

The area of family planning demonstrates the possibility of increasing awareness, expanding services, and facilitating the adoption of new technologies and behaviors. This success relied on the range of formal, informal, and media communication strategies now being mobilized to address HIV/AIDS. HIV prevention has much to learn from these efforts, which saw global use of contraceptives quadruple over 40 years and several countries (for example, Taiwan and Iran) go from restricted information and services to full scale-up of effective programs within a decade (Larson 2002; Mason and Westley 2002).

LoveLife in South Africa combines sophisticated media campaigns with adolescent-friendly health services and outreach

Programs focused on youth. Young people are especially vulnerable to HIV/AIDS infection for many reasons, and it is estimated that half of new infections are occurring among 15- to 24-year-olds (UNAIDS 2002d). In some regions, sexual relations between older men and younger women have been identified as an important driver of the epidemic (see the section on gender below) (MAP 2002; UNAIDS 2002d; van der Staten 2002). Many general prevention campaigns are aimed in large part at young people, but a comprehensive approach should also involve programs in schools; youth-friendly health services; community-based projects for young people not in school; and programs to reach young men in the army, in the workplace, and in prisons (UNICEF/UNAIDS/WHO 2002). These projects should provide information and motivation for safer behavior, but also teach relevant life skills and provide condoms. Trained peer educators can be a powerful way to reach young people.

In Uganda, prevalence among young people has declined considerably, apparently as a result of delaying the start of sexual activity, reduction in the number of sexual partners, and greater use of condoms, as discussed later in the text and in box 2.3 (Bessinger and Akwara 2002). It is difficult to know to what extent these promising changes can be attributed to specific programs, however, and we still know too little about what works in protecting young people.

One of the most ambitious—and highly publicized—youth prevention programs in Africa is LoveLife in South Africa. LoveLife combines sophisticated media campaigns aimed at influencing sexual behavior and promoting "healthy life styles" with adolescent-friendly health services and outreach and support programs (Stadler 2001). It is too early to say if the program is working, but it is certainly reaching many young people: 85 percent of South Africans between 15 and 24 had heard of LoveLife in 2003, and more than a third had participated in one of its programs (Pettifor and others 2004). LoveLife seeks to encourage more open communication about sex and sexuality as a necessary foundation for behavior change. But the program has been criticized for shying away from discussion of the suffering caused by AIDS in order to maintain a positive message attractive to young people (Epstein 2003).

Programs focused on populations at high risk. In much of the world, including almost all of Latin America and Asia, HIV epidemics are strongly concentrated in specific populations, including injecting drug users, sex workers, men who have sex with men, and in some circumstances migrant workers, truck drivers, and other mobile populations. Programs directed at these groups are among the most important prevention measures in these settings (see below) (Garnett and Anderson 1995; MAP 2002; Van Vliet and others 1998; World Bank 1999). Mathematical models demonstrate that targeted interventions remain vital even in generalized epidemics, although they are clearly no longer sufficient (Boily and others 2002). In that case, prevention efforts must also reach a much broader population at risk.

There is strong evidence to support a set of approaches, collectively known as harm reduction

Three keys to success in targeted prevention are good local information on groups at risk, strong involvement of the affected groups themselves in design and implementation, and protection from discrimination and police harassment.

Four groups that deserve particular attention are:

- *Sex workers.* Prevention programs for sex workers have generally focused on increasing condom use and on diagnosis and treatment of sexually transmitted infections. Some programs, such as the sex worker collectives in the Sonagachi District of Kolkatta, in India, have emphasized mobilization and collective action by sex workers themselves, while national programs in Thailand and Cambodia have relied more on legal and policy changes and measures directed at brothel owners and sex worker clients (Cohen 2004b; MAP 2004; UNAIDS 2001a). Initiatives in Abidjan, Ivory Coast, and elsewhere have had a more clinical focus, emphasizing prompt treatment of sexually transmitted infections (Ghys and others 2002). All three approaches have been effective in certain settings.

- *Men who have sex with men.* Although the HIV epidemic first came to light among gay men in the developed world—and these communities achieved the first prevention successes—the importance of transmission among men who have sex with men in the developing world has often been overlooked. These communities, which differ considerably in their nature and identity, are strongly stigmatized and difficult to reach in much of the world. Yet the principles of successful HIV prevention in this population are well established and include peer outreach, protection from abuse and imprisonment, and promotion of condoms and reduction in the number of partners.

- *Injecting drug users.* Injecting drug users share the burden of stigma and discrimination with other vulnerable populations, but require prevention services tailored to their predominant mode of HIV transmission: sharing of blood-contaminated needles and syringes. Prevention and effective treatment of drug addiction would reduce HIV transmission among drug users and should be part of a comprehensive strategy.

  But eliminating drug use has proved an elusive goal, and there is strong evidence to support a set of approaches, collectively known as harm reduction, that seek to minimize the harm caused by drug use while recognizing that complete abstinence may not always be possible (Open Society Institute 2001). Needle-exchange programs have been shown to reduce incidence of HIV and other blood-borne diseases without increasing drug use (Health Outcomes International 2002; Hurley and others 1997; Normand and others 1995). Long-term substitution therapy with methadone is also effective in reducing injection and can give addicts access to other medical services and to voluntary testing and counseling (Ball 1998; WHO/UNODC/UNAIDS 2004d).

The main obstacle to harm reduction is national and international drug enforcement policies

Despite the proven effectiveness of these interventions, they are not available to the great majority of those who need them (Global HIV Prevention Working Group 2003). The main obstacle to harm reduction is not lack of resources or technical know-how, but national and international drug enforcement policies that drive users farther underground, increase stigma, and criminalize the prevention measures themselves (Human Rights Watch 2004b; Reid and Costigan 2002; Wolfe and Malinowska-Sempruch 2003). Controlling the galloping AIDS epidemic among drug users in China, the former Soviet Union, South and Southeast Asia, and elsewhere will require moving away from failed criminal enforcement policies toward an approach founded on evidence-based drug treatment and harm reduction. These issues are discussed in more detail below.

- *Partners of people living with HIV.* People whose husbands, wives, or regular partners are HIV-positive constitute a large population at very high risk. This category includes women married to men who frequent sex workers or who have other casual partners, but also men and women whose spouses were infected before marriage.[3] Preventing infection in marriage or in stable partnerships poses formidable challenges. In almost all settings condom use is much lower with regular than with casual partners, and women are in many cases unable to require condom use even when they suspect that their partners are unfaithful. Abstinence is generally not a viable option, and the desire (or pressure) to have children is another barrier to using condoms. Microbicides may represent the best hope for protecting women (and potentially men as well) in these situations, especially if they allow conception (see the section on new ideas below). It should be noted that monogamous partners of people with HIV (as well as infants of HIV-positive mothers) are at high risk of becoming infected, but not of transmitting the virus to others. Thus, prevention services targeted to these groups could have a high payoff in infections directly averted without having the same impact on the epidemic as a whole (including infections indirectly averted) as services for sex workers or injecting drug users. The term "vulnerable populations" has the disadvantage of blurring this distinction.

Voluntary counseling and testing

Voluntary counseling and testing acts as a gateway to other AIDS services, providing access to psychological support, care, and treatment (if available). Counseling can put people into contact with programs for harm reduction, for preventing mother-to-child transmission, and for diagnosing and treating tuberculosis and sexually transmitted infections: these links must be strengthened. Finally, people who know their HIV status are more likely to change

The effectiveness of enhanced STI treatment in preventing HIV may depend on epidemiological circumstances

their behavior and respond to counseling on preventive practices. A randomized trial in Kenya, Tanzania, and Trinidad found that voluntary counseling and testing reduced unprotected sex significantly more than health information alone; the effect was greater among those who tested positive (Voluntary HIV-1 Counseling and Testing Efficacy Study Group 2000).

With the prospect of greater access to treatment, increasing testing is becoming a much higher priority. Affordable testing services should be far more widely available and should be more integrated into healthcare settings. There is growing support for moving away from some aspects of the traditional voluntary counseling and testing model by having healthcare providers offer testing on a routine basis in a variety of clinical circumstances (see the section on this issue below). Testing must always remain voluntary, however. Pre-test counseling may be shortened and in some cases be done in groups, but individual post-test counseling remains essential. Clinics that provide testing must also provide prevention services, including condoms and advice on their use and links to family planning information and services (box 2.1). It will be important to evaluate the prevention impact of changes in the context and format of testing.

Diagnosis and treatment of sexually transmitted infections

Sexually transmitted infections (STIs) can contribute significantly to the spread of HIV, enhancing transmission several-fold (Population Council

Box 2.1

Linking reproductive health and AIDS services

Source: UNFPA/UNAIDS 2004.

Reproductive health and HIV/AIDS are deeply entwined. The great majority of HIV infections are transmitted sexually or during pregnancy, childbirth, or breastfeeding. The prevention, diagnosis, and treatment of sexually transmitted infections are core reproductive health concerns as well as important HIV prevention interventions. Gender inequality, poverty, and social marginalization are root causes of both AIDS and reproductive ill health. Moreover, family planning programs have developed considerable knowledge and tools for conveying information and influencing sexual behavior. Thus, there are abundant reasons to foster strong links between reproductive health and AIDS programs and services. Yet, these ties have generally been weak.

Two recent high-level consultations, in Glion, Switzerland, in May 2004 and in New York in June 2004, reaffirmed the importance of ensuring that AIDS and reproductive health programs are mutually reinforcing. These consultations specifically called for:

- Provision of an essential package of sexual and reproductive health information and services to all people reached by AIDS programs, including voluntary counseling and testing and services to prevent mother-to-child transmission of HIV.
- Provision of an essential package of HIV/AIDS information and services to all people reached by sexual and reproductive health programs.
- Greater emphasis on HIV prevention among women and prevention of unintended pregnancy among HIV-positive women as elements of a strategy for reducing HIV infection among infants.
- Recognition of the links between reproductive health and HIV/AIDS programs in budgets and poverty reduction strategy papers.

There are
now effective
methods for
preventing
mother-
to-child
transmission

2001). Three large community trials in Uganda and Tanzania on the effectiveness of enhanced STI treatment in preventing HIV at the population level gave conflicting results, suggesting its value may depend on epidemiological circumstances (Grosskurth and others 1995; Kamali and others 2003; Wawer and others 1999). Subsequent analysis suggests that this intervention is most important among high-risk groups and where high-risk behavior and STIs are common in the general population. It should be stressed that prevention and prompt diagnosis and treatment of STIs are important health services in their own right. Diagnosis and treatment of STIs should be available whenever possible and certainly wherever antiretroviral therapy is offered; counseling on STIs and appropriate referral should also be incorporated into family planning services. STI programs are thus a critical aspect of integrating prevention and treatment. Counseling in conjunction with HIV testing, as well as broader communication campaigns, offer opportunities to promote STI awareness and prevention.

The primary obstacles to better management of sexually transmitted infections are stigma and inadequate health systems. Another problem is inadequate diagnosis: treatment of STIs in the developing world is compromised by reliance on syndromic management. Cheap and affordable diagnostic kits should be a research priority.

Finally, there is the problem of HSV-2, which is the single largest cause of genital sores worldwide and was found to be a major determinant of differences in HIV prevalence among four African cities (Buve and others 2001). HSV-2 is not generally treated in resource-poor settings; treatment can alter the duration of symptoms, but does not eradicate infection. A large trial of the effectiveness of acyclovir treatment of HSV-2 in preventing HIV is planned.

Prevention of mother-to-child transmission

In the absence of any intervention, babies born to HIV-positive mothers have a 15–35 percent chance of becoming infected in utero, during birth, or through breastfeeding. UNAIDS estimates that 630,000 children became infected in 2003, the majority of them by this so-called vertical route (UNAIDS 2004a). However, there are now effective methods for preventing mother-to-child transmission. In the rich world, transmission rates as low as 1–2 percent are achieved with a combination of triple antiretroviral therapy, sound obstetrical management, and substitution of formula for breastfeeding. In the developing world an influential clinical trial demonstrated that it is possible to decrease transmission by 50 percent with a single dose of the antiretroviral drug nevirapine administered to the mother at the onset of labor and another given to the infant within the first three days of life (Guay and others 1999).[4] This intervention, which can be incorporated into routine antenatal care along with voluntary testing and counseling, is becoming more available in the developing world. Yet, the great majority of

Stigma is an additional barrier and may deter substantial numbers of women from being tested

HIV-positive women in the poorest countries do not have access to effective mother-to-child prevention services (Policy Project 2004).

The main barrier to providing these services in the poorest countries is shortage of trained personnel and the lack of HIV testing. Stigma is an additional barrier in some areas and may deter substantial numbers of women from being tested, returning for test results, or accepting the intervention (Policy Project 2004). Yet a survey of antenatal clinics offering mother-to-child preventive services in 14 African countries found that, on average, 90 percent of women were counseled and 80 percent of women accepted voluntary testing.[5] These services are also a promising entry point for antiretroviral therapy, providing an opportunity for treatment of the family. The MTCT-Plus Initiative uses prevention of mother-to-child transmission as an entry point for providing lifelong HIV care, including antiretroviral therapy when necessary, to mothers, their partners and children, and other family members in eight African and Asian countries (Mailman School of Public Health 2002).

Transmission during breastfeeding is a continuing challenge to preventing vertical transmission (Mbori-Ngacha and others 2001). Replacement feeding could eliminate this component of mother-to-child transmission, but formula feeding is highly stigmatized in some settings. Moreover, breastfeeding is the cheapest and safest way to ensure adequate nutrition and to protect against common respiratory and gastrointestinal infections. At present no proven strategies exist for reducing postpartum transmission, but studies of providing antiretrovirals to either the mother or the infant throughout breastfeeding are underway (Fowler and Newell 2002). Some evidence suggests that exclusive breastfeeding carries less risk of transmission than mixed feeding (Coutsoudis and others 1999).

An additional issue concerning the most common mother-to-child intervention in resource-poor settings is the possibility of compromising future antiretroviral therapy for the mother by inducing resistance to nevirapine, a component of one of the most widely recommended first-line antiretroviral regimens. Resistant strains appear in a high proportion of women who receive a single dose of nevirapine to prevent vertical transmission, and a recent study found that in women carrying these strains viral replication was less likely to be suppressed to very low levels after six months of antiretroviral therapy with nevirapine-containing regimens (Jourdain and others 2004; Martinson and others 2004). But the study did not observe any effect on CD4 counts (a measure of immune system function) or clinical outcomes, and the long-term effect of single-dose nevirapine on treatment effectiveness or duration remains unknown. Studies are underway to address this issue more definitively.

The ultimate goal must be to provide all HIV-positive pregnant women with the more effective three-drug regimens used in the developed world to prevent vertical transmission and to ensure that all HIV-positive women identified during pregnancy also have access to antiretroviral therapy when they

Improved family planning services can also reduce mother-to-child transmission

need it to prolong their own lives. This more sophisticated intervention cannot immediately be scaled up to reach all women in need, however, and the drawbacks of single-dose nevirapine must be balanced against the need to bring an effective, if imperfect, intervention to as many women as possible.

Two additional intermediate options should be considered in some settings. First, a regimen of one antiretroviral, zidovudine, in the third trimester, plus a single dose of nevirapine at the onset of labor has been shown to be more effective than either drug alone and might reduce the risk of resistance (Lallemant and others 2004). Since this protocol involves a longer course of treatment, it would represent a substantial challenge in many settings.

Second, vertical transmission depends strongly on viral load, and it might be possible to prevent a large share of infections in infants by focusing on those women in the most advanced stages of infection. In particular, bringing triple therapy to the relatively small proportion, perhaps 15 percent, of HIV-positive pregnant women who already qualify for treatment according to WHO criteria might avert a large share of transmission even where multiple-drug regimens cannot yet be offered to all.

Finally, improved family planning services can also reduce mother-to-child transmission by preventing unwanted pregnancies among HIV-positive women. Although there are no data specific to women living with HIV, it is estimated that about one third of pregnancies globally are unwanted and that 63 percent of women in Sub-Saharan Africa at risk for unwanted pregnancy have an unmet need for contraception (Singh and others 2003b; UNFPA 2000). Thus, the need to expand access to reproductive health services takes on a particular urgency in high-prevalence areas. Women should be offered family planning information and referral to reproductive health services during post-test counseling in conjunction with mother-to-child preventive services. A recent study concluded that adding family planning to these services would double their impact in averting HIV infections among infants, and that it would be very cost-effective (Stover and others 2003). Family planning services must remain voluntary, and the right of HIV-positive women to have children must be respected. More broadly, better integration of HIV and reproductive health services would bring considerable synergies (see box 2.1).

Health system precautions and blood safety

HIV transmission by blood contamination, nonsterile injections, and other unsafe medical practices has been documented in many settings. A recent series of publications argued that unsafe injections may play a major role in the epidemic in Africa (Brewer and others 2003). WHO and others, however, while acknowledging that unsafe injections are widespread, estimate that they account for no more than 2.5 percent of infections and insist that the great majority of infections occur by sexual transmission (Schmid and others 2004). The working group believes that the evidence at present does not warrant

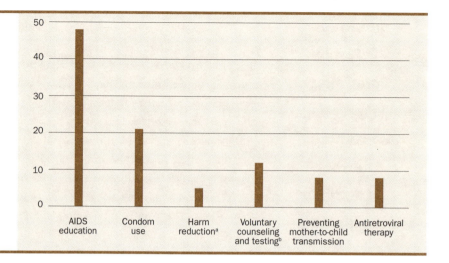

Figure 2.1

HIV/AIDS services reach a small share of the total population in need

Percent of those in need reached

a. Less than 5 percent; exact data are not available.
b. More than 12 percent; exact data are not available.

Source: Based on data from Policy Project 2004; WHO 2002, 2004.

a major shift in prevention emphasis. What is clear is that transmission by unsound medical practices has caused several serious local outbreaks, such as the epidemic among children in Romania and the recent outbreak in China's Henan province resulting from unsafe practices during plasma collection and sales (Hersh and others 1991; Kaufman and Jing 2002). Lack of health system capacity and proper control over blood banks are the major challenges to eliminating these sources of transmission, since the necessary technical steps are well understood (CDC 1999; WHO, UNAIDS, and International Council of Nurses 2000).

Current coverage of prevention services

Access to (or coverage of) most of the basic services described in the last section remains very low in much of the developing world (figure 2.1). Coverage of health services (equated rather loosely here to the fraction of the population in need of the service that has access to it) is difficult to define and even more challenging to measure. The most reliable information on the use of services comes from population surveys such as the Demographic and Health Survey, while the most complete data on service availability comes in theory from surveys of facilities. Data are poor and difficult to interpret. Yet information on coverage is critical for assessing the state of health services and for planning for scaling up, and should be a high priority as health information systems are strengthened.

The most complete set of estimates for a range of HIV prevention services are those developed by the Policy Project of the Futures Group for USAID and UNAIDS, using a combination of service statistics and assessment by local experts in 73 countries in 2003 (Policy Project 2004). For some services (such as voluntary counseling and testing), these data are best thought of as estimates of utilization, while for others (harm reduction for injecting drug users) they are closer to estimates of access or availability. This study expands and updates estimates from 2001, allowing comparison of coverage levels for a few

In only a small minority of countries did more than 30 percent of young women correctly answer five questions on basic prevention methods

services (WHO 2002a). Some information on coverage of other services is available from other sources, including efforts to monitor the 2001 UNGASS Declaration of Commitment (UNAIDS 2003b).

Information and behavior change programs for youth and the general population

The Policy Project study surveyed the availability of AIDS education in schools. Globally, AIDS education was reported to be part of the primary school curriculum in 46 percent of countries and in the secondary school curriculum in 86 percent of countries, although estimates of the percent of students actually receiving this service (50 percent and 48 percent) were lower. These data suggest that coverage of this prevention intervention is relatively high but tell us nothing about the quality or completeness of the AIDS education that children are receiving or about the availability of education and information services for out-of-school youth. According to one estimate, only 8 percent of out-of-school youth in Africa have access to prevention programs (Global HIV Prevention Working Group 2003).

"Percent of schools with trained teachers providing life-skills education" is one of the UNGASS indicators. Few countries (34, including only 12 from Sub-Saharan Africa) reported on this indicator, however, and the data are difficult to interpret (UNAIDS 2003b).

The reach of mass-media AIDS awareness campaigns is still surprisingly poor. The Global HIV Prevention Working Group (2003) estimated coverage at 43 percent in Sub-Saharan Africa, 33 percent in Latin America and the Caribbean, and around 20 percent elsewhere.

Knowledge about HIV transmission and prevention can be considered a key output of information and education programs, although people learn about HIV/AIDS from many sources. By this standard, most countries, even in highly affected regions, are still doing poorly, at least with young people. Household surveys reveal that in only a small minority of countries (7 of 38) did more than 30 percent of young women correctly answer five questions on basic prevention methods and common misconceptions, although majorities answered many individual questions correctly (UNAIDS 2003b). For example, majorities in 13 of 23 African countries, including all those with high-prevalence epidemics, knew that condoms reduce HIV risk (data mostly from 2000). Since condom use remains low in many of these countries—only in Botswana did a majority of young women report using a condom the last time they had sex with a nonregular partner—these data illustrate the gap between information and behavior change.

Information and behavior change programs for special populations

The Policy Project study estimated that only 16 percent of sex workers and 11 percent of men who have sex with men were being reached by targeted prevention programs in 2003. These are disturbing findings, since services

Coverage of basic harm-reduction services for injecting drug users is very low

for these populations are among the most important and demonstrably effective of HIV prevention services.

Condom distribution

The number of condoms distributed by governments and nongovernmental organizations is fairly well known, but it is much harder to define and estimate the number of condoms that are needed for HIV prevention. A UNAIDS costing study estimated that condom distribution in 2001 covered 42 percent of need in low- and middle-income countries, while another UNAIDS report put coverage at below 25 percent (UNAIDS 2002a, 2002d). The Policy Project estimated coverage at 21 percent globally (19 percent in Africa) by dividing the number of condoms distributed for disease prevention (the total minus those used primarily for family planning) by the number of risky sex acts, estimated from survey data.

These estimates suggest that there is still a very large "condom gap." But distribution numbers do not distinguish between insufficient supply and lack of demand, which is probably the main obstacle in many settings. What is really needed is a measure of the extent to which lack of convenient and affordable access to condoms hinders their use for disease prevention.

Harm reduction for drug users

The Policy Project concluded that coverage of basic harm-reduction services for injecting drug users is very low, below 5 percent globally. For example, in the Western Pacific region, where needle sharing is the most important mode of transmission in many countries and where the number of injecting drug users is estimated at 4.3 million, only 5,300 are benefiting from needle and syringe exchange and only 50 are in drug substitution programs (Policy Project 2004). UNAIDS put coverage of harm-reduction services at 19 percent in a 2002 costing study; the source of this estimate is not clear (UNAIDS 2002a).

Diagnosis and treatment of sexually transmitted infections

No source provided a global figure for access to diagnosis and treatment of sexually transmitted infections, but the Global HIV Prevention Working Group (2003) provided regional estimates, all between 15 and 20 percent. These numbers describe access to services but say nothing about utilization or quality. Ideally one would want to know what fraction of sexually transmitted infections are correctly diagnosed and successfully treated: this is one of the UNGASS indicators, but few countries have reported, and data are poor (UNAIDS 2003b).

Voluntary testing and counseling

Estimates of access to voluntary testing and counseling vary considerably, primarily because of differences in the way the denominator in the coverage fraction,

Low voluntary counseling and testing numbers may reflect lack of demand as much as insufficient supply

need for testing, is defined and calculated. WHO put coverage at 12 percent for 2001, using a formula for need based on prevalence. The more recent Policy Project study reached the much lower figure of 0.2 percent, defined as the number of voluntary counseling and testing clients in 2003 divided by total adult population. Although coverage is clearly still low—in Africa, which has higher than average coverage, the numbers imply that only 1.5 percent of adults have been tested in the last three years—the number of tests provided has doubled since 2001.

Two caveats should be kept in mind. First, these numbers do not include diagnostic testing in clinical settings or other types of testing that are not initiated by the client. These kinds of testing are likely to increase substantially, especially as treatment is scaled up. Second, as with many other services, low voluntary counseling and testing numbers may reflect lack of demand as much as insufficient supply. Low awareness of risk, stigma, cost, and low motivation in the absence of treatment could all contribute to low demand for testing.

Prevention of mother-to-child transmission

Globally, only 8 percent of pregnant women are offered services for preventing mother-to-child transmission; in Africa, coverage is only 5 percent. The situation is even worse than this already very low figure suggests, however: many women, especially in Africa, choose not to be tested, and many who test positive do not receive nevirapine or other antiretrovirals to prevent transmission. Thus, the percentage of HIV-positive women who receive the actual prevention intervention is less than 4 percent (Policy Project 2004). There are few data on uptake of the other half of the standard intervention, the antiretroviral dose given to infants at the time of birth.

Safe injection

A recent review estimated that almost 40 percent of medical injections in the developing world are performed with unsterilized, reused equipment, and are thus unsafe (Hutin and others 2003). The rate of unsafe injection in Africa is lower but still high, about 20 percent.

Targets

There are three reasons for the working group to endorse prevention targets and to propose new ones where necessary. The first is to give specificity to the Millennium Development Target for AIDS, which is vague and lacks meaningful benchmarks against which progress can be measured (see chapter 1). A second reason is to infuse new vigor into global prevention efforts. In contrast to the international campaign to expand treatment, which has been energized by the "3 by 5" target, global prevention lacks clear momentum. Compelling goals might help. The working group believes that simple but ambitious overall outcome targets, supplemented by coverage targets for a few key interventions,

Simple but ambitious overall outcome targets, supplemented by coverage targets for a few key interventions, would be the most useful combination

would be the most useful combination. Third, intervention coverage targets are important for estimating resources requirements.

Overall outcome targets for 2015

- Reduce prevalence among young people to 5 percent in the most affected countries and by 50 percent elsewhere by 2015.
- Reduce prevalence by 50 percent in key vulnerable populations by 2015.

We begin by reaffirming the UNGASS target of reducing prevalence among young people by 25 percent in the most affected countries by 2005 and globally by 2010 (UN General Assembly 2001). Unfortunately, neither the date from which reductions would be measured nor the class of "most affected" countries has been defined, and reliable systems for measuring prevalence among young people are not in place in many countries. Perhaps partly as a result of these omissions, this central UNGASS goal is not at the moment attracting sufficient attention. We suggest that reductions be measured from 2000 levels and that "most-affected" countries be defined as those with adult prevalence above 10 percent in 2000.[6]

As the UN Millennium Project Working Group on HIV/AIDS, we need to set a clear goal for 2015. Since the UNGASS target for prevalence among young people has been agreed to by the international community, it makes sense to use it as the starting point in choosing a target for 2015. Moreover, prevalence among young women is also one of the official Millennium Development Goal indicators. Thus our proposed 2015 target builds on UNGASS and at the same time uses one of the official indicators to give specificity to the Millennium Development target for HIV/AIDS.

Prevalence among young people. The UNGASS target focuses on young people (ages 15–24) not only because they are critical to the epidemic, but because their prevalence rate is considered a good proxy for incidence, which is hard to measure directly. Restricting the target to prevalence among young people rather than all adults also lessens the potential conflict with treatment goals. Treatment will reduce mortality and thus may obscure the effect of falling incidence on prevalence. But this effect should be small among young people, whose infections are generally more recent and whose mortality rates should therefore be lower. A target expressed in terms of infections averted would reflect more exactly the ultimate aim of prevention and might be more intuitively compelling, since it would make immediate the connection to lives saved. (This is part of the appeal of the "3 by 5" target.) But it would be much more challenging to define and to monitor.

The examples of Uganda and Thailand demonstrate that a 50 percent reduction in youth prevalence is attainable in 15 years. In the most affected countries (adult prevalence above 10 percent) it is not ambitious enough, as it would leave prevalence among young people much too high. For these countries the proposed target is 5 percent.[7]

Intervention coverage targets are a way to link outcome targets to concrete action

Prevalence among vulnerable populations. In countries with concentrated epidemics, a distinct target for prevalence in vulnerable populations will help to focus prevention efforts where they are most needed and would do the most good. UNAIDS has already suggested that these countries track prevalence in vulnerable populations as part of their Millennium Development Goal monitoring (UNDG 2003). Restricting the target formally to concentrated epidemics, however, would leave out an important class of countries with general adult prevalence between 1 and 5 percent. For the sake of this target, vulnerable populations (or "high-risk groups") would be defined explicitly as injecting drug users, sex workers, and men who have sex with men; the target would only apply to the groups that are important to each country's epidemic. Monitoring progress toward this target will require reinforcing epidemiological surveillance programs in many countries.

Intervention coverage targets

- Ensure that by 2015 affordable HIV testing and appropriate counseling are offered at all sexually transmitted infection, tuberculosis, and antenatal clinics globally, and at all medical facilities in high-prevalence countries.
- Ensure that 100 percent of patients receiving HIV treatment and care have access to effective "prevention for positives" by 2015.
- Ensure that 80 percent of injecting drug users have access to harm-reduction services by 2015.
- Ensure that 80 percent of pregnant women have access to services for preventing mother-to-child transmission by 2015.
- Ensure that 100 percent of young people have access to reliable information about the epidemic and how to protect themselves by 2015.

Intervention coverage targets are a way to link outcome targets to concrete action. Moreover, access to essential services can be seen as a right in itself. These five targets have been chosen for their importance to the overall prevention objective and to highlight key messages of the working group.

Testing and counseling. Access to testing is critical for both prevention and treatment. It is clear that many people who would like to learn their status cannot, either because the service is not available or too expensive, or because confidentiality is not ensured. A target formulated in terms of availability of testing at medical facilities avoids the difficulty of defining and measuring population in need and emphasizes the importance of integrating testing into clinical care. In contrast, the coverage estimates cited above consider only traditional client-initiated voluntary counseling and testing.

Prevention for positives. This target would serve to underscore the importance of integrating prevention and treatment. Giving it substance will require defining what constitutes effective "prevention for positives" (described in the

**Success
will always
require acting
on several
fronts at once**

section below on integrating prevention and treatment). One possibility is to monitor the percentage of HIV patients who receive counseling on reducing risky behavior within the clinical setting or as part of a community adherence monitoring program, or both.

Harm reduction. Harm reduction could be defined explicitly as needle and syringe exchange or opiate substitution, along with adequate information. UNAIDS set a target of 60 percent coverage by 2007, but current coverage is almost certainly much lower than the estimate of 20 percent used in that study (UNAIDS 2002a).

Mother-to-child transmission. A more demanding target for preventing mother-to-child transmission would define coverage by the number of women who actually receive the intervention, thus taking into account the problems with uptake where the service is offered. The target as worded is ambitious in that it is not restricted to women who have access to antenatal services. Thus, the target can only be met by substantially expanding access to antenatal care or by developing ways to provide mother-to-child prevention services outside conventional antenatal care.

UNGASS does not set a specific target for prevention of mother-to-child transmission, but requires that information, counseling, and "other HIV services" be available to 80 percent of pregnant women accessing antenatal care by 2005. It also calls for the proportion of HIV-infected infants to be cut by 20 percent by 2005, and by 50 percent by 2010. Given the relatively low uptake of services where they are offered and the unsolved problem of transmission by breastfeeding, meeting even the 2005 goal would require levels of access that will almost certainly not be achieved.

Information for young people. This is an extension of a 90 percent target from UNGASS. Progress in this area could be measured using the suggested Millennium Development Goal indicator "comprehensive correct knowledge," perhaps supplemented by condom use at last risky sex.

It would be possible in principle to link intervention coverage targets to outcomes, using established methods (Stover and others 2002). Although this would provide a satisfying justification for the coverage targets, it would involve many quite arbitrary assumptions. Moreover, expanded coverage of basic prevention interventions is required on human rights as well as instrumental grounds. Thus, we will not attempt a quantitative linkage of intervention coverage and outcome targets.

Priorities

No single prevention measure can stop the spread of HIV; success will always require acting on several fronts at once. Yet, it is clear that the right mix of interventions depends on local conditions and that some measures are especially important in some circumstances. Moreover, although the ultimate goal may be to achieve universal coverage of all effective prevention interventions,

Some measures are especially important in some circumstances

in practice choices must be made. Even with unlimited funding, other critical resources, especially the time and attention of leaders, managers, and health-care workers, will remain in short supply. Thus, it is essential that developing countries—and donors—place greatest emphasis on those prevention services that are most important in their circumstances.

There is a considerable literature on setting prevention priorities, much of it taking the form of cost-effectiveness analyses of prevention interventions, based in turn on simple epidemiological models (Ainsworth 2000; Creese and others 2002; Jha and others 2001; Kumaranayake 2002; Walker 2003; World Bank 1999). This approach has a number of drawbacks and must be interpreted with care, but it can provide useful insights. One of the most robust conclusions, reached by numerous studies, is that in countries with concentrated epidemics, interventions focused on vulnerable, high-risk populations—peer education, condoms, and management of sexually transmitted infections for sex workers and men who have sex with men; needle exchange and opiate substitution for injecting drug users—are vitally important and very cost-effective. These measures are also important in generalized epidemics, but in those circumstances they are clearly not sufficient to bring the epidemic under control. Priorities in high-prevalence epidemics are discussed below.

The relative importance of different vulnerable populations varies considerably among countries with concentrated epidemics, as do the links among high-risk behaviors, such as injecting drug use by sex workers. Thus, prevention policy must be based on the best possible local information on the size, geographical distribution, and behavior of those most at risk for HIV.

It is important to emphasize that focusing on programs for those at greatest risk does not mean focusing only on the technical interventions themselves. For these programs to be effective, governments must also address the legal and structural factors that often prevent marginalized populations from protecting themselves, even where the tools of prevention (condoms, clean needles) are in theory available.

Unfortunately, the public health consensus on the importance of prevention programs targeted at high-risk populations is often not reflected in national plans and, more to the point, actual resource allocations. For example, a study of expenditures in 12 countries in Latin America and the Caribbean found that only 7 percent of prevention funds were spent on targeted programs, although all but one of the countries had concentrated epidemics (prevalence in the general population below 1 percent) (Opuni and others 2002).

This problem is particularly vivid in many places where HIV transmission is largely driven by injecting drug use. Governments spend their resources on prevention programs for the general public, while ignoring (or actively impeding) proven harm-reduction approaches to reducing transmission among addicts. Some countries recognize the importance of one vulnerable population, while ignoring or pursuing counterproductive policies toward others.

Punitive approaches not only violate human rights, but also worsen HIV transmission

Thailand, where a highly successful 100 percent condom use program for sex workers and their clients is a model of targeted prevention, has taken a diametrically opposed approach to injecting drug users, engaging in harsh crackdowns that have resulted in the deaths of hundreds. Very few injecting drug users have access to needle and syringe exchange, HIV prevalence among injectors reaches as high as 50 percent in Bangkok, and transmission in this population now accounts for a quarter of new cases in Thailand (MAP 2004; UNDP 2004).

Why do programs for vulnerable populations receive less attention and resources than they should? Lack of information may play a role: governments may not fully appreciate the importance of these efforts to controlling the epidemic. But political and ideological considerations are surely the more important factors in many cases. In almost all cases, high-risk groups are already marginalized and highly stigmatized. Governments are often reluctant to admit that these populations exist at all and may find providing services to them politically unpalatable. To the extent that governments acknowledge AIDS as a problem, they often prefer to devote their efforts to campaigns aimed at young people or the general public. These measures are important, since everyone, especially every young person, has a right to basic information about HIV/AIDS, its prevention, and reproductive health more generally, even if his or her risk is low. But they must not be allowed to substitute for providing services to those most in need.

It is important to stress that government attention to HIV transmission among vulnerable populations is only a good thing if it translates into effective and humane services. A more common response is to crack down further on these already persecuted groups, "solving" the problem by imprisoning drug users and harassing commercial sex workers and men who have sex with men. These punitive approaches not only violate human rights, but also worsen HIV transmission among the affected populations by driving them further underground. Even when central governments support appropriate prevention for vulnerable populations, these programs can be blocked by police harassment at the local level. Recent studies by Human Rights Watch documented the ways in which prevention programs in India and Kazakhstan are being undermined by widespread abuse of sex workers and drug users by police and local officials (Human Rights Watch 2002, 2003). Another study showed how violence against men who have sex with men, widely condoned or even perpetrated by local police, fuels the epidemic in Jamaica (Human Rights Watch 2004a). Ultimately, this is a human rights issue—governments are denying basic services, including treatment and care, as well as prevention, to populations that desperately need them—and the solution will ultimately have to be political. But the problem can also be framed as a critical and terribly costly public health mistake, a missed opportunity to make decisive progress against the epidemic.

Epidemics evolve and so must prevention priorities

Epidemics evolve and so must prevention priorities. Specific patterns of behavior and vulnerability are constantly changing, and prevention programs must carefully track these changes and respond quickly, a point made with particular clarity in a recent report on Asia by the Monitoring the AIDS Pandemic Network (MAP 2004). In addition, concentrated epidemics can turn into generalized ones. Indeed, much concern has been expressed in recent years that the countries of Asia could "follow in the path of Africa" if appropriate action is not taken, with nascent or concentrated HIV epidemics evolving into high-prevalence epidemics. Although the danger cannot be dismissed, the rhetoric is imprecise (is the "path of Africa" that of Swaziland or that of Senegal or Ghana?) and misleading (why should any or all of the very diverse Asian epidemics become like those of southern Africa, instead of, say, those of South America?). Moreover, excessive emphasis on the possibility of generalized spread of HIV could actually be counterproductive, encouraging governments to focus on broad prevention initiatives instead of on those that can help the people most at risk, thus making the feared outcome more likely. Finally, too much stress on the danger of spread into the "general population," while perhaps intended to motivate government action, could worsen the situation of already marginalized populations by focusing attention on preventing transmission from "them" to "us" rather than among those most at risk.

In countries with generalized epidemics driven by heterosexual transmission, prevention priorities are quite different. While it is still important to focus special attention on those at greatest risk, both of becoming infected and of passing the virus on to others, a much greater share of the population is at real risk and must be reached by effective services. Where prevalence is high, broad-based behavior change must be the highest prevention priority. Addressing gender inequities, involving communities as a whole, and strong links between family planning and HIV prevention services become essential, as does prevention of mother-to-child transmission. In a broad sense, young people become the most important segment of the population for prevention. But young people are not a homogeneous group and here too detailed, local information can be critical to reaching those whose circumstances or behavior puts them at greatest risk.

Integrating prevention and treatment

The prospect of greatly expanded treatment in the developing world offers an enormously important opportunity for prevention, as well as significant risks. In the most affluent nations, where antiretroviral therapy is widely available, links to prevention have often been poorly developed. Prevention programs have focused on helping HIV-negative people to protect themselves from infection, while prevention has not been systematically incorporated into clinical care for people living with the virus. It is now widely recognized, however, that prevention efforts targeted at HIV-positive people should be strengthened, and

Knowing that treatment is available provides a strong motivation for learning one's status

that this will require much stronger integration of prevention and treatment. This is the essential message of the Center for Disease Control's influential (and controversial) new prevention strategy for the United States (CDC 2003a). In the developing world this is a critical moment, when ambitious new treatment programs are being planned, to ensure the integration of prevention from the outset (Global HIV Prevention Working Group 2004).

This section will outline briefly the ways that treatment and prevention interact and sketch some preliminary recommendations for making the most of the opportunities opened by increased treatment. These issues are discussed in greater detail in the recent report of the Global HIV Prevention Working Group, *HIV Prevention in the Era of Expanded Treatment Access* (2004), whose findings and recommendations we strongly endorse.

How treatment helps prevention

There are a number of ways that increasing the availability of effective treatment could help prevention. Although the evidence is mostly from small pilot programs, it is nonetheless encouraging.

Increased demand for testing. Knowing that treatment is available provides a strong motivation for learning one's status. Testing is in turn an important opportunity for prevention counseling, as well as a link to other prevention services, including prevention and treatment of sexually transmitted infections and prevention of vertical transmission. Several small-scale treatment programs in developing countries have reported large jumps in testing. For example, Médecins Sans Frontières reports that the number of people coming forward for testing has increased twelvefold since 1998 in the district surrounding the South African township of Khayelitsha, where it has operated a pioneering treatment program since 1999 (MSF South Africa and others 2003). Similarly, voluntary testing increased threefold in the first two years of Partners in Health's HIV care project in rural Haiti (Mukherjee and others 2003).

Decreased stigma. Increasing access to treatment may reduce stigma, by mitigating the fear that is one of the sources of stigma and by demonstrating that the lives of people living with HIV are valued. This effect is hard to measure, but it makes intuitive sense, and there seems little doubt that stigma has decreased in the developed world since the advent of treatment. Decreasing stigma would help prevention in many ways.

More efficient targeting of prevention programs to people living with HIV. There is much interest at the moment in developing stronger prevention programs aimed at HIV-positive people. These measures, which could include various kinds of group and individual counseling as well as help with partner notification, would ideally be integrated into treatment and care but need not occur in clinical settings (International HIV/AIDS Alliance 2003b). There is as yet little evidence on the effectiveness of these interventions (CDC 2003b). Expanded treatment can give this "prevention for positives"

The most powerful benefits of treatment will come through mobilizing communities to take responsibility for fighting the epidemic

approach an important boost by encouraging more people to know their status and by bringing them into contact with the health system.

Reduced transmission. Infectivity—the likelihood that an infected person will pass the virus to an uninfected individual during sexual intercourse—is thought to depend in part on viral load, the concentration of viral particles in the blood or semen (Quinn and others 2000). Antiretroviral treatment routinely decreases viral load by several orders of magnitude and has been shown to reduce transmission in serodiscordant couples (Musicco and others, 1994). This biological effect, however, would reduce transmission at a population level only if it were not offset by increased risky behavior (see below). Moreover, the issue is complicated by the fact that the period of highest infectivity may occur soon after initial infection, when viral loads are very high. These newly infected individuals will in general not know that they carry the virus and will not be on treatment. There is very little data yet on the effect of widespread treatment on transmission at the population level, although a study in Taiwan concluded that free access to antiretroviral therapy had decreased incidence per prevalent case by 53 percent (Fang and others 2004). A recent modeling study concluded that treatment could indeed significantly lower transmission, but that the effect could be negated by changes in behavior (Blower and others 2003). Another study modeling the possible effects of expanded access to treatment in Sub-Saharan Africa also found mixed effects on new infections in the absence of concurrent expansion of prevention, but argued that if both are scaled up, the availability of treatment might greatly enhance the effectiveness of prevention (Salomon and others 2005).

Community mobilization. It may turn out that the most powerful benefits of treatment will come through mobilizing communities to take responsibility for fighting the epidemic. Low-Beer and Stoneburner (2003) have argued that caring for people with AIDS has been a basic element of community response to the epidemic where prevention has succeeded, in Uganda as well as in the segments of the Western gay community. Strong community involvement in treatment programs, in decision making as well as in important aspects of delivering care, could reinforce this broad community response and set in motion a virtuous cycle of decreased stigma, open discussion, and changed behavior. This is what appears to be happening in Khayelitsha, according to Médecins Sans Frontières (MSF South Africa and others 2003). But for these powerful forces to be unleashed, treatment programs must build strong ties to communities. Where this careful preparation has not happened, the benefits have not materialized.

Treatment and risky behavior

There is thus much reason to hope that expanded treatment will give prevention a powerful boost. But there are risks as well. The most important danger is that the introduction of treatment will cause people to behave in a more risky

Making the most of the opportunities for prevention offered by treatment will require action in several areas

fashion. One way that this could happen is if some people come to believe that AIDS is no longer as grave an illness and therefore take fewer precautions to protect themselves or others. Another possibility is that people on antiretrovirals could believe that they are no longer able to transmit the virus to others, either because they feel healthy again or because they are aware of the possible effect of lower viral load (Ostrow and others 2002). There is some evidence that risky behavior has increased in vulnerable populations in Europe and North America since the advent of effective treatment, although it is not easy to know whether this has happened *as a result of* treatment (Chen and others 2002; Dodds and others 2000; Dukers and others 2002).

There are many reasons why the impact of treatment on behavior may be very different in the very different social and cultural contexts of the developing world. But it would be foolhardy not to plan carefully for the possibility that risky behavior may increase. One important precaution would be to carefully monitor behavior and attitudes as treatment is introduced, so that worrisome changes can be detected early. For example, such a surveillance system in Tamil Nadu, India, recently detected a fall in the percentage of sex workers (among those who practiced unprotected sex) who said that they were at risk for HIV (MAP 2004). Investigators concluded that this change was due in part to increased awareness of antiretroviral therapy and the resulting misperception that AIDS was curable. Surveillance of the kind, which should cover the general population as well as groups at special risk, would allow prevention messages to be quickly modified to respond to such new threats.[8] Although prudence requires planning for the possibility that risky behavior may increase in response to treatment, this hypothetical danger must not be used to justify denying or delaying the expansion of treatment.

Opportunities for integration

Although some of the prevention benefits of treatment may occur more or less automatically, most will come only with careful planning and deliberate action. Since integration of prevention into treatment has not until now been a high priority, relatively little is known about what works. It is clear in general terms, however, that making the most of the opportunities for prevention offered by treatment will require action in several areas.

Testing. In many ways, HIV testing is the key point at which prevention and treatment interact. Reaching far more of those who could benefit from treatment in the developing world, and reaching them when they can be helped most easily, will require a drastic increase in testing. This will require scaling up access to voluntary counseling and testing and, at least in the high-prevalence countries, changes in testing policy, in particular adoption of routine offer of testing in certain clinical settings (see the section on this issue below). As discussed earlier, broader knowledge of serostatus could bring many benefits for prevention, including changes in risky sexual behavior and prevention of

Poverty can powerfully constrain people's freedom to make safer choices

mother-to-child transmission. But for these benefits to be realized, testing will have to be well linked to appropriate services.

Prevention in the clinical setting. HIV care and especially antiretroviral therapy bring HIV-positive patients into regular contact with healthcare providers, offering an important opportunity for prevention. This can take several forms (CDC 2003a, 2003b; International HIV/AIDS Alliance 2003b). First, counseling on reducing risky behavior and protecting one's partners should be built into treatment protocols. Help with notifying partners can also be provided. This can be done by lay counselors, including people living with HIV, as well as by nurses and other trained care providers. Second, clinical HIV care should include diagnosis and treatment of sexually transmitted infections. Although the ability to provide this critical service should not be a prerequisite for beginning antiretroviral therapy, its availability at every facility providing antiretrovirals should be an important goal (WHO/UNAIDS 2004b). Third, treatment sites should provide referral to other reproductive health services, including family planning, safe motherhood, and services to prevent gender-based violence (see box 2.1). Finally, condoms and education on how to use them should be readily available at every treatment site.

Integration in the community. Community outreach will be critical to the success of treatment programs in resource-poor settings (International HIV Treatment Preparedness Summit 2003). Community understanding and involvement in treatment (sometimes called "treatment preparedness") should be tightly linked to understanding and participation in prevention. One way to reinforce these ties is through community outreach mechanisms for monitoring adherence to antiretroviral therapy (Walton and others 2004).

Harmonization of messages. Finally, prevention and treatment programs will have to ensure that the messages they seek to communicate serve to reinforce each other. Prevention messages should reaffirm the value and importance of treatment while guarding against increases in risky behavior, while treatment education should reinforce the importance of prevention.

Gender and HIV prevention

It has become increasingly clear that attempts to prevent HIV by changing sexual behavior (encouraging condom use and reducing the numbers of sexual partners) will have only limited success in many settings unless they take into greater account the economic, social, and cultural environment in which individual choices are made. Poverty can powerfully constrain people's freedom to make safer choices, for example by obliging men to migrate far from their families to find work or by forcing women to enter or remain in unsafe relationships. All individual choices are strongly influenced by cultural and community values and norms, making lasting change in sexual behavior as much a matter of social as individual transformation. These broader considerations are particularly relevant in countries with generalized epidemics, where

Gender inequality and gender roles are in many settings the most important underlying influences on vulnerability to HIV

clinical and narrowly focused prevention interventions, although important, will not be sufficient to reverse the epidemic and broad-based behavior change will be necessary.

Gender inequality

Gender inequality and gender roles are in many settings the most important underlying influences on vulnerability to HIV. In fact, the AIDS epidemic cannot be understood, nor can effective responses be developed, without taking into account the fundamental ways that gender influences the spread of the disease, its impact, and the success of prevention efforts. On one hand, AIDS is a gender issue because women and girls bear a disproportionate and increasing share of the suffering caused by the epidemic. But gender and AIDS are entwined in much deeper ways, since gender differences, and particularly the subordinate position of women in most societies, increase risk for both men and women. At a minimum, the crucial links between gender and HIV/ AIDS require that prevention and treatment programs must take gender into account. Decisive success against the epidemic, however, will require attacking gender inequities themselves. This section will first outline the causes of women's greater vulnerability to HIV/AIDS, then address the broader influence of gender on HIV transmission, and finally recommend some concrete actions that could lessen the epidemic's disproportionate impact on women and facilitate HIV prevention more broadly by combating gender inequities.

The relative powerlessness of women and girls in most societies, together with socially constructed gender roles and attitudes, render women more vulnerable to the epidemic in a variety of ways (Rao Gupta 2000; UNAIDS/UNFPA/ UNIFEM 2004; Weiss and Rao Gupta 1998; WHO Department of Gender and Women's Health 2003). First, lower levels of education, coupled with cultural attitudes surrounding women and sex, make it more difficult for women to obtain information about HIV. Second, subordination to men in marriage and elsewhere, reinforced by fear of violence (see below), can make it difficult or impossible for women to refuse sex or to demand the use of condoms. Third, lack of economic opportunity can oblige women and girls to enter into and remain in dangerous relationships. Biology plays a role as well, as the virus is more easily transmitted from men to women during intercourse. As a result of these factors, the proportion of people living with HIV who are women is rising steadily, from 41 percent in 1997 to 48 percent at the end of 2003 (UNAIDS 2004a).[9] This global average conceals considerable geographic variation (map 2.1). The share of women is highest where heterosexual transmission predominates, reaching 57 percent in Sub-Saharan Africa (UNAIDS 2004a).[10]

Young women are at particular risk. In Sub-Saharan Africa, rates of HIV infection are more than three times as high among women ages 15–24 than among boys of the same age (UNAIDS 2004a). In parts of eastern and southern Africa, HIV-infected girls ages 15–19 outnumber boys five or six to one in

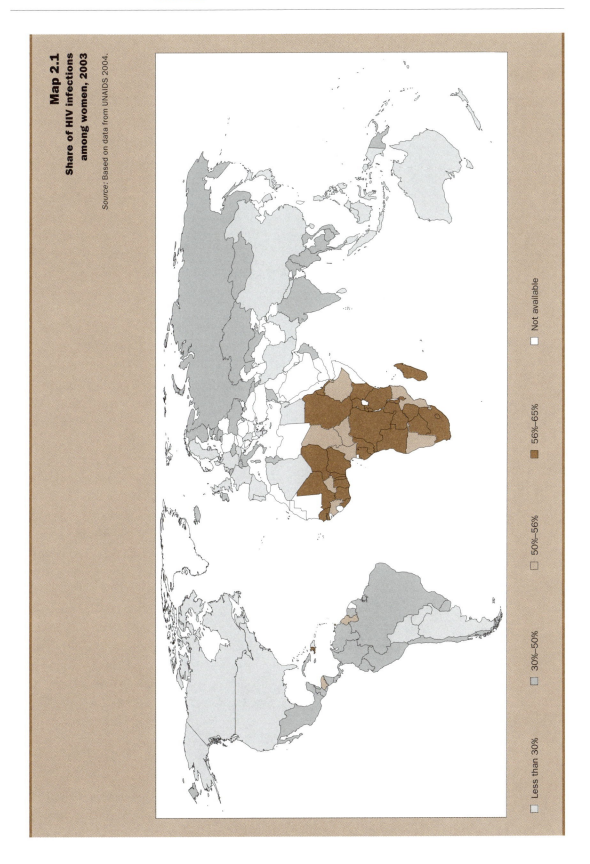

Map 2.1
Share of HIV infections among women, 2003

Source: Based on data from UNAIDS 2004.

Less than 30%   30%–50%   50%–56%   56%–65%   Not available

this age group (UNICEF and others 2002). Prevalence reaches its peak 5 to 10 years earlier among women than among men (Schmid and others 2004). These dramatic figures suggest that intergenerational sex, between girls and older men, is playing an important role in driving the epidemic in these countries (Gregson and others 2002; Luke and Kurz 2002). Although motivations for these relationships are varied, they are often rooted in disparities in economic opportunity (Luke and Kurz 2002; Rao Gupta 2002).

Women also suffer more than men from the economic and social consequences of the disease. Women are often blamed for the spread of HIV and for its introduction into families. Unequal inheritance rights can leave women widowed by AIDS destitute (Global Coalition on Women and AIDS 2004; Strickland 2004). Moreover, women shoulder a disproportionate share of the burden of caring for sick and dying family members (see chapter 3).

Violence

Violence underpins the vulnerability of women and girls to HIV/AIDS. Surveys show that around the world one woman in three has been beaten, coerced into sex, or otherwise abused (Heise and others, 1999). The direct role of sexual violence, including coerced sex in marriage, in HIV transmission is difficult to estimate, but it is likely to be considerable (Gordon and Crehan 2000; Maman and others 2000). In conflict situations, mass rape may be a major force fueling the epidemic. In Rwanda, organized rape was used systematically as an instrument of terror and is widely believed to have contributed to jump-starting the epidemic (Donovan 2002). An organization of widows of the genocide found that two-thirds of surveyed victims of sexual assault during the genocide were HIV-positive (AVEGA n.d.). But it is likely that violence and the threat of violence contribute to the epidemic most powerfully by restricting the freedom of women and girls to enter into and leave relationships, to choose when and how to have sex, to use condoms, and to benefit from prevention and treatment services (Fleishman 2002; Karanja 2003).

Moreover, the threat of violence serves to enforce the broader range of gender inequities which themselves put women at greater risk of HIV infection. Violence against women, especially within marriage, is condoned by many cultures; even where laws against the abuse of women exist, they are often not enforced. The practice of female genital mutilation, widespread in Africa as well as in parts of the Middle East and Asia, represents another form of socially sanctioned violence against girls that may contribute to HIV transmission (Brady 1999; WHO 2000).

Risks for men

While gender roles and expectations increase women's vulnerability to HIV/AIDS, they put men at risk as well, for example by sanctioning promiscuity and encouraging risk-taking (Rao Gupta 2000). After all, where HIV

Developing an affordable and effective microbicide would address the difficulty women face in using condoms

transmission has remained high in spite of widespread awareness, one must also ask why men are failing to protect themselves. Although the constraints that men and women face to safer behavior may be quite different, both must be addressed if prevention is to succeed.

An in-depth study of a failed prevention program among miners and sex workers in the South African town of Carletonville documented the forces that impeded change in each arm of the program (Campbell 2003). While among the women failure could be attributed largely to the sex workers' lack of economic power and to a shortage of social capital in their fragmented and demoralized community, among the miners progress was blocked by attitudes toward sex and risk, as well as by disinterest on the part of their union. In the broadest sense, attitudes toward gender and sexuality shape the entire realm of behavior within which sexual transmission of HIV occurs, and reversing the epidemic may require broad-reaching societal reconsideration of gender roles and relationships. One aim of HIV prevention programs should be to stimulate and support such a discussion, including by encouraging greater openness about matters relating to sex and reproduction. This kind of broad conversation, which may be beginning in parts of Southern Africa (Epstein 2004), will be critical to sustainable, broad-based behavior change.

Gender in prevention strategies

What does gender inequality mean for the fight against HIV/AIDS? At a minimum, prevention and treatment programs should avoid reinforcing harmful attitudes (Rao Gupta and others 2003). For example, Rao Gupta has expressed concern that a common approach to condom promotion, in which condom use is associated with sexual prowess, may do more harm than good (Rao Gupta 2000). Beyond this, programs must take into account the constraints that women and girls face. Thus, developing an affordable and effective microbicide would address the difficulty women face in using condoms by giving them an option more under their control. Cheaper or more convenient female condoms could also give women an additional option; several products are under development. The way that HIV/AIDS services are delivered can have important implications for women's access, and could even contribute to lessening discrimination and stigma. Treatment programs such as MTCT-Plus, which build household access to antiretroviral therapy around women, may serve as an important test of this concept.

More gender-sensitive HIV/AIDS services can reduce women's vulnerability and make HIV prevention more effective. But ultimately the most powerful solutions will be those that address the root cause of the problem: gender inequality itself. Thus, promotion of equal access to education, economic opportunity, and political power; enforcement of equal property rights; and aggressive prosecution of domestic and sexual violence may be among the most important ways to fight AIDS. These issues are largely beyond the scope of the

Working Group on HIV/AIDS, but the UN Millennium Project's Task Force on Education and Gender Equality has identified seven strategic priorities for national and international action. We strongly endorse these priorities, each of which relates directly to HIV/AIDS (box 2.2). We will return to several of these themes later in this report.

The Global Coalition on Women and AIDS

In February 2004 UNAIDS convened a Global Coalition on Women and AIDS that brings together a broad range of regional and global civil society

---

Box 2.2

Priorities of the Task Force on Education and Gender Equality

Source: UN Millennium Project 2005d.

The Task Force on Education and Gender Equality has identified seven strategic priorities. Progress toward each would help to combat HIV/AIDS.

1. *Strengthening opportunities for postprimary education for girls, while simultaneously meeting commitments to universal primary education.* Girls' education can reduce vulnerability to HIV directly, by providing information on HIV/AIDS and relevant life skills, and indirectly, by increasing economic opportunity and thus choices and bargaining power in relationships.

2. *Guaranteeing sexual and reproductive health rights.* These rights include access to services for prevention and treatment of sexually transmitted infections, family planning (including access to condoms), and promotion of open discussion of sexuality and gender roles. All three contribute to HIV prevention.

3. *Investing in infrastructure to reduce women's and girls' time burdens.* Women and girls often spend many hours a day in routine household tasks, such as gathering firewood and water and walking long distances to markets. Relieving this burden through investments in modern fuels, water systems, and roads could allow girls to stay in school and free women to take jobs outside the home. Access to education and economic opportunity reduces HIV risk. Furthermore, these improvements would lessen the burden on women caring for sick family members.

4. *Guaranteeing women's and girls' property and inheritance rights.* Protecting inheritance and property rights makes women safer from HIV by increasing their bargaining power. Ensuring these rights would also reduce the impoverishment of women widowed by AIDS.

5. *Eliminating gender inequality in employment by decreasing women's reliance on informal employment, closing gender gaps in earnings, and reducing occupational segregation.* Greater economic opportunity reduces HIV risk by providing income for health services, by increasing women's status and bargaining power, and by reducing the impoverishment of women widowed by AIDS or living with HIV/AIDS themselves.

6. *Increasing women's share of seats in national parliaments and local government bodies.* Greater political power would give women more influence over policy and legislation affecting women's vulnerability to HIV and allow them more easily to lead community and national reexaminations of gender roles and their links to AIDS.

7. *Significantly reducing violence against girls and women.* Violence against women increases their risk of HIV by increasing their vulnerability to coercive sex and by restricting their ability to demand use of condoms or other protections against infection.

Broad social mobilization leading to locally driven behavior change will probably be required

organizations and UN agencies (UNAIDS 2003a). This informal partnership has identified seven priorities:

- Prevent HIV infection among girls and young women.
- Reduce violence against women (promote "zero tolerance").
- Protect the property and inheritance rights of women and girls.
- Ensure equal access by women and girls to care and treatment.
- Support improved community-based care, with a special focus on women and girls.
- Promote access to new prevention options for women, including microbicides.
- Support on-going efforts toward universal education for girls.

Community involvement

The experience of successful HIV prevention programs has demonstrated again and again the importance of community involvement and social mobilization. The example of Uganda has often been invoked to show the importance of political leadership or of particular prevention messages—and both arguments have merits—but the most important lesson of Uganda may be the critical role of community mobilization against the epidemic and local ownership and propagation of prevention messages (box 2.3). It has recently been argued that these were also features of other well-documented large-scale prevention success stories (Low-Beer and Stoneburner 2003). The working group believes that broad social mobilization leading to locally driven behavior change will probably be required if the high-prevalence countries of southern Africa are to follow Uganda's example. Only communities themselves can bring about the changes in sexual and gender norms that this will entail. The prevention efforts of donors and national governments should focus in substantial part on stimulating and supporting this kind of broad, indigenously developed response.

Community involvement, although of a somewhat different kind, is just as important to combating the epidemic where it is concentrated in special populations, such as injecting drug users, sex workers and their clients, and men who have sex with men. Here involvement of the vulnerable populations themselves, including through peer outreach, is critical to winning their trust and drawing on their special knowledge of their circumstances and of the approaches most likely to be effective. It is important, however, to be aware of the limits to the power of these fragile and marginalized "communities," acting alone, to change their circumstances in order to protect themselves (Campbell 2003).

This report cannot do full justice to the rich and complex topic of community participation and mobilization. This section will outline some of the strategies and processes that can fall under this broad and rather vague rubric, review some of the benefits they can bring (as well as some of the risks), and spell out some practical implications for HIV prevention.

Box 2.3

Lessons from Uganda

Source: Bessinger and Akwara 2002; Konde-Lule 1995; Low-Beer and Stoneburner 2003; Mbulaiteye and others 2002; Singh and others 2003a.

Uganda remains the only country where a very high prevalence rate has fallen substantially. As a result, there has been much discussion—and some quite heated debate—about what happened in Uganda and how its success can be replicated elsewhere. We will probably never understand exactly why this dramatic turnaround occurred when and where it did. But several points are clear.

First, there seems little doubt that prevalence has indeed fallen dramatically, from 15 percent in 1991 to 5 percent in 2001, according to UNAIDS estimates. At the end of 2003, adult prevalence was 4.1 percent, although this estimate may not be directly comparable to the earlier figures.

Second, there is evidence that incidence also fell during the 1990s, although perhaps not enough to explain the large drop in prevalence. Directly measured incidence fell 37 percent between the early and late 1990s in one rural cohort; significant declines in prevalence among women ages 15–24 suggest a broader fall in incidence. But incidence may have already fallen substantially in the late 1980s, perhaps after a spike associated with conflict and civil disorder. Since declines in prevalence can lag well behind changes in the rate of new infections, some of the fall in prevalence since 1990 may result from changes that occurred before major prevention efforts began.

Third, survey data suggest that there were significant changes in sexual behavior during the 1990s that could at least in principle account for declining incidence. These changes were consistent with all three arms of Uganda's "ABC" strategy: A for abstinence, or later sexual debut; B for being faithful, or having fewer sexual partners; and C for condoms. Partner reduction may have contributed the most to the decline in new infections, at least during the early 1990s; condom use increased mostly in the later 1990s.

The ABC message has dominated discussion of the Ugandan success story, with much of the more polarized rhetoric focused on the role of abstinence. This oversimplifies a multifaceted prevention strategy by dismissing the significant role of greater condom use and by overlooking other elements of Uganda's strategy, including expansion of voluntary counseling and testing, treatment of sexually transmitted infections, screening of the blood supply, and campaigns to combat stigma. Moreover, the key to Uganda's success may have been less the behavior change message itself than how and by whom it was communicated. Prevention messages similar to ABC have been tried elsewhere in Africa without notable success. What may have made Uganda different was the combination of early and vigorous political leadership on AIDS and impressive community involvement. In the absence of either, the message may not have mattered.

Taking this analysis further, Low-Beer and Stoneburner hypothesize that Uganda's prevention campaign shared with several other notable prevention successes (including that of the San Francisco gay community in the 1980s) a reliance on indigenously developed approaches and transmission of knowledge through community networks rather than more formal channels. They argue, moreover, that these examples of success also had in common community mobilization to care for the sick.

Thus, the lesson of Uganda may be more the importance of genuine community mobilization and locally developed strategies than a particular behavior change message, although the ABC approach, when flexibly applied, may be appropriate for many settings.

Definitions

The term *community* can cause considerable confusion. While it often refers to a group of people living in a defined geographic area, such as a village or urban

Community mobilization generally refers to a broader process of increasing awareness, concern, ownership, and activity

neighborhood, it is also used to refer to larger populations or in a vaguer sense to "the people" at a grassroots level (as opposed to government officials, elites, or outsiders). Sometimes the term is used for groups of people sharing ethnic identity, lifestyle, profession, or other characteristics. In HIV/AIDS work, reference is often made to communities of sex workers, injecting drug users, or men who have sex with men. Clarity in particular applications is important, since the benefits and pitfalls of community approaches will be quite different for the different types of communities.

Community involvement can take a number of forms, ranging from the use of focus groups and other forms of consultation to inform project design and evaluation, to formal participation in decisionmaking structures, to the assumption of various roles in implementation. Community mobilization generally refers to a broader process of increasing awareness, concern, ownership, and activity.

Benefits

Local information. Community members and organizations have a privileged understanding of local circumstances, culture, and capacities that can be vital to the design of programs. Drawing on this knowledge is most valuable when local specificity is particularly important and less critical when a standard approach can be expected to work in most environments. In the case of HIV prevention, local knowledge is critical to identifying vulnerable groups, choosing approaches for reaching them, developing culturally appropriate messages, and to evaluating the effectiveness of programs.

Local capacity. Communities are a reservoir of skills and capacity for implementing AIDS programs. Community involvement in delivering services can relieve shortages of healthcare workers or other highly trained personnel and thus allow programs to extend their reach. Examples include the use of paid or volunteer community health workers to provide home care for people living with AIDS, adherence support for antiretroviral therapy, and support to orphans and vulnerable children. Moreover, community members may be uniquely suited to some tasks, such as peer outreach to young people or marginalized populations. People living with HIV are a particularly important resource and can bring valuable personal experience and a compelling perspective as well as special motivation to various aspects of AIDS work. Finally, community-based organizations, drawing on these advantages and others, are often in a position to deliver a variety of AIDS services more effectively—and at lower cost—than governments or international organizations.

Local ownership. It is a truism in development work that a sense of local ownership is vital to the success and sustainability of development projects ranging from water wells to disease control initiatives: initiatives that are perceived as originating from and controlled by outside interests will often be allowed to fail. But local ownership is especially vital when sustained change

In the context of AIDS, people living with HIV constitute one of the most important communities

is required in deep-seated community attitudes and practices, such as sexual behavior and gender norms.

Local channels of communication. In promoting behavior change, the way a message is transmitted matters as much as the message itself. There is considerable evidence that people are more likely to respond to what they hear from family, neighbors, and friends than from impersonal, distant sources like the mass media, billboards, and leaflets. Community members and organizations thus have a natural advantage in spreading HIV prevention messages and in stimulating broader community discussion of HIV risk, sexuality, relationships, and gender roles. This is one of the most important lessons of the Uganda prevention success story (Epstein 2004; Low-Beer and Stoneburner 2003).

Local autonomy and self-determination. Finally, community participation in decisions affecting citizens' well-being and relationship to government must be seen as a right, a manifestation of local self-determination and full citizenship. Communities and civil society organizations should also be able to hold governments (and NGOs) accountable for the quality and availability of health services. To play this role they must have access to relevant information and meaningful recourse when governments do not deliver.

In the context of AIDS, people living with HIV constitute one of the most important communities (or segments of a community). They can bring special knowledge to the planning and monitoring of prevention and treatment programs and to roles as counselors and outreach workers. Moreover, genuine and visible involvement of people living with HIV can be an important way to combat stigma. Their formal representation on the Country Coordination Mechanisms of the Global Fund to Fight AIDS, Tuberculosis, and Malaria is a promising example of meaningful participation at a high level. The principle of involvement of people living with HIV was emphasized in the UNGASS Declaration of Commitment.

People already living with HIV are not the only constituency with a powerful stake in prevention and treatment programs. It is important that the views and interests of those at risk of infection are also taken into account in priority-setting and planning.

Possible costs and risks

While community involvement can bring many benefits (and is a goal in itself), it can also impose costs. First, genuine community involvement and mobilization is laborious and time-consuming, potentially delaying the planning and implementation of new programs and adding to demands on overburdened health personnel. Second, communities may not always reach the same conclusions as program managers or experts: they may set different priorities or favor approaches that have proved less effective in other circumstances. In some instances communities may make choices that violate outsiders' standards of equity, for example by favoring men over women or one ethnic group

Community involvement can also impose costs

over another, or by excluding groups whose behavior goes against community values. For example, if communities (defined geographically) are given responsibility for determining access to antiretroviral therapy, they may give low priority to sex workers or injecting drug users. This illustrates the importance of clarity in defining "community" and suggests limits to community control. A related risk is that successfully mobilized communities may be able to demand more than their share of resources. Since better-off and more stable communities are generally more able to organize themselves, this scenario has equity implications.

Implications for HIV prevention
These considerations have several implications for HIV prevention. Many apply as well to treatment and care and to support for vulnerable children.

- In high-prevalence settings, raising awareness and communicating basic information about AIDS through the mass media and other public channels is important, but prevention efforts by community groups and local NGOs may be more important in the long run. These efforts can be supported by providing technical assistance, funding, or help in building larger networks of local organizations. Moreover, donors, international NGOs, and national governments should seek to stimulate broad conversation at the community level about HIV and AIDS, sexual behavior, relationships, and gender.
- Communities should be involved in the design of prevention programs in order to draw on local knowledge and ensure that local priorities are reflected. This is important both for programs aimed at the general population and for those focusing on marginalized populations. Participation can take the form of informal consultation or establishment of formal community boards or local AIDS councils.
- Affected constituencies, including but not only people already living with HIV, should be represented on higher level decision-making bodies, as they are now on Country Coordinating Mechanisms.
- Civil society, including community groups, larger NGOs, and organizations of people living with HIV, should be supported in holding governments (and also donors and powerful NGOs) accountable. This will require access to relevant government information and to the media, as well as other political freedoms.
- Marginalized populations at special risk should be involved in prevention programs targeted at them and supported in organizing themselves to protect themselves. But it will often be just as important to involve or ensure the cooperation of brothel owners, police officers, local government officials, and others. Moreover, in many cases legislative or policy changes will also be necessary to protect the rights of these populations and to remove barriers to effective prevention (see below).

- Community volunteers and paid community health workers can play important roles in HIV prevention as well as in treatment and care, particularly as outreach workers and as peer counselors. People living with HIV are particularly well suited to these roles.

Links to other parts of the HIV/AIDS response

Community involvement in HIV prevention can be part of a broader local response to the epidemic. In fact, this response may focus initially on caring for the sick and for vulnerable children, but community groups can be encouraged to integrate prevention (and support for antiretroviral therapy when it becomes available) into their work. In their analysis of the Ugandan experience, Low-Beer and Stoneburner (2003) argue that care for the sick was an integral part of the local mobilization to combat the epidemic that led eventually to reduced transmission. It should be noted that antiretroviral therapy was not broadly available in Uganda when incidence began to decline (and is still available to only a small minority today.) Thus prevention can succeed in the absence of effective treatment, as this and many other examples demonstrate. But the importance of care to the prevention response here and elsewhere provides another strong reason to believe that broad access to antiretroviral therapy can greatly strengthen the forces driving change, especially if treatment is strongly linked to prevention in the community as well as in the clinic.

Issues and controversies

Among the most controversial issues concerning HIV/AIDS prevention are the relative merits of promoting abstinence versus condoms; the potential benefits and risks of moving toward routine, provider-initiated testing; and the policy and treaty barriers to harm reduction among injecting drug users.

Abstinence and condoms

Many successful prevention campaigns among gay men and among sex workers and their clients in Thailand, Cambodia, and elsewhere have had at their core the promotion of safer sex, particularly the use of condoms. There is thus abundant evidence that condoms can be a powerful prevention tool. Social marketing of condoms through the mass media and by other routes has been a mainstay of donor-funded prevention programs. More recently, however, there has been a shift, led by the U.S. government, toward an approach to behavior change that emphasizes abstinence, especially among young people, and reducing the number of sexual partners, as well as condoms. This approach, sometimes called ABC ("Abstain, Be faithful, use Condoms when necessary") owes much of its momentum to an interpretation of Uganda's striking success in lowering prevalence (and, apparently, incidence) over the last 15 years. The evidence indeed suggests that all three kinds of behavior change contributed to the drop in new infections in Uganda, although the unusual combination

"Abstain, Be faithful, use Condoms when necessary"

of community involvement with strong leadership from the top may have been more important to Uganda's success than the particular prevention message (see box 2.3).

The example of Uganda, and those of other regions where prevalence has apparently begun to decline, such as the Kagera District in Tanzania and eastern Zimbabwe, clearly show that abstinence (at least in the form of delayed sexual debut) and partner reduction can be effective in certain circumstances (Lugalla and others 2004; Mundandi and others 2004). Reduction in the number of partners, in particular, should be a central part of behavior change strategies in the high-prevalence epidemics of southern and eastern Africa (Shelton and others 2004). In much of the world, however, where the epidemic remains largely concentrated in high-risk populations, condom promotion must remain the mainstay of behavior change programs.

Moreover, the evidence does not support campaigns based on abstinence only. Studies in the United States show that young people exposed to abstinence-only sex education in schools are abstinent for relatively short times on average and are more likely than adolescents receiving more comprehensive information to practice unsafe sex later (Bearman and Bruckner 2001; Jemmott and others 1998). Moreover, remaining abstinent until marriage offers no guarantee of protection: data from Uganda, Zambia, and Kenya show that married young women are more likely to be HIV-positive than their sexually active unmarried peers (Glynn and others 2001; Kelly and others 2003). Although it cannot be known from these data whether these women contracted HIV in marriage, another study found that husbands of married girls in Kenya and Zambia were three times more likely to be HIV-positive than boyfriends of unmarried girls (Clark 2004). These statistics illustrate the risks faced by married adolescents, especially girls, who are often ignored by prevention campaigns.

In summary, the working group believes that each of the three kinds of behavior change can have a role in particular populations in particular circumstances. Partner reduction is likely to be critical to reversing generalized epidemics. In young people, delayed sexual debut should be promoted only as part of comprehensive campaign that also includes information on condoms; programs that encourage abstinence while denigrating or ignoring condoms may do more harm than good. Most important, the choice of strategy and emphasis should be based on evidence and on local conditions, not on ideological considerations. Earmarking a large share of prevention funds for abstinence-only campaigns is a bad idea, as it prevents managers from designing strategies on the basis of the best information.

Routine offer of testing: beyond voluntary counseling and testing

Voluntary counseling and testing is often called the gateway to both prevention and treatment. If so, it is striking how few people are passing through the gate. It is a nearly universal feature of HIV epidemics that few people know

A nearly universal feature of HIV epidemics is that few people know their HIV status

their status. In Botswana, for instance, it was estimated in 2003 that of perhaps 300,000 HIV-positive people, only about 8 percent knew that they were infected (KaiserNetwork.org 2003b). Not knowing their status keeps people from learning how to protect their partners and children and from accessing treatment. More widespread awareness of status would also almost certainly reduce stigma. Early knowledge of status will become even more important when treatment becomes more widely available, since it is far better (and cheaper) to begin antiretroviral therapy before patients are desperately ill.

At least three factors currently limit testing in much of the developing world. The first is lack of affordable treatment: without treatment there is far less incentive to learn one's status. The second is a shortage of trained counselors to do the extensive pre- and post-test counseling mandated by the standard voluntary counseling and testing model. The third is fear of stigma and discrimination, which inhibits people from coming forward to be tested. The first factor could be changed by scaling up access to treatment, while the second two could be alleviated by modified approaches to testing.

The current model of voluntary counseling and testing arose from the early experience of the epidemic in the developed world, out of concern over stigma and discrimination and the threat of coercive approaches to AIDS control. HIV/AIDS came to be treated differently from other infectious diseases—a phenomenon that has been called "AIDS exceptionalism" (Bayer 1991)—with testing limited by an unusual emphasis on informed consent and counseling, and little focus on partner notification or prevention services targeted at HIV-positive people.

It has recently been argued that these and other features of the response to the epidemic are not well suited to the African emergency, with its generalized, high-prevalence epidemics, and should be revised in favor of a more traditional public health approach (De Cock and others 2002). A central element of such a public health response would be a greatly increased testing program and a recognition that testing serves a variety of purposes, calling for a variety of approaches. Traditional voluntary counseling and testing, initiated by people wanting to know their status, should be made far more available. WHO estimated access to this service in 2001 at 12 percent globally and 6 percent in Africa (WHO 2002a); a more recent study using a different definition of need arrived at an even lower estimate (Policy Project 2004). In addition, however, testing should be offered routinely in clinical settings to several classes of patients, including pregnant women, tuberculosis patients, and patients at sexually transmitted infection clinics.

In November 2003 Botswana became the first country in Africa to adopt a policy of routine offer of testing in clinical settings (KaiserNetwork.org 2003b). The testing rate has apparently quadrupled as a result (KaiserNetwork.org 2004c). In July 2004, WHO and UNAIDS announced a policy on testing that embrace this new thinking (UNAIDS/WHO 2004a). The new policy recommends three forms of testing:

**We urge
countries to
put in place
mechanisms
for monitoring
testing
practices
and ensuring
that testing
remains
genuinely
voluntary**

- Traditional voluntary counseling and testing.
- Diagnostic testing, to be offered when a patient shows symptoms or indications of HIV/AIDS. This would apply to all patients with tuberculosis, for whose proper care knowledge of HIV status is essential.
- Routine offer of testing to patients at high risk of HIV and to all patients in high-prevalence areas when treatment or services for preventing mother-to-child transmission are available.

Unlike voluntary counseling and testing, the second and third forms of testing would be initiated by healthcare providers and might involve substantially shorter pretest counseling. According to the WHO/UNAIDS policy, however, they would remain strictly voluntary. Patients would retain the right to refuse or "opt out," and the provider would be responsible for ensuring that this option is clear. Confidentiality must be strictly maintained in all forms of testing.

The working group endorses this modified policy and urges national governments to adopt guidelines consistent with routine offer of testing in appropriate clinical settings, particularly sexually transmitted infection and tuberculosis clinics, antenatal clinics providing prevention of mother-to-child transmission, and at all medical facilities in high-prevalence countries. Infrastructure, particularly the capacity for post-test counseling, must be scaled up dramatically.

At the same time, we recognize the real danger that in many settings "routine offer" of testing may become, in practice, involuntary if providers do not adhere to guidelines requiring informed consent or mandatory because their perceived authority makes it difficult for patients to refuse. We urge countries to put in place mechanisms for monitoring testing practices and ensuring that testing remains genuinely voluntary.

Policy and treaty barriers to harm reduction among injecting drug users

Transmission among injecting drug users is increasing globally and is driving several of the fastest growing national epidemics (see chapter 1). Harm-reduction measures, such as needle exchange and opiate substitution, have been proved to reduce transmission among injecting drug users, but are impeded almost everywhere by punitive government policies toward drug users (WHO/UNODC/UNAIDS 2004a, 2004b; Wolfe and Malinowska-Sempruch 2003). Almost all the countries of the former Soviet Union and Asia where injecting drug use is driving the HIV epidemic criminalize possession of even tiny amounts of drugs, carry out mass arrests of addicts, incarcerate users for long terms in prisons and forced treatment centers, and in many cases, execute even low-level traffickers. These measures are often part of a "war on drugs" or "social evil" campaign, featuring highly stigmatizing and dehumanizing media images. These harsh approaches drive users further underground, block their access to prevention and care, and encourage needle sharing. Needle exchange and methadone maintenance programs are either illegal or blocked by police harassment and addicts' fear of arrest. Moreover, mass incarceration of addicts

Mass incarceration of addicts contributes directly to the spread of HIV

contributes directly to the spread of HIV, since needle sharing and unprotected sex continue in prisons and treatment camps.

Other groups vulnerable to HIV, such as sex workers and men who have sex with men, experience social stigma, discrimination, police harassment, and imprisonment. For example, recent reports have documented the consequences for HIV prevention of violence and police harassment of men who have sex with men (in Jamaica) and sex workers (in India), even where central government policies are positive (Human Rights Watch 2002, 2004a). But only in the case of drug users are punitive government policies encouraged and even required by international treaties. A series of international conventions require signatory nations to adopt aggressive measures to reduce demand and supply of illicit drugs. While some have argued that the language of these treaties is flexible enough to permit harm reduction, the conventions are often interpreted as mandating punitive, law enforcement-centered approaches to users and as forbidding harm-reduction measures, such as opiate substitution and needle exchange. National governments in any case often invoke the conventions in defense of harsh policies, although there are in most cases strong domestic pressures for these policies as well.

The conflicting imperatives of the fight against AIDS and the international war on drugs as currently conceived have led to an inconsistent response on the part of the United Nations system. On the one hand, UNAIDS and WHO, taking a public health perspective, have for some time endorsed harm reduction as the best way to prevent HIV transmission among injecting drug users. On the other hand, the International Narcotics Control Board (INCB), the United Nations Office on Drugs and Crime (UNODC) (a UNAIDS sponsor), and its United Nations International Drug Control Program (UNDCP) have in the past consistently supported punitive approaches centered on criminal enforcement and have ignored or actively discouraged harm reduction.

There has recently been some progress in reconciling these conflicting messages: UNODC has issued a position paper with WHO and UNAIDS formally endorsing substitution treatment, as well as documents acknowledging the value of needle and syringe exchange for HIV prevention and the importance of creating an enabling environment for outreach to drug users (WHO/UNODC/UNAIDS 2004a, 2004c, 2004d). The INCB confirmed in March 2003 that providing sterile injection equipment and substitution therapy does not contravene the international drug control conventions (INCB 2003). Yet, the INCB continues to warn against the dangers of harm reduction, stating in its annual report that these measures "may sometimes be positive for an individual or for a local community while having far-reaching negative consequences at the national and international levels" (INCB 2004). Moreover, the UN has yet to work with bilateral donors or national governments to bring a single harm-reduction program to scale.

There have been some promising developments at the national level over the past year (box 2.4). Perhaps most significantly, in May 2004 Russia decriminalized possession of small amounts of narcotics (Human Rights Watch 2004c). Methadone remains illegal in Russia, however, and drug users are excluded from AIDS treatment, at least in some cities (Human Rights Watch 2004b). For its part, China has announced plans to legalize methadone, and provincial authorities in Yunnan, site of the country's largest HIV epidemic, are now promoting a range of harm-reduction measures, including needle and syringe distribution and methadone substitution (Cohen 2004a; KaiserNetwork.org 2004a).

The working group believes that the evidence overwhelmingly supports needle exchange and other harm-reduction approaches as the most effective way to prevent HIV infection among injecting drug users and urges both national governments and the UN system to remove obstacles to and rapidly increase access to these proven interventions. We propose a target of ensuring that 80 percent of injecting drug users have access to harm-reduction services by 2015. In addition, we recommend that:

- The international drug control conventions should be revised to explicitly support the full range of HIV prevention services for drug users, including needle exchange and substitution treatment. In the meantime, the UN, with the support of its drug control arms, should actively

---

Box 2.4

HIV services for drug users: the Iranian model

Source: WHO 2004g; personal communication from Dr. Kamiar Alaei, one of the founders of the original Triangular Clinic, to Paul Wilson, November 2004.

Although HIV prevalence in the Islamic Republic of Iran is low, it appears to be rising sharply, and the country faces a significant epidemic among its estimated 280,000 injecting drug users. Unlike many of its neighbors, however, Iran has adopted a balanced approach to the linked epidemics of HIV and drug use, combining drug prevention, harm reduction, and prevention and care services for people with HIV.

At the heart of the emerging Iranian model are the Triangular Clinics, which integrate harm reduction, treatment of sexually transmitted infections, and HIV care and support. The first Triangular Clinic opened in Kermanshah in the western part of the country in 2000. The clinic offers free needles, syringes, and methadone treatment for drug users; voluntary HIV testing and counseling, services to prevent mother-to-child transmission, and antiretroviral therapy for HIV patients; and diagnosis and treatment of sexually transmitted infections. Condoms and a variety of other HIV prevention services are also provided. The clinic has also worked hard, and successfully, to win support for this balanced approach among policymakers, law enforcement officials, and religious leaders at both the provincial and national level. The provincial governor chairs a provincial council on HIV/AIDS.

The approach developed in Kermanshah is now being replicated elsewhere in Iran. Several dozen Triangular Clinics have now been established, including 25 in prisons. The provision of harm reduction and other HIV prevention and care services in prisons is a particularly important element of the Iranian model, since in Iran, as in many countries, much HIV transmission occurs in jails and prisons through needle-sharing and unprotected sex. Religious authorities have ruled that harm reduction programs are consistent with Islam, and policies and legislation concerning drug users are being revised. More broadly, the Ministry of Health is integrating HIV programs into primary healthcare.

Iran's approach to the AIDS epidemic among drug users provides a compelling model of innovative and comprehensive service delivery, a supportive legal and policy environment, broad involvement of civil and religious authorities, and rapid scaling up.

**We propose
a target of
ensuring that
80 percent
of injecting
drug users
have access
to harm-
reduction
services
by 2015**

promote the expansion of harm-reduction programs as a necessary part of a comprehensive HIV prevention strategy.

- Methadone should be reclassified to a less restrictive category under the drug conventions. In addition, methadone and other substitution therapies should be included on the WHO essential drugs list along with other critical HIV/AIDS medications.
- At the national level, syringe and needle possession should be decriminalized and imprisonment for possession of small quantities of drugs should be ended.

New ideas and technologies

Although the working group believes the HIV epidemic could be brought under control by deploying more fully the tools we already have in hand, new strategies and technologies could greatly assist HIV prevention. We will consider briefly the status of research into vaccines, microbicides, and the use of antiretroviral drugs to block infection.

Vaccines

Vaccines are responsible for some of the most spectacular successes of international public health, and they are often viewed as the ideal answer to the prevention of infectious disease. There is no doubt that an effective and affordable HIV vaccine would be an enormous advance, fundamentally transforming the battle against AIDS and perhaps even offering hope of eradication. But such a breakthrough is a long way off: under the best circumstances a useful vaccine will not be available in fewer than 10 years. There is little hope that an AIDS vaccine will contribute significantly to achievement of the Millennium Development Goals. Research continues on many fronts, and a number of candidate vaccines are in clinical trials, although only one has reached phase III efficacy trials (International AIDS Vaccine Initiative 2003).

Although many workers in the field believe an effective vaccine will eventually be developed, several considerations should be kept in mind.

- There is no guarantee that a vaccine is possible. There are many diseases for which no effective vaccine has been developed, ranging from malaria to the common cold.
- If vaccines are developed, it is likely that they will offer only partial protection. Although such a vaccine may be useful, the protection it offers would have to outweigh any increases in risky behavior. The value of a vaccine will also depend on how long the protection it confers lasts.
- It may prove difficult to develop a single vaccine that would protect against the many strains of HIV.
- The clinical trials necessary to prove both safety and effectiveness can be very expensive, since large numbers of people must be followed for long periods of time. These trials also pose complex ethical dilemmas.

Research on vaccines must remain a high priority but not be allowed to monopolize research funding

These challenges must be weighed against the enormous benefit that an effective vaccine could bring. On balance, the working group believes that research on vaccines must remain a high priority but must not be allowed to monopolize research funding.

Microbicides

A microbicide is a substance that can kill or neutralize an infectious agent and, in the case of HIV, prevent infection in the vagina or rectum. An ideal vaginal microbicide would be undetectable, long lasting, easy to use, and effective against other sexually transmitted infections, as well as safe and affordable. Moreover, there would be great value in having in hand both spermicidal microbicides and alternatives that allowed conception. One of the main attractions of microbicides is that they would in theory be under the control of women, who are often unable to require that their partners use condoms. One study estimated that a 60 percent effective microbicide could avert 2.5 million infections over three years (Watts and others 2002).

Several microbicides are now in clinical trials. The Rockefeller Foundation has made microbicides a priority and the Gates Foundation has committed $60 million to the International Partnership for Microbicides, a public-private partnership. Microbicides are likely to be available well before effective vaccines and could be a very important new prevention tool.

Antiretroviral drugs for prevention

Antiretroviral drugs are currently used for post-exposure prophylaxis after needle-stick and, in some cases, after sexual exposure. Recently, however, the idea of using low doses of antiretroviral drugs for on-going prevention in high-risk groups has been drawing attention. Studies in monkeys have shown that the antiretroviral drug tenofovir can block infection by a retrovirus closely related to HIV. Clinical trials are now planned in several countries (Cohen 2003).

Recommendations

- Global and national prevention efforts need to be reinvigorated by ambitious new goals. National governments and the UN system should commit to two parallel targets as part of the Millennium Development Goals process:
  - Reducing prevalence among young people to 5 percent in the most affected countries and by 50 percent elsewhere by 2015.
  - Reducing prevalence within key vulnerable populations by 50 percent by 2015.
- HIV testing must be made far more widely available and must be more integrated into routine clinical care. By 2015 affordable HIV testing and appropriate counseling should be offered at all sexually transmitted infection, tuberculosis, and antenatal clinics globally and at all medical

Global and national prevention efforts need to be reinvigorated by ambitious new goals

facilities in high-prevalence countries. Testing must remain voluntary and strictly confidential.

- Prevention must be strongly integrated into HIV treatment and care. All patients receiving HIV care should have access to effective "prevention for positives," including counseling, condoms, and management of sexually transmitted infections.

- Prevention and treatment messages disseminated through the media and other channels must be carefully harmonized. Prevention messages should contribute to treatment awareness, while treatment literacy campaigns should reinforce prevention. The introduction of treatment on a large scale should be accompanied by increased monitoring of behavior, so that possible increases in risky behavior can be detected early.

- No single prevention message is appropriate for all settings: prevention strategies should be designed on the basis of accurate local information and evidence of effectiveness, not ideology. Donor funds should not be earmarked for abstinence-only campaigns.

- Where HIV epidemics are largely concentrated in high-risk groups, national governments must make prevention services for these vulnerable populations—peer outreach and harm reduction for injecting drug users, programs to increase condom use by sex workers and their clients and by men who have sex with men—the central priority of HIV/AIDS programs. Provision of prevention services should be accompanied by legal measures to ensure the rights of these marginalized populations and to remove barriers to effective prevention.

- Harm-reduction measures such as needle and syringe exchange and methadone substitution have been shown to reduce HIV infection among injecting drug users. By 2015, at least 80 percent of injecting drug users should have access to harm-reduction services. The UN system, with the support of its drug control arms, should actively promote the expansion of harm-reduction programs as part of a comprehensive HIV prevention strategy. At the national level, syringe and needle possession should be decriminalized and imprisonment for possession of small quantities of drugs should be ended.

- The fight against AIDS and the broader struggle for reproductive health should be mutually reinforcing. National governments should incorporate universal access to reproductive and sexual health services and information as an integral part of their AIDS responses. In addition, there should be greater integration of HIV and other reproductive health services, including voluntary counseling and testing, services for preventing mother-to-child transmission, family planning, and safe motherhood services.

Chapter 3

Treatment

Treatment and care must stand alongside prevention as fundamental pillars of a comprehensive response to the epidemic. On the most basic level, care for the sick is a moral imperative, all the more so now that the means are at hand to forestall death and alleviate suffering. Moreover, although prevention is ultimately the key to bringing the epidemic under control, only treatment can prolong the lives of the almost 40 million people who already carry the HIV virus and allow those who are already ill to return to productive work. In the highest-prevalence countries, only urgent expansion of treatment will forestall continued catastrophic rates of illness and death and the attendant social and economic devastation. AIDS is already wreaking havoc on families and communities, contributing to famine, threatening economic devastation, and leaving tens of millions of AIDS orphans in its wake (Bell and others 2003; UNAIDS 2002d). Loss of healthcare workers and critical personnel in other sectors to HIV/AIDS threatens the achievement of all the Millennium Development Goals (Cohen 2002; WHO 2003a). Only treatment can prevent their deaths and avert a multifaceted catastrophe.

Moreover, the current situation, in which access to life-saving treatment is primarily determined by ability to pay, is both fundamentally unjust and dangerous. Recent data indicate that lack of affordable access to antiretroviral therapy creates an environment where resistance can flourish by encouraging dose skipping, sharing with family members, and the use of dual and single therapies (Brugha 2003). This desperate situation also leads to the proliferation of "gray" markets selling vitamins, immune boosters, and other unproved HIV therapies (Plusnews 2003).

More broadly, care and support for those affected by HIV/AIDS, including home-based as well as clinical services, palliative care as well as antiretroviral therapy, constitute perhaps the most elemental response to the epidemic

The expansion of effective treatment represents an important opportunity for prevention

and the suffering it causes. This response, encompassing orphans and vulnerable children along with the sick themselves, serves as a measure of the commitment of communities and societies to those who suffer from HIV and AIDS, closely tied to repudiation of stigma and discrimination and critical to a broader mobilization against the epidemic.

Finally, as discussed in chapter 2, the expansion of effective treatment in the developing world represents an important opportunity for prevention, if treatment and prevention programs are carefully designed to work together at all levels: in the community, in the clinic, and in the media.

After years of contentious debate, a broad consensus has emerged that treatment can and should be rapidly expanded in the developing world. Even institutions such as the World Bank and the U.S. government, which had long argued that antiretroviral therapy was neither feasible nor cost-effective in the poorest countries, are now in the forefront of this gathering effort. The WHO/UNAIDS initiative to bring antiretroviral therapy to 3 million people by the end of 2005 ("3 by 5") has done much to mobilize support for ambitious treatment goals. National governments have announced bold treatment plans. In fact, it is fair to say that the drive to expand access to treatment now dominates the HIV/AIDS agenda at both the international and national levels.

This report will not dwell further on the case for treatment, which we consider to have been well made by others and largely accepted. Moreover, we will not focus on technical aspects of HIV care in resource-poor settings, except where they are relevant to the larger policy themes of this report. WHO and UNAIDS have issued and will continue to issue guidelines for antiretroviral therapy and other aspects of HIV care in resource-poor settings that address these technical issues (UNAIDS/WHO/International HIV/AIDS Alliance 2003; WHO 2003k; WHO/UNAIDS 2004b). Our discussion will concentrate instead on the practical challenges to meeting the working group's target of bringing equitable and sustainable access to antiretroviral treatment to at least 75 percent of those in need by 2015.

This goal implies more than the provision of antiretroviral drugs to a target number of patients. Equity requires that no group is excluded by deliberate policy or neglect, that access is not determined by the patient's ability to pay, and that benefits do not accrue only to those who already have better access to health services. Sustainability has three elements. First, individual sustainability implies a reasonable prospect that provision will continue without interruption for the lifetime of the patient. Second, both individual and program sustainability require that the development of viral resistance be kept to a minimum. Third, program sustainability, especially in the hardest-hit countries, requires that expansion of treatment be accompanied by and closely linked to aggressive prevention, without which the numbers of people requiring treatment will overwhelm health systems and budgets.

If done badly, treatment scale-up will damage health systems and hinder the attainment of other health objectives

None of these dimensions of sustainability should be confused with financial sustainability in the narrow sense: treatment programs cannot be expected to pay for themselves nor, in the poorest countries, should national governments be expected to pay for them without international assistance.

The launch of ambitious treatment programs cannot wait until these elements can be guaranteed. But the urgency of expanding treatment as rapidly as possible must be balanced against the equally strong imperatives of equity and sustainability, and these considerations must be reflected in planning and program design. Failure to do so will bring widespread treatment failure and escalating new infections and will squander a historic opportunity for decisive progress.

Fair and lasting expansion of access to effective treatment will depend above all on building stronger health systems. If it is done well, the effort to provide HIV treatment to millions can help to strengthen provision of all health services and contribute to the achievement of each of the Millennium Development Goals related to health. If done badly, treatment scale-up will damage health systems and hinder the attainment of other health objectives. The challenges are great, but with a sustained sense of urgency, increased resources, effective partnership, and careful planning, they can be overcome.

Essential care and treatment interventions

Comprehensive care services for people living with HIV and AIDS include diagnosis, prophylaxis, and treatment of opportunistic infections; palliative care; and antiretroviral therapy, as well as counseling and a variety of support services. This report will focus primarily on antiretroviral treatment, since this intervention has far more potential than other interventions to significantly and rapidly decrease AIDS-related morbidity and mortality and to decrease the need for other services. We include a section on home-based care, however, because families and communities bear by far the greatest share of the burden of caring for the sick and dying. This will remain the case even if the most ambitious targets for expansion of treatment are met, and far more must be done to support overwhelmed caregivers and their families. Moreover, we will address the links between HIV and tuberculosis, the most important opportunistic infection in many settings, since it is vital that these two great epidemics be tackled in a coordinated way.

Effective treatment of HIV/AIDS became available in 1996 with the discovery that certain combinations of three or more anti-AIDS drugs could substantially suppress the virus for sustained periods. Although not a cure, triple antiretroviral therapy (ART) increases the quality of life of people living with HIV/AIDS, in addition to easing the burden of their care on families and health systems (Beck and others 1999; Dore and others 2002; Egger and others 2002). Antiretroviral therapy reduces mortality by up to 90 percent and the risk of major opportunistic infections by 55–80 percent (Dorrucci and others

1999; Jones and others 1999; Palella and others 1998), at least in the first years of treatment. While it may be that treatment will eventually fail in most people, as the virus becomes resistant to all available drugs, many individuals continue to do well after many years. Survival may be shorter in resource-poor settings because, at least as currently planned, most treatment programs will offer fewer alternative drug regimens. A study in Brazil, however, found that average survival after AIDS diagnosis increased from 18 to 58 months between 1995 and 1996, with the change primarily explained by the introduction of antiretroviral therapy (Marins and others 2003). Most modeling exercises assume that ART will prolong life by three to six years on average, but these estimates are speculative and may prove too conservative.

The advent of effective therapy can in principle bring substantial benefits to health systems in the form of averted infections and decreased hospital stays, which can be set against the costs of therapy: Brazil estimated these savings at $1 billion (Gadelha and others 2002). It is not yet clear whether these benefits will prove lasting, since if and when treatment fails, patients and health systems may again incur some or all of this burden of illness.

Drug toxicity and difficulty in adhering to complex drug regimens, long invoked as arguments against extending treatment to the developing world, have proved much less of a problem than many anticipated. Evidence so far suggests that first-line drugs have been relatively well tolerated; where adherence has been examined closely it has been at least as good in the developing world as in the rich countries (AHF Global Immunity 2003a, 2003b; Coetzee, Bouille, and others 2004; Farmer and others 2001; Laniece and others 2003; McNeil 2003).

As a result, there is a growing consensus that antiretroviral therapy should be given priority as treatment and care are expanded. Yet, other services remain vitally important. Even in the most optimistic scenarios ART will remain beyond the reach of some for years, and even when antiretroviral therapy is available other services remain integral components of a comprehensive care package (WHO/UNAIDS 2004b).

Treatment and prophylaxis of major opportunistic infections are especially important, because they reduce morbidity and mortality both among people clinically eligible for antiretroviral therapy and among those living with HIV who have not progressed far enough in their illness to meet standard criteria for ART (Grimwade and Gilks 2001; McNaghten and others 1999). Many common opportunistic infections can be effectively managed in resource-poor settings. Prophylaxis and treatment of tuberculosis are particularly high priorities and are discussed later in this chapter.

While clinical services, especially antiretroviral therapy, are scaled up, home-based care will remain essential. In the developing world today, the majority of seriously ill AIDS patients are cared for at home, both because hospital care is not available or too expensive and because most would prefer to be

**Dramatic
price
reductions
and sustained
advocacy
have changed
attitudes
toward
treatment**

at home if effective treatment is not available. The burden of caring for the sick is borne almost entirely by family members, usually women and girls. While programs to support caregivers exist in many communities, often managed by community groups, faith-based organizations, or local nongovernmental organizations, they generally remain small and underfunded. Strengthening these programs and building links to the formal health system must be a high priority (see the section below on home-based care).

Current coverage of care and treatment services

In spite of recent progress, most of those who urgently need antiretroviral therapy are not receiving it. Access to other essential treatment and care services is also very low.

Antiretroviral therapy

Since its introduction, antiretroviral therapy has been widely available mainly in industrialized countries, which account for only about 4 percent of the global burden of HIV/AIDS, and in a few middle-income countries (UNAIDS/WHO 2003; WHO 2003h). The initial barrier to the provision of ART in low- and middle-income countries was the cost of antiretroviral drugs. At more than $10,000 per person per year in the first years after its introduction, this therapy was far beyond the reach of national health services and the great majority of individuals.

Except in Brazil, where the government made universal access to treatment an early priority, antiretroviral therapy was available in the developing world only to the tiny minority who could afford to pay for it and through a handful of mostly small initiatives. In the past few years, however, differential pricing by research-based manufacturers, generic competition, partial easing of intellectual property restrictions, and aggressive negotiation by the advocacy and development communities have caused the price of triple-drug therapy to fall drastically to less than $0.55–$1.00 per person per day in some countries (MSF 2003; WHO/UNAIDS/UNICEF/MSF 2003). Recently the Clinton Foundation has negotiated even lower prices, about $0.38 per person per day (Altman 2003; KaiserNetwork.org 2004b). These prices have not yet been broadly realized, however, and costs of about $1.00–$1.50 are more typical (WHO 2004a).

Dramatic price reductions and sustained advocacy have changed attitudes toward treatment and increased availability of antiretroviral therapy in the developing world. The 2003 UNGASS progress report indicated that 80 percent of responding countries have strategies in place to provide ART and drugs for the prevention and treatment of opportunistic infections; 76 percent reported having national strategies to provide comprehensive care services (UNAIDS 2003b).

Despite these important advances, access to effective treatment in the developing world remains very low. As of June 2004 the number of people on

Access to treatment for infants and children in resource-poor settings is even lower than among adults

treatment in developing countries was estimated at approximately 440,000, which constitutes only 8 percent of the estimated 5.5 million people in urgent need (WHO 2003h, 2004a). Moreover, more than half of those on treatment were in Latin America (mainly in Brazil, Mexico, and Argentina), while in Africa, where about 70 percent of those in need live, only 4 percent had access (map 3.1).

Although the number of people on antiretroviral therapy has grown considerably in recent years—perhaps by twofold in the past two years (WHO 2004f)—the increase in the first six months after the launch of the 3 by 5 initiative in December 2003 has been somewhat slower than hoped, only about 10 percent. Unpublished data from WHO suggest that expansion of access to treatment may be accelerating, with coverage reaching 500,000–550,000 by October 2004. Access to treatment for infants and children in resource-poor settings is even lower than among adults, although there are few data on coverage (MSF 2004a).

There is hope to be gained from those countries that are succeeding in scaling up treatment. The government of Brazil, the first developing country to commit to universal access, provides comprehensive treatment services through the public sector to approximately 140,000 people. In 2002, Botswana launched Africa's first national, public sector program to provide antiretroviral therapy to all citizens who need it. Although Botswana is still far from its goal of universal access, the national initiative was treating over 21,000 people in September 2004 and remains the largest free public sector program in Africa.[1] Many countries have announced ambitious plans for expanding access to antiretroviral therapy, and universal access has been achieved or is within reach in several Latin American countries as well as in Thailand. It should be emphasized that no high-prevalence country is close to this ultimate goal.

Despite the relatively modest gains in access itself over the past year, there is no doubt that there has been substantial progress on several fronts, and there is reason to hope that the groundwork has been laid for an acceleration of access. At the international level, guidelines have been developed, drug prices have continued to fall, and partnerships have been built, while in the affected countries plans are being developed and healthcare workers trained to deliver antiretroviral therapy, thanks in part to impetus and assistance provided by the WHO/UNAIDS 3 by 5 initiative. The U.S. government's large bilateral initiative, the President's Emergency Plan for AIDS Relief, is beginning to provide treatment in its 15 focus countries, reaching about 25,000 patients by September 2004, although here too progress has been slower than hoped (AIDS Healthcare Foundation 2004; Office of the U.S. Global AIDS Coordinator 2004). Considerable new resources have become available, from the U.S. initiative and other bilateral efforts, from the World Bank, and from the Global Fund, which has approved grants that could eventually fund treatment for as many as 1.6 million people (GFATM 2004b).

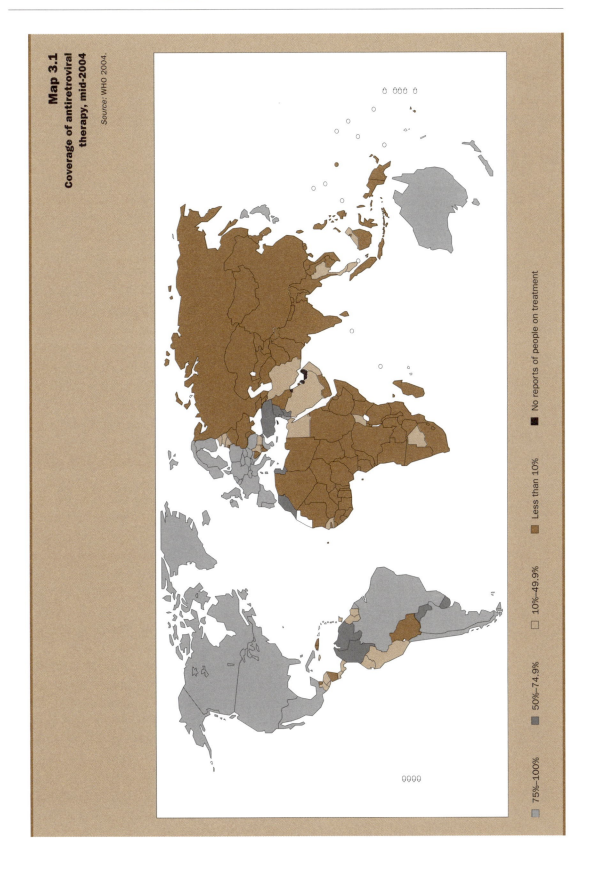

Map 3.1
Coverage of antiretroviral therapy, mid-2004

Source: WHO 2004.

75%–100%　　50%–74.9%　　10%–49.9%　　Less than 10%　　No reports of people on treatment

Other treatment and care services

Data on coverage of other care services are even less reliable than those for antiretroviral therapy, but access is clearly very poor. The recent Policy Project coverage report estimated that only 14 percent of those in need (defined as those in the last two years of life and not on ART) were receiving some kind of external support for home care in 2003, although the small size and informal nature of many home care programs may make this an underestimate. Cotrimoxazole prophylaxis against bacterial infections and isoniazid prophylaxis for tuberculosis are available to only tiny minorities of people living with HIV—4 percent and 1 percent worldwide (Policy Project 2004). Oral morphine for palliative care is also poorly available in Africa (University of Wisconsin 2002).

Targets

The UNGASS Declaration of Commitment recognized treatment and care as "fundamental elements of an effective response" and demanded that national strategies be developed to strengthen healthcare systems and address the factors impeding provision of antiretroviral drugs (UN General Assembly 2001). It set no numerical targets for antiretroviral therapy, but called for urgent efforts to provide the "highest attainable standard of care" for AIDS, including treatment of opportunistic infections and ART where possible.

In April 2002, the WHO announced the 3 by 5 target of placing 3 million people on treatment by the end of 2005, which constitutes about half of those in urgent need (WHO 2002c). The 3 by 5 target was adopted by UNAIDS' cosponsors in November 2003. The WHO also proclaimed a long-term objective of universal access, but did not set a date for achieving this goal (WHO 2003h). Although the target will be challenging to achieve, the 3 by 5 initiative and the accompanying WHO strategy are bold and important steps forward. If successfully implemented, 3 by 5 would be a dramatic advance toward the ultimate goal of universal access.

Overall antiretroviral therapy target for 2015

- Ensure equitable and sustainable access to antiretroviral therapy to at least 75 percent of those in need by 2015.

As discussed in chapter 1, the Millennium Development Goal for HIV/AIDS and its accompanying target lack specific benchmarks, and none of the official indicators covers access to treatment. The working group believes that only a comprehensive and ambitious response to the epidemic is consistent with the spirit of the Millennium Development Goals. We therefore propose the target of achieving 75 percent access to antiretroviral therapy by 2015 to set alongside the target of reducing prevalence among young people by 50 percent or more. We emphasize moreover that this access must be equitable and sustainable. Standards for equity in access are discussed later in this chapter; individual and program sustainability has three components:

It is critical that antiretroviral therapy not be interrupted

Reasonable assurance of uninterrupted and long-term access. It is critical that antiretroviral therapy not be interrupted—by drug stock-outs, by inability to pay, by lack of access to health facilities—once it is begun. Furthermore, once someone begins treatment, he or she should be able to continue for an extended period. While it is unreasonable to require that treatment programs in the developing world guarantee lifelong access before enrolling patients, they should plan to ensure provision of therapy for years rather than months.

Minimization of viral resistance. The development of resistance to commonly used antiretrovirals is a disaster for individual patients; widespread resistance at the population level could be disastrous for treatment programs. Slowing the development of resistance depends, on one hand, on strong adherence support and assured and affordable provision and, on the other, on strong prevention for positives to avert transmission of resistant strains. It will not be possible to avoid resistance altogether, and without better data it is probably not useful at present to set a quantitative target for resistance. This may be possible when we have more experience with large-scale treatment in resource-poor settings. The issue of resistance is discussed further below.

Strong links to prevention. Unless treatment is accompanied by effective prevention, the numbers of people in need will overwhelm treatment programs in the most affected countries. Thus, for these programs to be sustainable, they must build in strong prevention elements (see chapter 2). We have set a target of ensuring that 100 percent of patients on antiretroviral therapy have access to prevention for positives.

Additional targets

- Ensure that by 2015 women, children under 15, and members of key vulnerable populations are receiving antiretroviral therapy in numbers proportional to their representation in the population in need. Ensure that by 2005 countries have in place a system for monitoring access to treatment among these populations in both the public and private sectors.
- Ensure that by 2005 all graduating—and by 2010 all practicing—doctors, nurses, and medical officers in high-prevalence countries are trained and certified to initiate and follow patients on antiretroviral therapy.
- Ensure that by 2015, 75 percent of patients with sexually transmitted infections are appropriately diagnosed, counseled, and treated.

These additional targets are intended to ensure that access to treatment is expanded fairly, that training of healthcare workers is at the center of scaling up efforts, and that other clinical services with strong links to prevention are not neglected.

- *Equitable access.* There is considerable concern that certain populations, particularly women, children, and the marginalized populations

Training healthcare workers is at the center of scaling up efforts

who bear the brunt of the epidemic in many countries—injecting drug users, men who have sex with men, and sex workers—will not have equal access to treatment as it is introduced (see the section on equity). Children, and especially infants, are already clearly underrepresented. A target of proportionate representation by 2015 will help to ensure that these fundamental equity concerns are addressed and that barriers to reaching these populations are overcome. A critical first step will be to put in place systems for collecting data on access among these groups. The resulting data would also be useful in planning prevention programs. Finally, requiring these data from private providers would be a first step toward stronger oversight of ART provision in the private sector.

- *Training for healthcare workers.* Training of both new and already practicing healthcare workers in delivering antiretroviral therapy will be one of the most critical requirements for meeting ambitious treatment goals. HIV prevention and care should be part of the basic curriculum for all healthcare workers. In the high-prevalence countries (defined here as those with adult prevalence above 5 percent), all nurses as well as doctors and medical officers should be trained and certified to provide ART, prevention of mother-to-child transmission, and basic HIV counseling.

- *Management of sexually transmitted infections.* The diagnosis and treatment of sexually transmitted infections is part of the essential package of HIV care services, as well as an important prevention intervention and a component of comprehensive primary healthcare. Including this target in the treatment section thus serves to reinforce the importance of integrating prevention and treatment in the clinical setting and the need to strengthen health systems generally. "Percentage of sexually transmitted infection patients receiving appropriate care" is already an UNGASS indicator, although the Declaration of Commitment did not set a specific target (UN General Assembly 2001). WHO estimated in 2001 that fewer than 18 percent of people in need of services for sexually transmitted infections were able to obtain them (cited in UNAIDS 2003b). The 2015 target of 75 percent reflects results that have been achieved where specific efforts have been made (UNAIDS 2003b). Higher levels might be possible if syndromic management could be replaced by affordable and convenient diagnostic technologies. Following progress toward this target will require deciding which sexually transmitted infections should be included, specifying what constitutes appropriate diagnosis and treatment, and developing improved monitoring systems.

Scaling up antiretroviral therapy

Now that pilot projects have demonstrated the feasibility—and the benefits—of providing antiretroviral therapy in the poorest reaches of the developing world, what remains is the great challenge of scaling up all the systems and

What remains is the great challenge of scaling up all the systems and services

services that will be required to expand access from less than 10 percent today to at least 75 percent by 2015. In addressing this challenge, countries and their international partners must balance urgent need against the requirements of sustainability, the crisis of HIV/AIDS against other health and development priorities. As the UNAIDS 2004 report on the epidemic stated, AIDS is both an emergency and a long-term development issue (UNAIDS 2004a). We cannot rely on conventional, incremental development approaches, yet we must expand treatment in a way that builds for the long term and does not buy progress toward narrowly defined AIDS goals at the expense of other health objectives or other sectors.

After considering the possible magnitude of future need for antiretroviral therapy, this section will outline the major challenges to scaling up and consider some possible solutions. We will focus primarily on the special challenges of scaling up treatment in high-prevalence areas, although many of the main points will be relevant elsewhere in the developing world. Our discussion, especially the sections on service packages and models of care, will make frequent reference to the documents developed by WHO to support its 3 by 5 strategy, which resulted from a broad consultative process.

Estimating future needs

Practical planning for widespread access to antiretroviral therapy in 2015 will require estimating the number of people who will need treatment, as this will determine the demand on healthcare facilities and personnel, as well as the cost. Projecting need this far in the future is obviously difficult. Simple simulations from WHO and UNAIDS, considering mostly the effects of demographic growth and the accumulation of people on treatment as access is expanded, suggest that between 9.5 million and 16.7 million adults will require ART in 2015, compared with about 5 million to 6 million today.[2] WHO estimates that 500,000 to 700,000 children require treatment today.

Three main factors will influence the future need for antiretroviral therapy, not all of them considered in these preliminary projections.

HIV incidence. Since most of those who will require treatment in 2015 have not yet acquired the virus, the success or failure of prevention efforts will be a critical determinant of future need. Thus, prevention is critical to reducing the future burden on health services. Recent simulations for Sub-Saharan Africa shed some light on the possible impact of prevention.

When treatment is scaled up without strengthening prevention, the estimated number of people requiring antiretroviral therapy in 2020 rises to 9.2 million, or almost 2.5 times today's need, even taking into account a modest direct effect of treatment on transmission (Salomon and others 2005). If prevention is scaled up together with treatment, however, and the anticipated synergies materialize, only 4.2 million people would need treatment in 2020, despite considerable population growth. Moreover, the comprehensive strategy

A comprehensive strategy of prevention and treatment would avert 29 million infections, 10 times more than treatment alone

would avert 29 million infections, 10 times more than treatment alone. Thus, choices about prevention—and how it is linked to treatment—have large implications for the feasibility and sustainability of treatment, as well as enormous human consequences.

Effectiveness of treatment. Future need also depends on how much treatment prolongs life, since patients who begin antiretroviral therapy each year join those who began in previous years. The WHO/UNAIDS projections consider the effect of varying year-to-year survival from 80 percent to 90 percent, corresponding to median survival on treatment of about three years to about seven years, respectively. Longer median survival implies greater numbers of people requiring treatment in 2015.

Evolution of access to antiretroviral therapy. For the same reason, need in 2015 also depends on the path by which access to antiretroviral therapy grows between now and then. A more rapid approach to universal access will mean more total patients on treatment in 2015. This effect accounts for much of the range in the WHO/UNAIDS estimates.

Challenges to scaling up

The published literature, recent consultative processes, and surveys of existing treatment programs point to five major obstacles to reaching ambitious treatment targets: weak health infrastructure in high-prevalence areas, particularly a shortage of healthcare workers; lack of secure long-term funding; lack of international and national coordination; stigma; and low knowledge of HIV serostatus (Chang 2003; WHO 2003f, 2003i). The relative importance of these factors varies with the nature and scale of national epidemics and the state of health systems.

Health system weakness. In most high-prevalence areas, health system weaknesses—inadequate physical infrastructure, unreliable drug distribution systems, poor management, weak information systems, and, most importantly, lack of appropriately trained staff—will pose the greatest nonfinancial challenge to scaling up treatment rapidly. In the hardest-hit countries, existing shortages of human and financial resources are compounded by the death toll and considerable financial impact of the epidemic itself (Cohen 2002; Joint Learning Initiative 2004). The proportion of health workers infected with HIV in Africa is especially alarming. The challenge of weak health systems can be overcome, however, by sustained investment in health systems (and human resources for health), coupled with innovative approaches to delivering antiretroviral therapy. Some key features of these approaches, designed to make the most of existing facilities and personnel, are outlined later in this chapter.

Lack of secure long-term funding. There have been enormous increases in international funding for HIV treatment in the past two or three years, particularly from the Global Fund, the World Bank, and the U.S. government's

Health system weaknesses will pose the greatest nonfinancial challenge to scaling up treatment rapidly

initiative. As a result, many of the hardest-hit countries have already received or have the prospect of substantial resources for treatment. In fact, some have found it difficult to spend the funds they have in hand, in part because of weak health systems and inadequate public sector management and in part because of burdensome donor procedures and requirements. This should not be taken to mean that current resources will be sufficient, however: all projections agree that more funds will eventually be necessary (see chapter 5). The most urgent need, however, is for more secure and predictable funding, since no responsible government can commit to a large expansion of antiretroviral treatment without considering how it will be paid for in five or even three years. Development aid in general should be more predictable and longer term—this is a key theme of the UN Millennium Project's synthesis report—but security of funding is particularly critical for HIV treatment, since interruption or suspension of therapy can have dire consequences not only for the individual patient but, by encouraging viral resistance, for the larger community.

Poor coordination. Large-scale treatment will require partnership among donors, international organizations, and national governments; among government bodies; and between the public and private sectors. This coordination has often been missing so far, especially at the national level, where as many as dozens of international entities—bilateral aid agencies and their contractors, international nongovernmental organizations, UN agencies—have pursued duplicative or conflicting agendas. Overstretched national governments have often lacked the capacity to follow all the players, let alone impose order, and have sometimes dissipated energy in internal turf battles. These issues are considered in chapter 5 of our report as they apply to HIV/AIDS, and more broadly in the synthesis report.

Stigma. In countries with concentrated epidemics (and often somewhat stronger health infrastructure), the critical impediment to access to treatment is likely to be stigma and discrimination against those populations, particularly injecting drug users, men who have sex with men, and sex workers, who constitute a disproportionate share of those in need. Stigma against people living with HIV/AIDS can be a serious deterrent to treatment in high-prevalence countries too, but there is much reason to hope that wider availability and awareness of treatment will help to diminish this form of stigma. National authorities should establish clear policies, backed by appropriate legislation, to combat discrimination within the health system.

Low knowledge of HIV status. Finally, lack of access to voluntary counseling and testing (and in some cases lack of demand), resulting in very low knowledge of status, is also an important obstacle to scaling up treatment. When few people know their status, patients are identified for treatment only when their illness is already advanced, which greatly increases the cost and complexity of care. This was apparently a major factor in the relatively slow initial growth of the Botswana national program, where during the first year the average person presenting for testing had a CD4 count of 50, corresponding to end-stage AIDS.[3] Thus, rapid expansion of testing is critical to treatment scale-up (see also chapter 2). It is probably fair to say, however, that no treatment program in Sub-Saharan Africa has been limited by lack of willing patients: even the Botswana program has struggled with long waiting lists.

The WHO/UNAIDS 3 by 5 initiative

Although the drive to bring treatment to those who need it will ultimately depend primarily on the efforts of countries themselves and on the sustained availability of donor funding, the WHO/UNAIDS 3 by 5 initiative has done much to mobilize support at all levels for ambitious scaling up, to strengthen international partnerships, and to lay essential groundwork for success. In December 2003 WHO announced a multifaceted strategy for assisting countries in achieving the 3 by 5 target. This strategy includes close on-the-ground country support and global advocacy as well as the more traditional WHO responsibilities of prequalifying drugs and developing technical guidelines and training materials (WHO 2003h). Results have been mixed: while the rate at which access has expanded has been disappointing so far, progress in other areas, including the training of healthcare workers, is ahead of target (WHO 2004a). WHO's own contribution to the 3 by 5 initiative has been hampered by lack of funds and in-country staff. This constraint has recently been eased by significant new contributions.

Although the 3 by 5 target will be very difficult to achieve—and has been widely criticized as unrealistic—the urgency and ambition of the goal have mobilized extraordinary efforts on many fronts, work which will undoubtedly contribute to substantially increased access to treatment in the coming years. Moreover, while the target was set without much consultation, efforts to achieve it have involved broad consultation and growing partnership. WHO must now extend this urgency and collaborative approach to its prevention work.

Essential services and minimum prerequisites for antiretroviral therapy

Until recently, antiretroviral therapy was viewed as one of the last interventions to be added to a traditional comprehensive package of HIV/AIDS treatment and care services (UNAIDS 2000). A broad range of services, including treatment of opportunistic infections and palliative care, were expected to be in place before ART could begin. However, in light of sharply lower drug prices and the drastic reduction of morbidity and mortality that antiretroviral therapy confers, as well as the de-mystification of ART by experience in resource-poor settings, WHO/UNAIDS issued in early 2004 a set of operational guidelines for high-prevalence settings that place a higher priority on the introduction of antiretroviral therapy. These guidelines were based on the recommendations developed during a consultative meeting on emergency ART scale-up held in Zambia in November 2003 (WHO/UNAIDS 2004b).

Basic prevention services should be provided as soon as treatment is introduced

According to the WHO recommendations, in high-prevalence areas antiretroviral therapy should be initiated in facilities at all levels of the formal health system as soon as they meet certain minimum requirements. These prerequisites for ART include the availability of HIV testing and counseling, personnel trained and certified to prescribe antiretroviral therapy and follow up patients clinically, an uninterrupted supply of drugs, and a secure and confidential patient record system. The WHO recommendations also call for adherence support and community education to be instituted as ART is begun. Other services, including treatment and prophylaxis of opportunistic infections, palliative care, psychosocial and nutritional support, and key prevention services, are to be phased in as capacity is developed in communities and health centers.

Several aspects of these recommendations might have seemed radical until quite recently, including the prioritizing of antiretroviral therapy over treatment of opportunistic infections, the initiation of ART without sophisticated laboratory capacity, and the provision of treatment at the health center level. But there can be no doubt that antiretroviral therapy is the intervention that can have by far the greatest impact. The feasibility of this slimmed-down approach has now been demonstrated by successful pilot projects. These bold choices represent the best chance of saving lives quickly in places where limited health system capacity would impede a more traditional approach. This re-prioritization should not be seen as reducing the standard of care. Most of those who currently receive care in the developing world are obtaining it through the private for-profit sector, which often fails to meet the WHO prerequisites for ART, much less the broader recommended services package (Brugha 2003).

The working group strongly endorses the WHO recommendations on the essential services package, with one caveat. We believe that basic prevention services, particularly safer-sex counseling and provision of condoms, should be provided as soon as treatment is introduced. By condoning the postponement of even such a minimal step toward integration of prevention and treatment, WHO risks sending a harmful message and missing a critical opportunity.

Other prevention services that should eventually be integrated into clinical care include prevention of mother-to-child transmission, treatment of sexually transmitted infections, and assistance with partner referral. These services form part of the larger "aspirational" services package outlined in the WHO guidelines.

Models of service delivery

While the WHO package of essential services defines which treatment services are appropriate at various stages of scale-up, the way these services are actually delivered will be critical to maximizing antiretroviral therapy coverage while ensuring equity and quality of care. The WHO recommendations for service delivery, based on lessons learned from a number of pilot programs and

The way services are delivered will be critical to maximizing antiretroviral therapy coverage while ensuring equity and quality of care

scale-up initiatives, emphasize the WHO's public health approach to scaling up antiretroviral therapy (WHO 2003h; WHO/UNAIDS 2004b). Key elements of this approach include standardized treatment protocols and simplified clinical monitoring, optimal use of existing physical infrastructure and human resources, the involvement of communities and people living with HIV in program design and implementation, simplified record-keeping, and cost minimization, including minimization of the costs of drugs and diagnostics (WHO/UNAIDS 2004b). Pilot programs operated by Médecins Sans Frontières (MSF) and several other organizations reflect many of these principles.

However, current models of service delivery in resource-poor settings are extremely diverse. Lessons are still emerging as to how the many different aspects of service delivery affect efficiency, equity, adherence, and quality of care. Some key variables include:

- The level of the health system at which services are provided (health center, district hospital, or central/tertiary facility).
- The spectrum of services provided and extent of integration with other health services.
- Staffing models and healthcare worker roles.
- Treatment regimens and protocols.
- Strategies for supporting adherence.
- Financing strategy, particularly cost to the patient.

We will touch briefly on each of these topics here; some are explored at greater depth in the working group working paper on human resources for treatment (Hirschhorn 2004).

Health system level. Most nascent public sector antiretroviral therapy programs in resource-poor settings propose to roll out treatment first in referral and district hospitals, where more of the necessary infrastructure is already in place. Although these facilities may be a sensible place to start, it is critical that a strategy be developed to allow treatment to be provided at lower levels of the system, both to reach greater numbers of those in need and to ensure that patients are reached closer to their homes. As the WHO guidelines emphasize, antiretroviral therapy should be provided at all levels of the health system as soon as the basic requirements are met. Although these requirements, such as an uninterrupted supply of drugs, will pose a challenge for many health clinics (and even for some district hospitals), they do not include some of the elements that have been invoked to restrict provision to higher-level facilities, such as the ability to measure CD4 levels or the availability of specialist physicians. Pilot programs, especially those of Partners in Health in Haiti and MSF in South Africa and elsewhere, have conclusively demonstrated that effective treatment can be provided at community health centers (Coetzee, Hildebrand, and others 2004; MSF South Africa and others 2003; Mukherjee and others 2003).

A possible compromise is to begin by initiating antiretroviral therapy at district hospitals, while allowing patients to be followed subsequently at

Integrating antiretroviral therapy into primary care has the potential to reach the most people

community clinics; this was the Botswana model, at least as originally conceived. But where many of those in need live far from the nearest hospital, even this approach is likely to greatly limit access. Functional referral links to higher levels of the system will be critical for managing complications, changing regimens, and handling more complex cases, as recognized in the WHO guidelines.

Spectrum of services provided and degree of integration. Models of ART delivery can be classified according to their breadth of coverage and degree of integration with other services. Three broad categories are antiretroviral therapy only, HIV care only, and full integration into primary care (Hirschhorn 2004). In the first model, antiretroviral therapy is separated from other services in space or time and services are provided only to patients eligible to begin or already on treatment. All other HIV-related care is referred, and HIV-negative persons are not treated. The Botswana national treatment program essentially works this way. Under an HIV care only model, antiretroviral therapy and comprehensive primary HIV services are provided in the same facility, although some specialized services, such as tuberculosis care, are sometimes referred. These services are not integrated into a broader framework of care, and HIV-negative people are not treated in these clinics. The MSF sites are an example of this approach. The third option is to integrate ART into existing primary healthcare services, as the pioneering and influential Partners in Health program in rural Haiti has done (box 3.1). The Rwanda national program has also chosen this approach. Other variants involve integrating ART into tuberculosis or antenatal services.

Integrating antiretroviral therapy into primary care in the public sector has the potential to reach the most people; much of the population in high-burden countries of Sub-Saharan Africa is rural and has little access to higher levels of the health system. For this reason the integrated approach can be considered more equitable.

Integration into primary care is also critical to ensuring that the expansion of antiretroviral therapy strengthens other health services rather than weakens them. The effort to bring primary care clinics to the level where they could provide treatment can benefit the broader health system by expanding the capacity of staff, building logistical and information systems, and strengthening referral links (Walton and others 2004). If treatment is instead provided primarily through specialized clinics, either in the public or nongovernmental sector, there is an increased danger that expansion of treatment will actually harm the rest of the health system by monopolizing resources and management attention and by competing with it for scarce staff.

No single approach will be right for all settings, of course, and less integrated programs may make sense in high-density urban settings, or where HIV patients are rare. Dedicated facilities allow for greater specialization of staff and other efficiencies. In general, however, the working group believes that

Box 3.1

Integration of HIV prevention and care into primary health: Partners in Health in Haiti

Source: Partners in Health; Behforouz and others 2004; Walton and others 2004.

In 1998, the Boston-based nongovernmental organization Partners in Health (PIH) launched a small pilot project in rural Haiti that integrates free HIV care and treatment with robust prevention efforts. Counseling, testing, care, and treatment are not delivered through free-standing HIV care facilities, but as part of a comprehensive primary health effort organized around the diagnosis and treatment of tuberculosis and other opportunistic infections associated with HIV, the diagnosis and treatment of sexually transmitted infections, and women's and prenatal healthcare. Partners in Health currently provides antiretroviral therapy to over 1,500 patients and monitors an additional 7,500 HIV-positive people. Mortality and opportunistic infections have been sharply reduced, demonstrating that high adherence to antiretroviral therapy regimens is possible in even the most resource-limited settings.

An essential feature of the PIH approach is an extensive network of community health workers (*accompagnateurs*) who provide daily directly observed therapy for tuberculosis and HIV as well as social support. *Accompagnateurs* are the essential link between patients—dispersed in rural villages throughout mountainous central Haiti—and the clinics and hospitals where HIV treatment is supervised. Moreover, their presence in the community helps renew faith in the healthcare system, stimulate demand for healthcare, reduce the stigma of HIV testing and treatment, enhance interest in prevention efforts, and involve local residents in the promotion and provision of health. PIH trains and employs over 700 Haitians as community-based health workers.

With support from the Global Fund, Partners in Health has now expanded its HIV treatment and prevention efforts to five new sites across Haiti's central plateau, in the process demonstrating that its model is replicable and can promote primary health goals. At each site, PIH partnered with other nongovernmental organizations and the Haitian Ministry of Health to refurbish clinics and hospitals, introduce essential drugs to the formulary, establish laboratories, train and stipend community heath workers, complement Ministry of Health personnel with PIH-trained staff, and begin aggressive case-finding and treatment of tuberculosis and sexually transmitted infections. Dramatic increases in the detection of tuberculosis and HIV cases and in the uptake of voluntary counseling and testing were documented at one PIH clinic within months of the start of an AIDS project. Patient visits skyrocketed, not only for HIV services but also for prenatal care and childhood vaccinations. While patients are more likely to come for HIV screening once treatment is available, the majority of HIV patients at PIH clinics present for help with symptoms rather than with the specific intention of seeking HIV testing. Firmly situating HIV testing and treatment in primary care eliminates the stigma attached to attending a freestanding AIDS clinic.

The experience of Partners in Health in rural Haiti suggests that integrating AIDS prevention and care into primary care can improve primary health services in general. Rather than siphoning resources from other health priorities, the focus on HIV can generate new sources of income, improve drug procurement and distribution, and spark new interest in applying first-world diagnostics in developing-world settings. Moreover, partnerships between nongovernmental organizations and the public sector can provide essential drugs, expertise, and incentives to staff and thus help to revitalize public clinics and improve both the utilization of services and the health of the community.

the goal should be to integrate AIDS treatment into primary care in high-prevalence countries to ensure greater coverage and maximize benefits to the health system as a whole.

Less integrated programs may make sense in high-density urban settings, or where HIV patients are rare

Staffing models. Since the shortage of doctors, nurses, and other health-care workers will pose the biggest obstacle to scaling up treatment in many countries, it will be essential to make the best possible use of existing staff, while investing now in building the health workforce for the longer run. Some aspects of treatment and care should be delegated from physicians to mid-level healthcare workers and to community and family members. In some programs, the role of physicians is restricted to initiating therapy, managing more serious conditions, and supervising staff, while clinical officers and nurses follow up, provide counseling, and diagnose and treat certain opportunistic infections.

It may be necessary to go even further in delegating tasks: the WHO/ UNAIDS operational guidelines recommend that nurses be trained and certified to initiate antiretroviral therapy in less complex cases. This may be the only logical way to reach the majority of the population in high-prevalence areas in the midst of a human resources crisis. Nurses are often the only medically trained staff at primary health clinics. In addition, although in most cases nurses have not yet been trained to initiate ART, they have been successfully trained to diagnose and manage acute infections through initiatives such as the Integrated Management of Childhood Infections (WHO 1997).

Just as nurses can take on many of the functions of doctors, trained and certified community health workers and people living with HIV can assume important roles in testing and counseling, distribution of medications, palliative care, and community education, thus freeing clinical staff to take on new responsibilities. The Partners in Health program in Haiti has made very successful use of a cadre of community health workers called *accompagnateurs* (see box 3.1). The involvement of community members, including people living with HIV, in delivering treatment has the added benefit of building ties between treatment programs and the communities they serve. Along with community education and participation in program design, these ties will be critical in reducing stigma and in ensuring the acceptability of antiretroviral therapy.

The use of standardized treatment protocols and simplified clinical monitoring is especially important when significant aspects of treatment and care are delegated to lower-level cadres of healthcare workers. The UNAIDS/WHO operational guidelines for ART recommend standardized first- and second-line treatment regimens and fixed dose combinations, simple rapid HIV tests, and clinical algorithms based on disease staging to initiate and monitor treatment where CD4 counts are not available. These approaches have been used successfully at several sites to simplify care (AHF Global Immunity 2003a; Farmer and others 2001; WHO 2003g). Adequate training and supportive supervision will also be critical to success.

Optimal staffing ratios are still unclear. UN Millennium Project analyses of data from existing ART sites suggest patient-provider ratios ranging from less than 100/1 to 1,000/1. But these numbers come from sites at various stages

Adherence to the prescribed regimen is critical to the lasting effectiveness of antiretroviral therapy

of scaling up and thus may not reflect ratios at full capacity. An analysis by WHO, extrapolating from two clinic sites in Kenya, suggests that 9–10 health-care workers are needed to treat 1,000 patients, including one doctor, one clinical officer, and two nurses (WHO 2003i). Data from existing sites and from projections are analyzed in greater depth in the working group working paper on human resource requirements for treatment (Hirschhorn 2004).

Strategies for supporting adherence. Adherence to the prescribed regimen is critical to the lasting effectiveness of antiretroviral therapy. An adherence rate of 95 percent or above is necessary to achieve sustained suppression of viral load and to minimize the development of resistance and the need to switch regimens (Bangsberg and others 2000; Montaner and others 1998). Several factors have been identified that influence adherence in all settings, including the complexity of the regimen, the type and severity of side effects, and the provider-patient relationship (WHO 2003b). In resource-poor settings, adherence is inversely linked to cost (Laniece and others 2003; Weiser 2002).

A variety of strategies have been used to increase adherence, including the simplification of regimens, patient counseling, the assignment of "treatment buddies," and the use of pillboxes and blister-packs (AHF Global Immunity 2003a; WHO 2003e). The Partners in Health program uses a modified system of directly observed therapy, in which *accompagnateurs* monitor patient compliance and provide psychosocial support (Leandre 2002). All sites surveyed by the UN Millennium Project that use one or more method of supporting adherence and provide free treatment reported compliance rates above 90 percent, but more research is needed in resource-poor settings on the best and most efficient methods of adherence support. The greatest challenge is likely to be maintaining high adherence after patients feel well again, both because they may be less motivated and because they may move away from the treatment site to look for work. Adherence requires repetitive counseling and training of patients and providers.

Payment policies. Payment systems used in resource-poor settings include insurance, especially in South Africa, sliding-scale user fees, and public and private single-payer systems. Affordability has been linked to both uptake and adherence (Laniece and others 2003; Weiser 2002; WHO 2003g). Although some believe providing drugs for free reduces their perceived value, encourages waste, and decreases adherence, there is no evidence to support this notion in the case of HIV treatment in resource-limited settings. Furthermore, sliding-scale user fees have proved difficult to implement successfully in Sub-Saharan Africa and rarely generate enough funds to contribute significantly to covering costs (Rowden 2001). For these reasons, and because making treatment free ensures more equitable access and reduces the threat of drug diversion, the working group believes that antiretroviral therapy should be provided free of charge whenever possible and should always be free to those who cannot pay.

Antiretroviral therapy should be provided free of charge whenever possible

The private sector

The private sector has a number of critical roles to play in scaling up AIDS treatment. First, although in Brazil and Thailand the public sector has played a major role in local production of antiretroviral drugs, the private pharmaceutical industry remains the only source of antiretrovirals for most countries. The research-based drug companies have been responsible for developing the drugs in use today and have provided many of them at considerably reduced prices in the poorest countries. This industry will remain essential for the development of new drugs. The generic industry, for its part, has contributed enormously to the feasibility of widespread treatment in the developing world by providing antiretrovirals at even lower cost and in the form of fixed dose combinations. The complex issues surrounding drug development, intellectual property, and availability to the poor are considered in the report of the Working Group on Access to Essential Medicines.

Second, some large private corporations provide antiretroviral therapy to their employees, either directly or through insurance coverage, although the Global Business Coalition estimates that fewer than 5 percent of companies have any kind of AIDS or antiretroviral therapy program. While especially in Africa only a small minority of workers are employed by firms with the resources to provide treatment, it may be possible to extend the benefits of corporate programs through public-private partnerships. For example, the Debswana Diamond Company in Botswana, jointly owned by De Beers and the Botswana government, began treating its employees in 2001. More recently, the Debswana facility was incorporated into the Botswana national antiretroviral therapy program and began treating other community members, with financial assistance from the government. In this way the national program extended its reach while making use of the capacity already developed in the private sector. Another example of public-private partnership is the World Bank's Treatment Acceleration Program in Ghana, Burkina Faso, and Mozambique, which will build on private sector treatment programs to expand access.

Third, the private sector, including the pharmaceutical industry, has contributed substantially to the HIV treatment in the developing world through corporate philanthropy. Examples include Merck's participation in the African Comprehensive HIV/AIDS Patnerships (ACHAP), a partnership with the government of Botswana and the Gates Foundation, and Abbott Laboratories' Step Forward Program.

In most countries, however, the largest role for the private sector in AIDS treatment has been provision by physicians in private practice. Although clinicians in private practice are an important resource, private sector provision also poses great risks to individual patients and to the public. In many settings, providers—whether physicians, pharmacists, or drug-sellers—are unlikely to be adequately trained in antiretroviral therapy and may prescribe inappropriate drug regimens. Moreover, difficulty paying the full cost of triple-drug therapy

Substandard therapy in the private sector poses dangers that cannot be ignored

may drive many patients to interrupt treatment or to mono- or dual-drug therapy. All of these factors could lead to treatment failure for the patient and to the spread of viral resistance in the population.

There is relatively little data on HIV treatment practices and patient outcomes in the private sector in Africa and other developing regions, but there are suggestions that the problem is serious (Brugha 2003; Livesley and Morris 2004). A recent World Bank survey in India found that most of the antiretroviral therapy received by 12,000 urban residents was "unstructured" (not conforming to standard guidelines) and that most patients were not adhering by the end of the first year, primarily because of cost. The study projected that unstructured therapy would continue to grow and would lead to widespread resistance (Over and others 2004). By 2033, according to this model, more than half of people living with HIV would be untreatable with the generic medications currently available in India. A study in Mumbai found high rates of resistance even though antiretroviral therapy came into widespread use only in 1999 (Hira and others 2004).

Thus substandard therapy in the private sector poses dangers that cannot be ignored. One solution, of course, is to expand high-quality, free provision in the public sector as rapidly as possible, giving patients an alternative and eliminating the incentive to purchase drugs through other channels. It will be several years at best before free ART is available to all, however, and some people may in any case prefer to seek treatment in the private sector.

Other solutions could include expanding training and certification of private providers in antiretroviral therapy, establishing and enforcing regulatory controls, and tightening control over drug supplies. The best approach in most cases will be to work with physicians' groups and other professional associations (Brugha 2003; Smith and others 2001).

Minimizing viral resistance

As the World Bank India study suggests and the experience of the developed world shows, viral resistance is a real threat to the long-term sustainability of antiretroviral therapy. Although many uncertainties remain, modeling studies, data from the developed world, and limited experience from resource-poor settings suggest several conclusions. First, the appearance and spread of resistant viral strains with the spread of ART is inevitable. Second, most of this resistance will be acquired (that is, it will develop in individual patients as a result of therapy). The prevalence of transmitted resistance (drug-resistant viral strains passed from one person to another) will always be lower, and in favorable circumstances can remain low, according to models of treatment in rich countries. Third, the development of resistance depends strongly on the effectiveness of therapy, which in turns depends on its quality and on adherence.

There is now strong evidence that adherence in well-structured programs in resource-poor settings can be as high or higher than in the developed world

Viral resistance is a real threat

(Coetzee, Boulle, and others 2004; Laniece and others 2003). Moreover, much of transmitted resistance in the developed world may result from treatment with substandard regimens in the era before triple-drug therapy. This is in theory less of a problem in the developing world, where access to any kind of therapy has been very low (but note the Mumbai results cited above). A recent study found low prevalence of resistance in Brazil, perhaps because treatment is free to patients and closely monitored by the federal government (Soares and others 2004).

Another recent modeling study focusing on Africa suggests that transmitted resistance is likely to remain below 5 percent as treatment is scaled up over the next decade, although overall prevalence of resistance (including acquired resistance) could be considerably higher (Blower and others 2005).

The rate at which resistance develops in individual patients depends on the quality of care, especially an appropriate choice of regimen, a continuous supply of drugs, and support for adherence. Thus, the keys to forestalling resistance will be ensuring that providers in both the public and private sectors are appropriately trained; improving drug distribution systems; developing effective strategies for monitoring and supporting adherence; and ensuring that ability to pay is not a barrier to adherence. It will also be important to minimize unregulated drug selling by increasing control over drug supplies and cutting demand through free public sector provision.

Keeping transmitted resistance low depends on these measures, which reduce the development of resistance in treated individuals, as well as on preventing transmission from patients who already carry resistant virus through effective prevention integrated into clinical care.

The specter of resistance cannot justify delaying the urgent expansion of treatment in the developing world. After all, these considerations were not allowed to delay access to antiretroviral therapy in the rich world in spite of much greater uncertainties. Yet there are strong reasons to try to delay the development of resistance as long as possible, both in individual patients and in the population as a whole, by emphasizing quality of care, adherence, and prevention for positives. These were also the conclusions reached by a high-level World Bank consultation in June 2003.

Strengthening health systems

The biggest challenge to scaling up antiretroviral therapy in high-prevalence settings—besides funding—will be poor health infrastructure, especially lack of skilled staff. Physical and laboratory infrastructure, drug and commodity logistics, information systems, and management at all levels will also have to be strengthened. Failure to invest adequately in health systems will not only block expansion of treatment, but could threaten the provision of other critical health services (Attawell and Mundy 2003; Barron 2003; Buve and others 2003; Morrison 2002).

In many settings lack of trained staff will be the single greatest constraint

In many settings lack of trained staff will be the single greatest constraint on expansion of antiretroviral therapy. WHO estimates that in the short term 100,000 staff will have to be trained to meet the target of placing 3 million people on treatment by 2005 (WHO 2003d). Training so many people to deliver ART is a great challenge, but WHO reports that this element of preparation to reach the 3 by 5 goal is ahead of schedule (WHO 2004a). The greater obstacle will be the absolute shortage of doctors, nurses, pharmacists, and other skilled professionals in most of the hardest-hit countries. While in the United States there is more than 1 doctor for every 500 people, in most African countries the ratio is 1 to 10,000 or higher, and in several countries it is over 1 to 30,000 (USAID/SARA 2003). Nurses and other healthcare workers, as well as managerial and administrative staff, are also often in short supply (Simms and others 2001).

Several factors contribute to these shortages, including low salaries, poor working conditions, recruitment to Western countries, and HIV/AIDS itself. One study found that health professionals in Africa are at least as likely to become infected as other people, and that mortality rates among nurses in Zambia jumped dramatically in the early 1990s (Buve and others 1994). Brain drain has robbed Africa of many of its doctors and nurses. At least 5,000 South African physicians have moved abroad; Zimbabwe lost approximately 70 percent of doctors trained in the 1990s; and in 1999 it was estimated that Ghana lost as many nurses to emigration as it trained every year (Physicians for Human Rights 2004; USAID/SARA 2003). A recent study concluded that Sub-Saharan Africa must add the equivalent of 1 million health workers through retention, recruitment, and training, if it is to achieve the Millennium Development Goals for health (Joint Learning Initiative 2004).

In many countries, formal or informal limits on public sector expenditure have exacerbated the problem.[4] In Tanzania, for example, the total size of the healthcare workforce has declined from 67,000 in 1994 to 54,000 in 2002, primarily as a result of a freeze in civil service hiring imposed in 1993. A careful analysis concluded that human resource requirements for meeting the Millennium Development Goals for health in Tanzania were likely to exceed availability by a factor of two or even three (Kurowski and others 2003). It is not clear how many health professionals are currently working in other professions and could be brought back into the health sector if spending limits were lifted or if salaries and working conditions were improved. Kenya is believed to have as many as 2,000 nurses who could in theory be rehired into the public sector (WHO 2003i). More information on these potential reserves of trained personnel is needed.

The number of healthcare workers who will be needed to provide antiretroviral therapy will depend on staffing ratios and other aspects of the service delivery model, as well as on the characteristics of sites, providers, and patients (Hirshhorn 2004). As mentioned above, patient-provider ratios may range from less

Regulations should be revised to allow greater flexibility in staff roles

than 100/1 to as much as 1,000/1 (WHO 2003i). These ratios—and thus the efficiency of service delivery—can be expected to grow initially, as staff acquire experience and as patients are stabilized. This trend may eventually reverse, however, as sites near capacity and the frequency of complications and treatment failure increase. A review commissioned by the working group found that the total number of dedicated staff required to meet the 3 by 5 target could be from 20,000 to more than 120,000, depending on the range of support personnel included in the estimates (Hirschhorn 2004). The number of staff needed to provide 75 percent (or universal) access by 2015 will, of course, also depend on the number of people who will need treatment by that date.

While the number of healthcare workers needed to deliver antiretroviral therapy will be large, expansion of treatment can be expected to relieve some of the existing burden of HIV care on the health system, at least initially: in high-burden countries patients with AIDS-related illnesses may be occupying up to 75 percent of hospital beds (Gadelha and others 2002; Nachega 2003).

Overcoming the shortage of clinical staff will require a two-pronged strategy. In the short term, hard-hit countries must make the best possible use of the personnel they have, as it takes three to six years to train new higher-level health workers. The key steps will be to train existing clinical staff in HIV care, to design models of care that allow nurses and other mid-level staff to assume responsibilities previously restricted to physicians, and to make greater use of community healthcare workers and other community members, including people living with HIV (see above). Relevant regulations should be revised to allow greater flexibility in staff roles and to expedite the training process. Training a cadre of workers in record-keeping and other administrative tasks might also help by freeing medical personnel to care for patients. An international medical service corps might be a way to bring much needed help to the hardest-hit countries, especially for training purposes.

In the longer term, a concerted effort will be required to ramp up the recruitment, training, and retention of health professionals, especially doctors and nurses, not only to deliver antiretroviral therapy and other HIV care, but to provide the full spectrum of basic health services. These efforts should commence immediately, as it takes several years to train higher-level medical staff, and should be guided by a comprehensive human resources plan. This plan should also address salaries and working conditions, including the need for supportive supervision. Steps must be taken at both country and international levels to reduce brain drain. Finally, the international financial institutions and national governments must find ways to relax restrictions on expenditure on health (and other social sectors) without compromising macroeconomic stability. This issue is addressed in the UN Millennium Project's synthesis report (UN Millennium Project 2005a).

Training of all personnel in antiretroviral therapy should be modular in design, should focus on the most critical training needs, and should disrupt

Management at all levels of health systems will have to be strengthened

existing services as little as possible. In high-prevalence settings, training should be integrated into all medical curricula as soon as possible. The working group calls for all graduating doctors, medical officers and nurses in these countries to be trained and certified to provide antiretroviral therapy by 2005 and for all already practicing staff to be trained by 2010.

Physical infrastructure will also have to be expanded and improved as treatment is scaled up. More research is needed to determine how much space is required to care for a certain number of patients on ART. As with human resources, space requirements will vary according to the range of services provided and the way they are delivered. Laboratory infrastructure, information systems, surveillance, and operational research must also be strengthened. Drug procurement and distribution will be a particularly high priority. In order to scale-up treatment, antiretrovirals and other drugs must be readily available, appropriately managed, secure, and affordable. Commodity management is problematic in many high-prevalence countries and stock-outs common. Capacity should be developed to monitor and forecast needs at all appropriate levels of the health system. Free provision of antiretroviral therapy could help ensure drug security by reducing the incentive for theft. In principle, strengthening the procurement system for AIDS drugs should strengthen procurement of all essential medicines.

Finally, management at all levels of health systems will have to be strengthened considerably, both to manage such a complex initiative as scaling up antiretroviral therapy and to manage the great increase in donor funding. Inability to plan, redeploy staff, procure drugs and commodities, and manage the flow of funds from donors to central ministries and from there to the periphery has been in large part responsible for the slow use of resources that have already become available to some of the hardest-hit countries. Onerous and poorly harmonized donor requirements have significantly exacerbated the burden on managers. Along with the shortage of healthcare workers, these management challenges probably account for much of the so-called absorptive capacity constraint (see chapter 5).

Research and development priorities
Some of the highest priorities for research and development are the development of new second-line drugs and pediatric formulations, cheaper technologies for monitoring treatment, and efficient and effective ways to deliver antiretroviral therapy in resource-poor settings.

Second-line drugs and pediatric formulations. Although the cost of the most common first-line regimens from both name brand and generic manufacturers has come down enormously, the prices of second-line and third-line drugs (which are less available in generic versions) have fallen far less. According to Médecins Sans Frontières, a typical second-line regimen costs 20 times as much as the cheapest first-line drugs (MSF 2004b). Moreover, second-line

The convergence of the global epidemics of tuberculosis and HIV is one of the most significant challenges

regimens are not available as fixed-dose combinations, making adherence more challenging, and often require refrigeration, limiting their use at lower levels of the health system (Chang 2003; MSF 2003). These problems will become more pressing as more people develop resistance to initial regimens.

More convenient and affordable antiretroviral formulations for children are another important priority. The available solutions and syrups for small children are expensive and difficult to use, while fixed-dosed combination pills in lower doses for older children are not available (MSF 2004b).

Cheaper technologies for monitoring treatment. CD4 and viral load tests are too expensive and impractical in many resource-poor settings. Although these measures may not be strictly necessary for the initiation of treatment, which can be done using clinical criteria, they are important to determining when treatment is failing and regimens should be changed. Several technologies are under development. Monitoring treatment—and even confirming HIV infection—in infants and children pose additional challenges.

Operational research. More research is needed to determine the most efficient and effective ways to deliver antiretroviral therapy in resource-poor settings. Important issues include adherence support, integration of prevention into care, and staffing models.

HIV and tuberculosis

The convergence of the global epidemics of tuberculosis and HIV is one of the most significant challenges to global public health. The interaction between HIV and tuberculosis is synergistic. On one hand, HIV promotes progression to active tuberculosis in people with either recently acquired or latent tuberculosis infection. In contrast to HIV-negative people, for whom the lifetime risk of progressing to active tuberculosis is 10–20 percent, up to 10 percent of coinfected individuals develop active tuberculosis *each year* (Corbett and others 2003). HIV also increases the rate of recurrence of tuberculosis after successful treatment, mainly because of an increased risk of disease following reinfection (Sonnenberg and others 2001; van Rie and others 1999).

On the other hand, tuberculosis is the most important and deadly opportunistic infection in AIDS patients in many settings, especially Sub-Saharan Africa, causing disease at any stage of HIV infection and accounting for 13 percent of deaths among HIV-positive people worldwide (WHO 2004e). Tuberculosis is the leading cause of death in HIV-infected individuals in Africa (Grant and others 1997; Rana and others 2000). It is estimated that 8 million of the 25 million Africans infected with HIV also carry the tuberculosis bacillus and that up to half will develop the active disease (WHO/UNAIDS 2004a). Tuberculosis rates among people living with HIV are particularly high in Africa (map 3.2).

But tuberculosis is not just part of the AIDS problem. Tuberculosis programs can be an important part of the solution, by providing a valuable entry point to

The management of HIV and tuberculosis coinfection poses special challenges

care for people living with HIV and by promoting and providing HIV testing and counseling for tuberculosis patients. In return, there is much that HIV programs can do to reduce the burden of tuberculosis among HIV patients.

HIV and the reemergence of tuberculosis

Tuberculosis, a disease forgotten by many, reemerged in the mid-1980s as a major global public health problem, thereby presenting the paradox of a disease that is fully treatable with affordable drugs, yet causes vast and increasing suffering and death. Indeed, the WHO estimates that there are 8 million new cases of tuberculosis every year, resulting in more than 2 million deaths annually (WHO 2004c). More than 95 percent of these cases occur in the developing world. Moreover, it is estimated that one-third of the world's population is infected with *M. tuberculosis*, although most of these latently infected people show no symptoms of disease (WHO 2004c).

The dramatic increase in tuberculosis rates in recent decades is largely attributable to the HIV epidemic, in the context of poorly organized control programs (Raviglione and others 1995). Annual tuberculosis case notification rates have risen up to fourfold since the mid-1980s in Sub-Saharan Africa, where three-quarters of HIV-infected people live. In some areas of Sub-Saharan Africa, over two-thirds of patients with active tuberculosis are coinfected with HIV (Dye and others 1999).

Diagnosis and treatment of tuberculosis in HIV-infected patients

The management of HIV and tuberculosis coinfection poses special challenges. To begin with, the most common methods of diagnosing tuberculosis, including sputum smear and chest radiography, work less well in immune-compromised HIV patients (Perlman and others 1997; Perronne and others 1988; Smith and others 1994). In addition, one of the most commonly used first-line antiretroviral drug regimens cannot be used with one of the standard tuberculosis drugs. Yet, the standard six-month tuberculosis chemotherapy also works well for HIV-coinfected patients, and ample evidence from pilot programs now demonstrates that tuberculosis in these patients can be cured readily with the standard DOTS approach (see below). All HIV patients with tuberculosis should have access to DOTS.

The optimal time to begin antiretroviral therapy in patients with tuberculosis is not clear, however. Mortality rates during the first two months of tuberculosis treatment are high, especially in patients with advanced HIV disease, and antiretroviral therapy in these settings might be life saving. Nonetheless, a paradoxical worsening of tuberculosis symptoms can occur when HIV-infected patients being treated for tuberculosis begin ART. Although these reactions appear to result from immune restoration rather than a failure to control infection, use of antiretroviral therapy might not be appropriate during the first weeks of tuberculosis therapy.

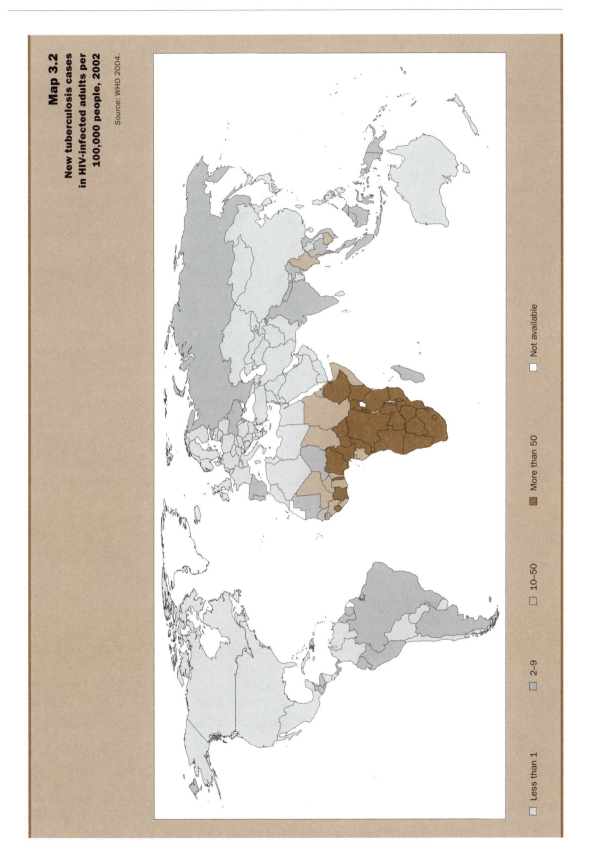

Map 3.2

New tuberculosis cases in HIV-infected adults per 100,000 people, 2002

Source: WHO 2004.

Less than 1

2–9

10–50

More than 50

Not available

AIDS treatment programs in the developing world have much to learn from tuberculosis programs

HIV-infected patients with latent tuberculosis are at high risk of progressing to active disease. As a result, those with a positive skin test for tuberculosis, as well as those who are in close contact with someone with untreated tuberculosis, should receive isoniazid prophylaxis, which can substantially decrease the likelihood of developing active tuberculosis (Bucher and others 1999; CDC 1998). Since it is not always feasible to carry out tuberculin skin-testing for all HIV-infected individuals, WHO recommends prophylaxis for all HIV patients in settings where the prevalence of tuberculosis infection is estimated to be above 30 percent (WHO/UNAIDS 1998). In all cases, active tuberculosis must be excluded before beginning treatment for latent tuberculosis.

The DOTS strategy

WHO declared tuberculosis a global health emergency in 1993 and launched DOTS, the directly observed therapy strategy for tuberculosis control. This comprehensive strategy includes case detection through passive finding using sputum smear microscopy, treatment using standard short-course chemotherapy, administered under direct observation by a healthcare worker for at least the first two months, and secure and regular supply of essential antituberculosis drugs. Its goals were to achieve a target of 70 percent detection of new cases and 85 percent cure of detected cases by 2000. Although these goals were not met, and debate continues on the appropriateness of DOTS as a universal policy (Jochem and Walley 1999), DOTS has been shown to be the best tool available in the fight against tuberculosis.

AIDS treatment programs in the developing world have much to learn from tuberculosis programs and the DOTS approach, which have demonstrated the feasibility of following patients during lengthy courses of treatment and illustrated the importance of standardized protocols. DOTS offers one model for monitoring and supporting adherence to antiretroviral therapy, and the Partners in Health program in Haiti has successfully adapted this approach to HIV care.

The WHO interim policy on collaborative activities

To address the suffering and death caused by the interaction of tuberculosis and HIV, the Global TB/HIV Working Group played a lead role in developing a strategic framework to decrease the burden of TB/HIV, an interim policy on collaborative TB/HIV activities, and guidelines for implementing these activities (WHO 2002b, 2003c, 2004d). The WHO documents recommend the establishment of a mechanism for collaboration between tuberculosis and AIDS programs and a set of activities aimed at decreasing the burden of tuberculosis in people living with HIV and the burden of HIV in tuberculosis patients.

Recommendations

The key to success in bringing the entwined epidemics of tuberculosis and HIV under control will be a greatly enhanced partnership between tuberculosis and

DOTS has been shown to be the best tool available in the fight against tuberculosis

HIV programs. In addition to joint planning and greater communication at all management levels, several specific steps will be particularly important:

- All tuberculosis patients should be offered HIV testing and counseling. Those who test positive should be referred for HIV prevention and care services, particularly antiretroviral therapy where it is available. Tuberculosis clinics offer one of the most important—and efficient—entry points for antiretroviral therapy, since the fraction of patients in this setting who test positive and qualify immediately for antiretroviral therapy will almost always be much higher than in other settings, such as antenatal clinics.
- All HIV patients should be screened for tuberculosis and referred for diagnosis and treatment if tuberculosis is suspected.
- All HIV patients with positive tuberculosis skin tests, as well as those who have been in close contact with someone with untreated pulmonary tuberculosis, should receive prophylactic treatment for tuberculosis.

Equity and human rights

In most of the developing world, the greatest equity issue surrounding treatment is the exclusion of the poor by the high cost of antiretroviral therapy. Unaffordable treatment also creates dangerous incentives for less effective one and two drug regimens and poses a proven obstacle to adherence (Brugha 2003; Laniece and others 2003; Plusnews 2003; Weiser 2002). Thus, both equity and sustainability require that HIV treatment be affordable to all who need it; in the poorest settings this will mean providing it free to many or most patients. Laboratory and transport costs will also have to be minimized or subsidized. In theory, sliding scales that base user charges on ability to pay can be established, as in the Rwanda national program. In practice, however, the complexity of such systems may outweigh any cost recovery or other benefits.

Rural populations in particular can also be denied access by failure to strengthen health systems and adopt appropriate delivery models, thereby preventing treatment from being provided at lower levels of the health system. While it makes sense to roll out treatment first at central and district hospitals, where infrastructure is stronger, there is a real danger that expansion will stop there, leaving many without access. The key to reaching everyone in need will be to choose a bold delivery approach that allows integration of antiretroviral therapy into primary care and then to invest heavily in building capacity at this level of the system. Thus, both the choice of delivery model and the commitment to investment in primary care have critical consequences for treatment equity.

An additional concern is that certain groups will be excluded, either by deliberate policy or by program design. For example, there is concern that women, who constitute the majority of those in need in Sub-Saharan Africa, may be put at a disadvantage by greater poverty, greater fear of stigma, and household priority decisions. There is much evidence that these and other factors have often conspired to leave women with less access to healthcare than

Children are already under-represented in treatment programs

men. It is worth noting, however, that women currently make up more than 60 percent of the patient population in the MSF and Botswana programs, both of which provide free access to antiretroviral therapy in most cases. In part, this reflects the preferential enrollment of pregnant women, one of the priority populations in the Botswana program, as in others. But other factors seem to be at work, and the higher enrollment—and better outcomes—of women in these programs is not well understood (Boulle and others 2004). Although women have been well represented in these and other small programs, there is no guarantee that problems will not emerge as programs are scaled up and other entry points, such as clinics for tuberculosis and sexually transmitted infections, become more important referral points for treatment.

Moreover, it is important that women who are not pregnant also have fair access. The representation of women in treatment programs should be closely watched, and the working group calls for systems to be in place at the national level by the end of 2005 to monitor the number of women and members of other potentially disadvantaged groups receiving treatment, in both the public and private sectors.

Children are already underrepresented in treatment programs (MSF 2004a). Treating children is more challenging, but recent experience in the developed world shows that children can be treated successfully and given a chance to reach adulthood. Diagnosis of children is more complicated, providers lack familiarity with their care, and cheap and convenient drug formulations are not yet available (MSF 2004b). The development of better tools and standardized protocols should be a high priority. Follow up and care of infants born to HIV-positive mothers will also be essential. The working group calls for the share of children receiving treatment to be monitored in all countries by the end of 2005 and for children to be on antiretroviral therapy in proportion to their need by 2015.

In concentrated epidemics, the greatest danger is that the marginalized populations most in need of treatment may be actively excluded by official or community discrimination or by fear of arrest or harassment. This is more than a hypothetical problem. In Saint Petersburg, for example, drug users are systematically excluded from antiretroviral treatment (Human Rights Watch 2004b). Thus, in these settings, access to treatment may be more a human rights issue than an issue of health system capacity and lack of resources. In many cases removing formal barriers may not be enough to ensure that injecting drug users, sex workers, and other vulnerable populations have fair access to treatment: special efforts will have to be made. Treating injecting drug users may also require somewhat specialized drug protocols (Dasgupta and Okhuysen 2001). For these reasons, it is essential that treatment access for these populations be watched closely.

Until universal access is achieved, communities, treatment sites, and national programs face difficult choices in deciding whom to treat first. Where

The greatest danger is that the marginalized populations most in need of treatment may be actively excluded

resources are highly constrained, it may be acceptable to use nonclinical as well as clinical criteria in prioritizing people for antiretroviral therapy. For example, the newly developed Rwandan guidelines on patient selection give priority to healthcare workers (Government of Rwanda 2003). However, every effort should be made to optimize the efficiency of antiretroviral therapy delivery before making this type of decision.

Cumbersome decision-making processes can themselves slow expansion of treatment. For this reason, Médecins Sans Frontières has now abandoned the use of community boards to screen candidates for treatment at its South Africa and Malawi sites. The working group does not take a position on how these difficult decisions should be made, beyond insisting that certain very basic equity principles must be upheld. Ultimately, these decisions must belong to communities and national governments. It is vital that community involvement not be sacrificed in the name of efficiency, since sustained support for treatment programs will depend on the sense that these life-or-death decisions are being made fairly. Finally, we also note that communities (or those who hold power in communities) may make choices that go against internationally accepted principles, for example by excluding certain ethnic groups or those perceived to violate community mores. Since many of those who need treatment may fall into these categories, this is more than a theoretical concern.

The expansion of HIV treatment in the developing world raises important equity issues beyond that of ensuring fair access (McCoy 2003). First, the balance of treatment and prevention has profound implications for those who already carry the virus and those at risk of infection, as well as for those who may be at risk 10 or 20 years from now. Only a truly comprehensive response, one in which both treatment and prevention are scaled up rapidly while strengthening the potential synergies between them, can be fair to all.

Second, an appropriate balance must be maintained between HIV treatment and other health priorities. The urgent effort to scale up treatment must not be allowed to divert funds or scarce staff from the drive to control malaria and tuberculosis or bring down maternal and child mortality, and, more generally, from the goal of building health systems capable of addressing the many health needs of impoverished populations. There are already indications that new treatment programs, especially the U.S. government's initiative, are pulling healthcare workers away from the other tasks. These concerns must not be used as arguments against the expansion of treatment. Instead, they reinforce the importance of making sure that treatment is scaled up in a constructive way, one that strengthens health systems instead of damaging them.

Home-based care

The great majority of people living with AIDS in the developing world are cared for at home by family members. Although many people may prefer to be home when they are sick—or when they die—they may also have little choice,

The great majority of people living with AIDS in the developing world are cared for at home

as they may not have access to or be unable to afford hospital care. Families are often hard-pressed to meet the basic needs of the patient, let alone provide necessary medical services, and caring for the sick can impose enormous financial and emotional strains on families and caregivers. There is great need to expand community-based home care programs, which can improve the quality of care for patients and provide vital support to their families. Home care for the sick shares many features, and should be governed by many of the same principles, as care for orphans and vulnerable children, which is discussed in chapter 4.

Although home care encompasses all forms of care and support that are provided at home, our discussion will focus mostly on programs that provide outside support to the patient and family. This support can include a variety of clinical and psychosocial services, as well as material help (see below). Some services may be provided by visiting nurses or social workers, but community health workers and volunteers are usually the backbone of home care programs. These initiatives are often organized and managed by nongovernmental organizations, church groups, or community organizations, although some governments have also established programs in the health sector, sometimes designed to follow and assist patients after they are discharged from hospitals.

There is little data on the scope of need for home care, but it is certainly great, and coverage with existing programs is poor. In its coverage report the Policy Project set the level of need at 5.8 million, corresponding to the number of people in the last two years of life who were not on antiretroviral therapy, and estimated coverage at 14 percent globally in 2003 on the basis of government service statistics (Policy Project 2004). These assumptions might be a little pessimistic: a survey in South Africa found that patients were chronically ill for a year on average before dying (Steinberg and others 2002), and coverage statistics may miss small community-based programs. But most of those who are currently reached by some kind of program almost certainly do not receive sufficient help or a full spectrum of support. And of course, need will continue to grow even where HIV prevalence has stabilized, because of the long lag between infection and progression to AIDS.

It should be emphasized that AIDS is not the only long-term illness that creates a need for home care services. Although AIDS is now the single greatest cause of adult mortality worldwide, many other conditions, including tuberculosis, cardiovascular disease, and cancer, can also cause long-term disability and illness, and in much of the world they impose a greater burden than AIDS (WHO 2003j). Moreover, many patients with AIDS are not aware of their status or are not willing to disclose it. Thus, in most cases it is neither fair nor sensible to target home care programs only to people with AIDS. In Africa, however, it may make sense to reach those areas hardest hit by the epidemic first, since families and communities are likely to be under the greatest strain there. Similar arguments apply to programs for orphans and vulnerable children.

**Most of
the burden
of care at
home falls
on women
and girls**

Comprehensive home care support would include:

- Medical and nursing care, including management of infections, relief of symptoms, and palliative care, including morphine, at the end of life.
- Referral to clinic or hospital-based services.
- Training for family caregivers, including education in avoiding infection.
- Basic nursing supplies, such as gloves and soap.
- Counseling, including HIV prevention counseling, and emotional and spiritual support.
- Help with other household work.
- Food, clothing, or other material support.
- Microfinance or help with income-generating projects.

Not all families will need all these forms of support, and of course not all programs will be able to meet all needs. An assessment of the most important needs should be the first step in planning a support program.

Most of the burden of care at home falls on women and girls (Ogden and others 2004). A survey in South Africa found that 68 percent of primary caregivers were female, while in a Ugandan study 86 percent were women. The responsibility to care for the sick can impose real opportunity costs, forcing women to leave paid employment or cut back on agricultural work and obliging girls to drop out of school. Thus, home care is an important gender issue and home care programs preferentially benefit women. In addition to expanding these programs, more efforts should be made to involve men in care: some programs of this kind have shown promise (Esu-Williams and others 2003).

The work of caring for the sick—and for children, the elderly, and family members generally—is sometimes considered to constitute a "care economy," part of a larger spectrum of work within the household, predominantly by women, that generally does not appear in national income statistics and has received too little attention from economists (Ogden and others 2004). The disproportionate burden of household chores, including caring for the sick, severely curtails the educational and employment opportunities of girls and women. As one way to reduce this burden, the UN Millennium Project Task Force on Education and Gender Equality recommends investments in infrastructure to reduce women's "time poverty." Such investments could include improved water supplies closer to home and alternative sources of fuel for cooking to reduce time spent searching for firewood.

The advent of widespread antiretroviral therapy in the developing world will not end the need for home-based care. But if will shift some of the responsibility of community health workers or volunteers away from palliative care and management of opportunistic infections toward patient referral, follow-up, and adherence support. Links between home care programs and the clinic-based health system must therefore be strengthened to ensure that home

Widespread antiretroviral therapy in the developing world will not end the need for home-based care

care workers have relevant information on patients' treatment and can in turn report back to the clinic.

While community members will continue to be the backbone of home care programs, extending coverage and expanding the role of home care will require government and, in the poorest countries, donor support. Even if a new cadre of community health workers cannot be created within the public sector, community volunteers must receive tangible support, including a small stipend. In many cases the best approach may be to sustain local initiative by channeling government and donor funds through grassroots organizations.

Recommendations

- Antiretroviral therapy should be given priority in expanding access to HIV care. It should be made available as soon as health facilities meet a set of basic prerequisites, as recommended by the WHO operational guidelines.
- Basic prevention elements, including safer-sex counseling and provision of condoms, should be incorporated into clinical care from the start. Treatment activities in the community, including education and adherence support, should be linked to prevention efforts.
- The working group endorses a public-health approach to treatment delivery in the developing world, as defined by WHO. Key elements of this approach are use of standardized treatment protocols and simplified clinical monitoring, optimal use of existing physical infrastructure and human resources, involvement of communities and people living with HIV in program design and implementation, simplified record-keeping, and cost minimization, including minimization of the costs of drugs and diagnostics.
- Strategies for scaling up treatment must be designed to strengthen health systems rather than circumvent their weaknesses. Failure to invest in health systems will endanger the sustainability of treatment and threaten the achievement of other health goals.
- Antiretroviral therapy should be integrated into primary care in high-prevalence settings as rapidly as possible. Even if this approach is initially less efficient, it has the potential to reach the most people, build capacity at this critical level of the health system, and increase access for the poor.
- The shortage of healthcare workers must be addressed as a fundamental element of national AIDS treatment strategies. In the short term, responsibilities should be reassigned to make the best use of existing staff. By 2005, all graduating—and by 2010, all practicing—doctors, nurses, and medical officers in high-prevalence countries should be trained and certified to provide antiretroviral therapy. In the long term, sustained efforts must be made to recruit and retain new staff at

The shortage of healthcare workers must be addressed as a fundamental element of national AIDS treatment strategies

all levels as part of a comprehensive human resources strategy for the health sector.

- Whenever possible, antiretroviral therapy should be provided to patients free of charge. Making treatment free will protect access among the poor, improve adherence, and reduce the incentive for drug diversion.

- National governments should do more to oversee and improve the quality of antiretroviral therapy in the private sector.

- All tuberculosis patients should be offered HIV testing and counseling, and those who test positive should be referred for HIV prevention and care services, particularly antiretroviral therapy where it is available. All HIV patients should be screened for tuberculosis and referred for diagnosis and treatment if tuberculosis is suspected. HIV patients with positive tuberculosis skin tests, as well those who have been in close contact with someone with untreated pulmonary tuberculosis, should receive prophylactic therapy against tuberculosis.

- To help ensure equitable access to HIV treatment, countries should have in place by 2005 a system for monitoring the proportion of women, children under 15, and members of key vulnerable populations among those receiving antiretroviral therapy in both the public and private sectors.

- The development of additional antiretroviral combinations appropriate to resource-poor settings, affordable clinical monitoring tools, and improved guidelines and drug formulations for children should be priorities for research and development.

- Home care programs providing clinical, psychosocial, and material support to patients and families should be a higher priority for national governments and donors. Although these services are often best delivered by community-based organizations, governments have the responsibility to provide financial support and oversight and to build strong links to the health system.

Chapter 4

Orphans and
vulnerable children

Although more than 2 million children are living with HIV, an even greater number have been affected by the illness and death of parents and family members and the economic and social devastation of communities. Disproportionately striking young adults—AIDS is now the leading cause of death worldwide of people ages 15–49—the epidemic is creating a terrible and rapidly growing new crisis of orphans and vulnerable children. In the highest-prevalence countries, the unprecedented number of orphans is threatening to overwhelm the capacity of extended families and communities to provide adequate care. In the long run, the epidemic's impact on children may pose risks to social stability, cultural continuity, and economic development, although there is so far little evidence to support the more alarmist scenarios.

The 2001 Declaration of Commitment on HIV/AIDS, promulgated by the UN General Assembly Special Session on HIV/AIDS (UNGASS), mandated care for orphans and other children made vulnerable by AIDS as a core element of a comprehensive response to the epidemic (articles 65-67) (UN General Assembly 2001). Yet the growing orphan crisis has received far too little attention and resources, perhaps because this aspect of the epidemic has been less pronounced in the developed world and because children have little or no political voice of their own. Although we focus primarily on prevention and treatment in this report, we also address the effect of the epidemic on children to draw attention to this neglected issue, while touching on the broader challenges of mitigating the impact of AIDS on families, communities, and societies. An additional reason for addressing this issue in our report is that children orphaned or otherwise affected by the epidemic are themselves more vulnerable to HIV infection. Thus, the humanitarian imperative—and obligation under international conventions—of caring for vulnerable children can also be seen as part of a comprehensive prevention strategy.

**A sense of
the scale of
the crisis is
beginning
to emerge**

Data on orphans have improved considerably in recent years, and a sense of the scale of the crisis is beginning to emerge. Before reviewing this evidence, some matters of definition must be addressed. First, this report will follow recent convention in defining orphans as children who have lost one parent (single orphans), as well as those who have lost both parents (double orphans). Although it may not correspond to common usage, at least in the West, this definition has been adopted by UNICEF and the other organizations leading the effort to gather and analyze data on children affected by AIDS.[1] While some children will be left very vulnerable by the death of a single parent, others will be far less affected—and of course many children who are not orphans live in single-parent households. But the death of a parent must always be a profound emotional trauma, and often has important, even devastating economic and legal consequences. Moreover, no simple definition of orphanhood could reliably identify the subset of children most affected by parental death.

Second, we will include in our discussion children up to the age of 18. While other reports have used lower cutoff ages, this is the definition used by *Children on the Brink 2004*, the UNAIDS/UNICEF/USAID (2004) report from which much of the statistical information in this chapter is drawn.[2] This is an important distinction, since adolescents make up the majority of orphans (see below).

Children orphaned by AIDS are children who have lost one or more parent to AIDS.[3] The broader category of vulnerable children, defined by *Children on the Brink 2004* as "children whose survival, well-being or development is threatened by HIV/AIDS," potentially encompasses children with sick family members, those who live in a household caring for orphans, and those who are living with HIV themselves, among others.

Scope of the crisis

Children on the Brink 2004 estimates that approximately 15 million children under 18 years old have been orphaned by AIDS worldwide (UNAIDS/UNICEF/USAID 2004). This number is not derived from any attempt at direct enumeration, but inferred from a country-by-country analysis of demographic data and mortality projections, validated when possible by survey data. There are many sources of uncertainty in this estimate—the report itself suggests that the true number is likely to lie between 13 million and 18 million—but it results from more sophisticated methods than previous estimates. The report also includes tables of national estimates. These data, together with subnational and community-level information, will be the most important for guiding policy.

Of the 15 million children orphaned by AIDS, 12.3 million, or more than 80 percent, are in Sub-Saharan Africa, reflecting not only the region's disproportionate burden of HIV infection, but also the African epidemic's relative maturity. AIDS mortality, and thus the number of AIDS orphans,

Globally, AIDS is responsible for only a relatively small share of orphaned children

lags well behind the number of people living with the virus as an epidemic grows. For this reason, the number of children orphaned by AIDS is projected to rise sharply in the coming years, even in regions where prevalence is stabilizing. *Children on the Brink 2004* estimates that by 2010 there will be 18.4 million orphans as a result of AIDS—and over 40 million orphans overall—in Sub-Saharan Africa.

Globally, AIDS is responsible for only a relatively small share, perhaps 10 percent, of orphaned children. Even in Sub-Saharan Africa, most children—more than 70 percent—are orphaned by other causes. But in the hardest-hit countries of southern Africa, AIDS is now the dominant cause of parental death. In Botswana, for instance, 77 percent of orphans have lost a parent to AIDS. Moreover, in Botswana an extraordinary 20 percent of all children are orphans, compared with 12.3 percent for Africa as a whole, and 8.4 percent for the world. The fraction of children who are orphans varies considerably across Africa, reflecting in large part the uneven impact of AIDS (map 4.1).

It is important for several reasons to place the crisis of children who have lost parents to AIDS in the broader context of children orphaned by all causes. First, a sense of how the numbers of AIDS orphans compares with the total number in a particular country or locality might give some indication of the degree to which traditional mechanisms for caring for children who have lost parents may be strained by the added burden imposed by AIDS. Second, this proportion might be an important factor in deciding whether and how to target services specifically to AIDS orphans, although the task force believes that in general this is not a good idea (see below).

Finally, examining how this share varies among countries and regions illustrates again how vital it is to consider local realities in any discussion of the impact of AIDS. To note that AIDS orphans are outnumbered by children orphaned by other causes, even in most of Africa, is not to diminish in any way the terrible suffering the epidemic has imposed on millions of children, nor to reduce the urgency of responding to the crisis, but only to inform policy choices and to emphasize the importance of developing a comprehensive strategy for ensuring that all vulnerable children are cared for.

The impact of AIDS on the number of double orphans (children who have lost both parents) is even greater, since the possibility of passing the virus from one parent to the other increases the chance that both will die. Of the estimated 7.7 million double orphans in Sub-Saharan Africa at the end of 2003, 60 percent lost one or both parents to AIDS; this fraction (and the total number of double orphans) will increase substantially by 2010 unless access to antiretroviral treatment is scaled up dramatically.

Much less data are available on children made vulnerable by AIDS in various ways. A recent costing study estimated that there are about 2.5 million children with a parent in the last year of life,[4] while the total number of vulnerable children is sometimes estimated at two to four times the number

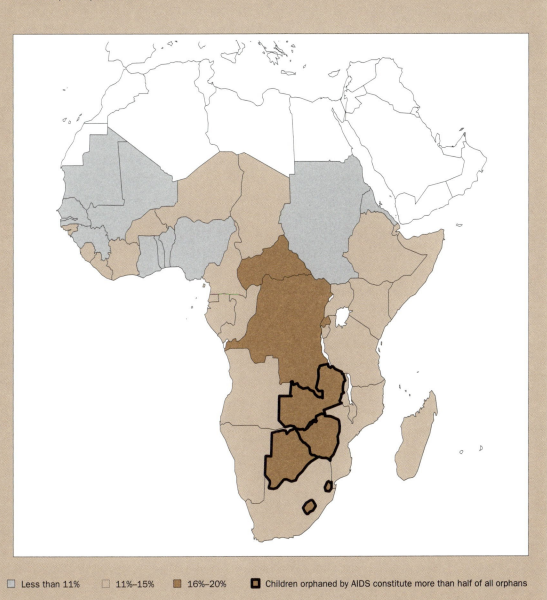

Map 4.1

The orphan crisis in Africa

Orphans as a share of children under 18, 2003 (%)

Source: Based on data from UNICEF/UNAIDS/USAID 2004.

☐ Less than 11%   ☐ 11%–15%   ▨ 16%–20%   ■ Children orphaned by AIDS constitute more than half of all orphans

of orphans.[5] Better information on children in these circumstances is critical, however, since in general programs for affected children should focus on

**Children who
have lost
parents to
AIDS are more
likely to carry
the virus**

reaching those in the greatest need rather than those who meet narrow definitions of orphanhood (or AIDS orphanhood).

Maternal and paternal orphans

In the hardest-hit countries, AIDS is leaving more children without their mothers than without their fathers, while in Sub-Saharan Africa as a whole paternal orphans outnumber maternal orphans, as is the general pattern elsewhere. The needs of children who have lost mothers and fathers are likely to be different in important ways, and the relative impact of these losses will depend on the cultural (and legal) environment.

Age

Data on the ages of orphans are critical for good planning, since orphans of different ages will have very different needs. The recent statistical data reveal that most orphans (55 percent) are adolescents between the ages of 12 and 17 (UNAIDS/UNICEF/USAID 2004). Another third are between 6 and 11, while only 12 percent are under 5. Two points should be kept in mind in interpreting these global estimates. First, they map the ages of children today, not at the time they lost their parents: ages at orphaning would, of course, be lower. Second, these data are for orphans from all causes. Children orphaned by AIDS might be expected to be younger on average than other orphans, since the death toll from the epidemic is still rising and thus contributes disproportionately to more recent parental deaths.

HIV infection

Children who have lost parents to AIDS are more likely to carry the virus themselves than other children, both because they may have acquired it from their mothers and because their circumstances may leave them more vulnerable to becoming infected by sexual transmission or through injecting drug use. There seem to be few data on rates of HIV infection among orphans, but a few considerations suggest that only a relatively small proportion of children orphaned by AIDS (and, of course, a smaller fraction of all orphans) are likely to be living with HIV acquired from their mothers. The overwhelming majority of children living with HIV in the developing world have no access to effective treatment; even where more adults are receiving antiretroviral therapy, access for children has lagged behind (MSF 2004a). Yet, without treatment the life expectancy of most infants living with HIV is tragically short, perhaps no more than two years in the developing world, although some live to primary school age and even to adolescence (Gray and others 2001; Newell and others 2004). Since women are less likely to conceive in the later stages of illness (Lewis and others 2004), relatively few HIV-positive infants will outlive their mothers.

The great majority of children who have lost a parent remain in the care of surviving parents or the extended family

Growing access to antiretroviral therapy and services to prevent mother-to-child transmission in Africa and elsewhere will change this picture in several ways. Most important, widespread treatment can prolong the lives of parents and thus delay or prevent orphaning altogether, while reducing the number of children made vulnerable in other ways. Second, mother-to-child prevention services can protect many children from acquiring the virus from their mothers. Finally, bringing treatment to children, especially infants, will give many a chance to reach adolescence and adulthood, as it now has in the rich world. This will mean an increase in the number of older orphans living with HIV, and countries will have to plan for meeting the complex needs of these children. In particular, it will be critical to develop strategies for ensuring equitable and stable access to treatment for this very vulnerable population.

The greater social and economic vulnerability of children orphaned or otherwise affected by AIDS means that as they enter adolescence they are also more at risk of becoming infected through unsafe sex or, where this is an important channel of transmission, through injecting drug use. Here, too, there are few data, but at least one study confirms the greater risk faced by these children (see below). Girls are at substantially greater risk than boys, in large part because of vulnerability to exploitative relationships with older men (see chapter 2).

Living circumstances

Although far too little is known about the living circumstances of orphans today, household surveys have shed some light on their situation in some African countries. The first conclusion from these data is that the great majority of children who have lost a parent—more than 90 percent—remain in the care of surviving parents or the extended family (UNICEF 2003). Single orphans generally live with the surviving parent, while double orphans are most commonly found in households headed by grandparents. The relative frequency of these arrangements varies among countries.

These data, although enormously valuable, have important limitations. By their nature household surveys will not find children who are living on the street. Surveys may also miss many child-headed households, although these are thought to be relatively rare in most countries (Monasch and Boerma 2004). Not surprisingly, there is evidence from some African cities that orphans are disproportionately represented among street children (Nkouika-Dinghani-Nikita 2000; Zambia Central Statistical Office and ILO 1999). A recent UNICEF study in Blantyre, Malawi, and Kingston, Jamaica, however, found relatively few orphaned children—less than 1 percent—living on the street or in institutions.[6] Although we clearly need more information on these children and their circumstances, it seems fairly clear that they represent a small proportion of vulnerable children, at least at present. There is a danger

Many households caring for orphans may be overstretched

that their numbers will rise as the strain on families and communities grows over the coming decade.

The most important limitation of the data that we have on the living circumstances of affected children is that they do not tell us much about how well their needs are being met. Many households caring for orphans may be overstretched, and some may not treat orphans as well as their own children.

Needs

All children need a safe and supportive home environment, adequate nutrition, access to healthcare and education, and protection from abuse and exploitation. While these basic needs are far from being met for millions of nonorphans, orphans and other children affected by AIDS are put at special risk in a variety of ways.

Poverty and malnutrition

AIDS can have a devastating impact on the economic situation of families, threatening their capacity to feed themselves and to provide for the basic needs of children. Impoverishment can begin with the illness of family members and can work in several ways. First, the illness of family members with paying jobs can reduce or eliminate the family's income. Second, illness in farming families can cause shortages of labor at critical points in the agricultural calendar, such as plowing and planting, leading to less land being cultivated and lower production (Barnett and Blaikie 1992; Munemo 2004; Shah and others 2002). Expenses for healthcare may be catastrophic and constitute a third channel of impoverishment. Finally, other family members may have to take time away from outside or farm work to care for sick members of the household. These effects translate into food insecurity either directly by reducing food production or indirectly by decreasing income with which to purchase food. Although it is difficult to disentangle its impact from those of drought and (particularly in the case of Zimbabwe) political instability, AIDS has been blamed for increasing food insecurity in southern Africa (de Waal and Whiteside 2003).

After the deaths of parents, other factors add to the risk of poverty that orphans face. Where women and children do not enjoy secure inheritance rights, paternal and double orphans may lose access to land and other property. Many orphans find themselves in households headed by women or elderly relatives who may have limited earning capacity (UNICEF 2003). Moreover, households with orphans may care for larger numbers of children or include fewer adults and thus suffer from high ratios of dependents to adults of working age. The data on the wealth and income of households caring for orphans relative to other households have been somewhat equivocal, perhaps because the effects outlined above are balanced to some degree by a tendency to place orphans with better-off relatives when possible (Bicego and others 2003). It is

One of the most important conse- quences of orphanhood can be loss of access to education

likely that the time of greatest economic vulnerability for many children may be when their parents are still alive but ill and no longer able to work, or soon after the parents have died and before stable arrangements for the children have been found.

Increased poverty can lead to reduced access to education (see below), malnutrition, and even reduced survival. There are little data on either the nutritional status or survival of orphans, but some studies have shown a link between mortality of children under 5 and death of the mother (Ainsworth and Semali 2000).

Disinheritance

Disinheritance of orphans or their widowed mothers can pose a grave threat to the economic security of orphans. Even where women enjoy equal property and inheritance rights under the law, legal systems may be weak or corrupt and these rights may be poorly enforced. Moreover, women are often unaware of their rights and may be disadvantaged in legal disputes by lack of education and lack of access to the justice system. Property rights, especially the right to own or make use of land, are often subject to customary as well as official law, and to traditions like wife inheritance. AIDS and the stigma associated with it have weakened traditional mechanisms for ensuring the livelihood of widows and orphans, while at the same time providing new justifications for land-grabbing and disinheritance (Global Coalition on Women and AIDS 2004; Strickland 2004).

Access to education

One of the most important consequences of orphanhood can be loss of access to education. Not only do orphans often find themselves in households that are less able to afford school fees and other expenses, but their schooling may be given a lower priority than that of other children in the same household. They may also face discrimination on the basis of perceived HIV status.

The ratio of school attendance of orphans to school attendance of nonorphans ages 10–14 is an UNGASS indicator as well as one of the core Millennium Development Indicators (see boxes 1.2 and 5.1), but most of the available evidence comes from household surveys. Data from a large set of African countries suggest that double orphans are less likely to be in school than nonorphans, but that the extent of the disadvantage varies considerably (UNAIDS 2003b; UNICEF 2003). In Mozambique orphans are half as likely to attend school, according to these data, while in Botswana the difference is apparently very small. (It is important to keep in mind that these surveys do not include the relatively small number of children living on the street or in institutions.) In general, household wealth has a much greater effect on school enrollment than orphan status (Ainsworth and Filmer 2002). A number of factors influence attendance rates: a recent study in Zimbabwe found that paternal orphans

**Orphaned
children are
also left with
emotional
scars**

did better than maternal orphans, even though they were more likely to be in female-headed and poorer households (Nyamukapa and Gregson 2004).

Psychosocial consequences

Orphaned children are also left with the emotional scars caused by the illness and death of family members, made worse in many cases by having had to care for the ailing parent and, in the case of AIDS, by the prolonged and difficult nature of the illness (Barnett and Whiteside 2002a; Monk 2002). This trauma can manifest itself in many ways, including anxiety, depression, aggression, loss of self-esteem and confidence, drug abuse, insomnia, poor performance in school, and malnutrition. Moreover, distress over the death of parents can last many years, as a survey in Lusaka showed (FHI and SCOPE OVC 2002). Orphaned children may lack a sense of identity or belonging, status, or self-respect, and may have difficulty integrating themselves into society or maintaining normal relations with others (Kelly 2002).

Vulnerability to HIV

The poverty and social marginalization experienced by orphans and other children affected by HIV put them at greater risk of becoming infected with HIV themselves, by denying them access to information and to preventative health services and by constraining their ability to protect themselves. These risks are particularly great for girls. A recent study in Zimbabwe confirmed these all too plausible speculations, finding that girls 15–18 (but not boys) who had a deceased or ill parent were more likely to be HIV positive (Wambe and others 2004). An HIV prevalence survey in South Africa also found a higher rate of HIV infection in double orphans than in nonorphans, although the contributions of vertical and sexual transmission could not be teased apart (Brooks and others 2004). Another study of factors influencing unsafe sexual behavior in KwaZulu Natal Province in South Africa found that being an orphan increased risk even after controlling for education and household wealth (Hallman 2004).

Social and economic consequences

Some have expressed concern that the large number of children orphaned by AIDS could threaten social stability by preventing appropriate socialization, leading to rampant crime and a breakdown of social institutions (Barnett and Whiteside 2002a; Schonteich 1999). Although these alarmist scenarios cannot be dismissed out of hand, there is to date little evidence to support them (Bray 2003). Moreover, these predictions may rest in large part on exaggerated projections of the numbers of children orphaned by AIDS relative to other causes (recall that AIDS accounts for less than 30 percent of orphans in Africa as a whole) and on the misconception that a large share of orphaned children find themselves on the street. The broader strain imposed by AIDS

**The best
solution to
orphaning by
AIDS will be
prevention of
HIV infection**

on families and communities in high-prevalence areas probably poses a greater danger in the long run, especially if food security or prospects for economic growth are threatened.

Studies of the economic impact of AIDS have reached widely varying conclusions. Some studies, relying on conventional analyses of labor supply and productivity, have predicted that even devastating epidemics might have only relatively minor effects on economic growth (reviewed in Haacker 2002).[7] In contrast, one of the most widely quoted studies argues that AIDS could cause far greater losses over the long run by disrupting transmission of human capital (skills and know-how) from one generation to the next (Bell and others 2003). This disruption is closely linked to the orphan crisis, since it is hypothesized to result from loss of parenting, as well as deprivation of schooling. The study asserts that South Africa's economy could virtually collapse over three generations if decisive action is not taken, both to prevent and treat HIV/AIDS and to mitigate its effects, especially by subsidizing education. Although these findings rely on many assumptions, they illustrate possible, even probable, ways that high rates of orphaning could have very damaging economic consequences and provide some guide to the kinds of policies that might best forestall these impacts.

In considering the possible impact of very high AIDS mortality in southern Africa, it may be instructive to consider the experience of Uganda, which experienced very high AIDS prevalence in the early 1990s and where rates of mortality and orphaning have already peaked. Although there has certainly been great suffering at the level of individuals, families, and communities, the economy has grown briskly and there has been no sweeping social breakdown. There is certainly no guarantee that the very different and even more affected societies of southern Africa will be able to match Uganda's remarkable resilience, but its example should be kept in mind in weighing the more apocalyptic scenarios.

Interventions and policies

In the long term, the best solution to the tragedy of orphaning by AIDS will be prevention of HIV infection itself. More immediately, rapid expansion of treatment can play a critical role by prolonging the lives of parents. In addition, comprehensive family-planning services should be available to all women, including those who are HIV-positive (UNFPA 2004; UNFPA/UNAIDS 2004).

But the most affected countries cannot wait for these measures to take effect. They must act now to meet the needs of children who have already lost or will soon lose their parents. Moreover, mobilizing communities around care and support for affected people, both children and adults, will be critical to involving communities in prevention and treatment as well. Effective responses to the orphan crisis must be multifaceted, addressing the various needs of vulnerable children, and locally tailored, drawing on knowledge of

Effective responses to the orphan crisis must be multifaceted

local circumstances. They will depend critically on community knowledge and involvement, and they should build close links to prevention and treatment programs, especially at the community level.

Broad strategies and general principles

A broad process of consultation led by UNICEF and UNAIDS has led to a consensus document, The Framework for the Protection, Care and Support of Orphans and Vulnerable Children in a World with HIV and AIDS, which lays out five broad strategies and a number of more detailed recommendations (UNICEF and others 2004). The Framework has been endorsed by a broad range of organizations brought together by UNICEF in the first Global Partners Forum on Orphans and Vulnerable Children in October 2003, and subsequently by UNAIDS. The five strategies are:

- Strengthen the capacity of families to protect and care for orphans and vulnerable children by prolonging the lives of parents and providing economic, psychosocial, and other support.
- Mobilize and support community-based responses to provide both immediate and long-term support to vulnerable households.
- Ensure access for orphans and vulnerable children to essential services, including education and healthcare.
- Ensure that governments protect the most vulnerable children through improved policy and legislation and by channeling resources to communities.
- Raise awareness at all levels through advocacy and social mobilization to create a supportive environment for children affected by HIV/AIDS.

The task force endorses these priorities. We highlight as well three broad principles, each of which is widely, if not universally, accepted. First, the task force believes that, in general, services should not be targeted specifically to children affected by AIDS. Singling out children affected by AIDS would be unfair, as children orphaned by other causes will experience many of the same deprivations. Although children affected by AIDS (or thought to be) face the additional burden of AIDS-related stigma, treating these children differently from others is likely to make this situation worse. Singling out AIDS orphans is in any case impractical, since in many circumstances the cause of the death of parents cannot be ascertained. Instead, services for orphans and other vulnerable children should be provided to those most in need.

The Framework suggests a two-phase strategy for directing assistance to where it is most needed in the context of a high-prevalence AIDS epidemic. First, planners should target the regions and communities with the greatest concentrations of orphans and other vulnerable children, which in the hardest-hit countries will tend be those most affected by the epidemic. Second, the affected communities themselves should take the lead in identifying children and families most in need. Although this is not an ideal solution—vulnerable

Planners should target the regions and communities with the greatest concentrations of orphans and other vulnerable children

children in less affected areas risk being deprived of assistance—it is a practical way to reach many of those in the greatest need without singling out children affected by AIDS within communities.

The second broad principle that the task force endorses is the importance of keeping children in families and assisting households to meet children's needs. The great majority of orphans and vulnerable children currently live with families, and these settings are in almost all cases better for their emotional and social development (International Save the Children Alliance 2003; Tolfrey 2003; UNAIDS/UNICEF/USAID 2004). Moreover, caring for children in institutions is considerably more expensive than supporting them in families and communities (Prywes and others 2004; USAID/UNICEF/UNAIDS 2002).

Although orphanages are neither a desirable nor practical answer for more than a fraction of orphans, they may have a role for children who would otherwise find themselves on the street or in abusive situations. Given the scale and diversity of need it seems unwise to rule out altogether any form of institutional care. At a minimum, governments have a responsibility to ensure that orphanages, where they do exist, provide adequate care and access to education.

A third broad principle of the response should be the leading role that must be played by communities. Although community participation will be critical to the success of prevention and treatment as well, a comprehensive effort to assist vulnerable children in the family setting is almost inconceivable without the commitment and participation of communities and community-based organizations, especially given the very limited reach of government structures in most of the hardest-hit countries. While national and local governments, with the assistance of donors, should build their capacity to plan, oversee, and finance child and family welfare programs, they will have to rely on community groups to identify families in need, determine the most important types of assistance, and deliver many services. Moreover, mobilization of communities and civil society to respond to the needs of vulnerable children can be a fundamental part of a broader response that can encompass care for the sick, support during antiretroviral therapy, and prevention.

The pivotal role of communities in the response to the orphan crisis does not absolve governments of their basic responsibility to enable, guide, and support this response and to intervene when local efforts founder or fail to meet basic standards of equity. Moreover, governments have primary responsibility for ensuring children's access to education and healthcare and for enacting and enforcing laws to protect the rights of vulnerable children. Finally, governments and donors will have to cover many of the costs of orphan programs.

National plans

At the national level, the first step in responding to the orphan crisis should be development of a comprehensive national strategy. Although UNGASS called for such strategies to be in place by 2003, only half of countries in Sub-Saharan

Governments must ensure a supportive legal environment for vulnerable children and their caretakers

Africa have met this deadline (Monasch and others 2004). Development of a national strategy should begin with a collaborative national assessment, involving a broad range of stakeholders and pulling together information on the geographic distribution and circumstances of orphans and vulnerable children, the impact and likely evolution of the AIDS epidemic, and the most urgently needed kinds of assistance (Williamson, forthcoming). This assessment should then inform the development of a national strategy or action plan outlining programs to meet the various needs of vulnerable children, detailing how much the programs will cost, and spelling out how they will be implemented and monitored, with appropriate roles for government at various levels, donors, nongovernmental organizations, and community groups.

Legal measures

As part of the national response governments must ensure a supportive legal environment for vulnerable children and their caretakers. The most important elements include laws protecting the inheritance rights of widows and orphans and the right of women to ownership or secure use of land. Even where such laws exist, they are often not well enforced or well understood (Global Coalition on Women and AIDS 2004; Strickland 2004). Efforts should be made to educate women and communities about these rights, especially where they may conflict with local custom, and to provide recourse to a trusted authority for the adjudication of disputes. A review of Save the Children's work in Uganda found that strengthening the capacity of district social welfare officers to settle property disputes had been one of its more successful programs (Witter and others 2004).

Governments must also work to protect orphans, including AIDS orphans, from discrimination in access to education and healthcare and from abuse and exploitation, including exploitative child labor. This will require substantial strengthening of local government capacity.

Birth registration is an important step in ensuring the rights of children. In many African countries fewer than 50 percent of births are registered (UNICEF 2003). More broadly, we join the Task Force on Maternal and Child Health in calling for investment in building national systems of vital registration, which will be critical to measuring progress toward all the Millennium Development Goals on health (UN Millennium Project 2005b).

Specific interventions

This report will not attempt a comprehensive review of the kinds of programs that have proved useful in meeting the needs of orphans and vulnerable children. Although nongovernmental organizations and community groups have now accumulated a considerable body of experience with small-scale programs of various kinds, much work remains to be done in extracting best practices from this experience. Development of a set of tested, replicable models for interventions of various types would greatly facilitate scaling up.

**A set of
tested,
replicable
models for
interventions
of various
types would
greatly
facilitate
scaling up**

Microeconomic strengthening, income-generating projects. Many households caring for orphans require economic support, which can be provided in several forms. Rather than offering cash grants, many organizations prefer to help households to increase agricultural production or to earn money through small businesses, by providing free or subsidized inputs, technical advice, or microcredit. Income earned in this way can be used to buy food, clothing, and other necessities and to pay school fees. In fact, profits from microcredit programs, especially those targeted to women, are often used to pay school fees (Williamson, forthcoming). Thus in theory microeconomic support programs could substitute at least in part for direct support of other kinds. But for programs of this kind to succeed, at least two conditions must be met. First, sufficient unexploited economic opportunities must exist locally. Second, the individuals or households needing help must be able to take advantage of these opportunities; this may not be the case for the most vulnerable families, those that are too unstable or include no healthy adults. These families will often require more direct support.

Although experience with these "income-generating activities" has been mixed (Williamson, forthcoming), this kind of support is in theory more sustainable than direct transfers. As with most child care and support activities, these kinds of programs require detailed local knowledge regarding economic opportunities and regarding the skills and capabilities of vulnerable households. As a result they are probably best implemented by community-based groups or local nongovernmental organizations, with funding from national governments and donors.

Many households that are not caring for orphans are also poor, of course, and there are dangers—and ethical issues—in using household composition as a criterion for financial support. Ideally, these forms of assistance would be provided as part of a broader system of support for disadvantaged households.

Education. Programs to ensure that orphans and other vulnerable children have access to education are among the most important. Since school fees are a critical barrier to access for children in the poorest households, as shown by the dramatic increases in enrolment seen in Uganda and Kenya when fees were abolished (Herz and Sperling 2004), the task force believes that the most effective and equitable way to increase access for vulnerable children would be to end school fees for all children. This will require increased funding, both to offset the loss of fees and to pay for expanding capacity to accommodate increased enrolment. In the poorest countries, substantial donor support will almost certainly be necessary. Where school fees cannot be eliminated for all children immediately, waivers for certain categories of vulnerable children should be considered. The major challenges to this approach are to equitably define and identify eligible children and to ensure that schools are compensated for the resulting loss of income. Swaziland recently announced a program under which the central government will pay the school fees of orphans and vulnerable children (IRIN 2004).

Supporting vulnerable children and households requires detailed local knowledge and strong community involvement

School feeding programs. School lunches offer a powerful way to support the twin objectives of alleviating hunger among children and keeping them in school. Although school meals may have to be supplemented by other forms of food support, they can provide a substantial share of a child's daily food requirement. Moreover, provision of free meals can significantly boost enrollment (WFP 2001). Finally, if school lunches are produced from locally grown food, they can boost local agricultural production. For these reasons, the UN Millennium Project Task Force on Hunger includes school feeding programs as one of the key interventions in its Early Action Plan for Africa (UN Millennium Project 2005c).

Psychosocial support. Psychosocial support programs should provide services both before and after the death of the parent. Before the death of the parent, one aim should be encourage open discussion between parents and children and to allow children to actively participate in decisions concerning their future. "Memory books" can help orphans to discuss their feelings and provide children with a physical reminder of their parents. After the death of the parent, children need a safe environment to talk about their feelings, either among peers or individually with a trusted adult. Several programs train teachers, religious leaders, community leaders, and other adults to provide support to orphans and other vulnerable children. One example is HUMULIZA, a pilot project in Nshamba, Tanzania. While HUMULIZA also provides school fees for orphans, its primary focus is psychosocial support (International HIV/AIDS Alliance 2003a; UNAIDS 2001b).

Psychosocial support programs can also further the socialization of affected children by creating opportunities for them to play with their peers or interact with and emulate the behavior of adults. An example of a successful program is the Zimbabwe Salvation Army Masiye Camp, which teaches children life skills using an Outward Bound approach. Other programs groups allow children to practice these skills in their own community by participating in peer support groups, community service, and income generating activities (International HIV/AIDS Alliance 2003a; UNAIDS 2001b).

Community involvement and mobilization

Supporting vulnerable children and households requires detailed local knowledge and strong community involvement. In many places, local groups are already trying to do what they can. If these efforts are to be brought to scale, governments and donors will have to find ways to nurture and support local initiatives without compromising local participation and ownership (Donahue and Williamson 1999).

Working with (and funding) community groups and local nongovernmental organizations can be challenging, since governments and donors have difficulty identifying and evaluating groups with the necessary capabilities, while grassroots organizations often lack experience with writing proposals,

Programs for vulnerable children should be part of a network of prevention, care, and support services

managing and accounting for funds, and monitoring and reporting on their work. Umbrella organizations or networks of community groups can help by linking donors to appropriate recipients or by channeling funds (Williamson and others 2001). Alternatively, donors can work through local committees. Organizations such as the International HIV/AIDS Alliance and its local partners can help to build the capacity of community groups. Developing better mechanisms for channeling resources to community organizations will become increasingly important as governments and donors seek to implement ambitious AIDS programs through local partners.

The Scaling-up HIV/AIDS Interventions Through Expanded Partnerships (STEPS) program in Malawi (formerly known as Community-based Options for Protection and Empowerment, or COPE), which is run by Save the Children (USA) and funded in part by USAID, is a promising example of donor and government assistance to community initiatives supporting vulnerable children and households (Hunter 2002). The program is built on a structure of village, community, and district AIDS committees established earlier by the Malawi government but strengthened and assisted by STEPS. Village committees develop and deliver a set of services, which can include home care; nutritional, emotional, and income support; and HIV prevention. The committees also identify local children and households most in need. STEPS works to mobilize communities through the local committees and provides training and supplies. As of 2002, the program had assisted more than 18,000 orphans and vulnerable children through almost 300 village committees in four districts (Hunter 2002; Opoku and Yamba 2001). By 2004, STEPS was supporting local activities in thirteen districts.

Links to other HIV services

In areas of high HIV prevalence, where AIDS is responsible for growing numbers of orphans, programs for vulnerable children should be part of a network of prevention, care, and support services. There should be strong links to treatment and care programs, especially those providing home care, to identify and help vulnerable children before they are orphaned. Programs for orphans can in turn identify and refer HIV-positive children for diagnosis and treatment. Orphan and home care programs may already have strong ties in some places, since both services are often provided by community and religious groups. The challenge will be to build stronger links to the formal health sector and to other arms of government.

At the same time, programs working with older children need to help them protect themselves against infection by providing information, condoms, and access to other prevention and reproductive health services. More broadly, prevention, care, and support for affected families and children should constitute interdependent elements of an integrated community response to the epidemic.

The challenge will be to build stronger links to the formal health sector and to other arms of government

State of the response

It is likely that most households caring for orphans and vulnerable children are not receiving substantial assistance of any kind, and that what help there is comes primarily from community groups, churches, and nongovernmental organizations with little financial or other support from governments.

Most countries in Sub-Saharan Africa have some kind of process under way to develop a national response to the needs of orphans and vulnerable children, but in most cases these efforts are still very preliminary. These are the conclusions from scores on the OVC Policy and Planning Effort Index, developed recently by UNICEF, USAID, and the Futures Group to measure national effort in this area (Monasch and others 2004). A majority of countries in Sub-Saharan Africa have conducted some kind of national assessment and established consultative processes and coordinating mechanisms; half have written national action plans. But the quality of most situation assessments is poor, and few plans are costed and resourced. The greatest weakness found by the survey was legislative review: few countries had implemented laws to protect the rights of vulnerable children, and even fewer had the resources to enforce such laws.

For almost all hard-hit countries, lack of funds will be an important obstacle to a comprehensive response to the needs of affected children. A recent UNICEF-sponsored analysis suggests that these efforts could be more expensive than previously thought. This study, based on data collected from organizations providing services to children in more than 20 African countries, found that providing a full set of services cost on average about $600 per child per year.[8] Providing this assistance to those orphans and vulnerable children in households in need, defined as those living below the poverty line, would cost perhaps $3.5 billion in 2004 and as much as $6 billion in 2010 for Sub-Saharan Africa as a whole. Some of the components of these cost estimates, especially for food, seem high, but a recent World Bank costing analysis in Benin and Eritrea reached roughly similar estimates (Prywes and others 2004).

There appear to be few data on current spending on care and support for orphans and vulnerable children. Until recently, few large international initiatives had specifically targeted this population. The U.S. government's AIDS initiative earmarks funds for AIDS-affected children, and the Global Fund hopes to reach 1 million children with funds from its first three rounds of approved grants (Save the Children 2004; U.S. Department of State 2004).

Recommendations

- National governments must recommit themselves to developing and implementing comprehensive strategies and detailed, costed plans for meeting the needs of orphans and other vulnerable children, as mandated by the UNGASS Declaration of Commitment. The United Nations should more effectively support countries in fulfilling this commitment and more boldly call to account those that fail to do so.

Singling out AIDS orphans is impractical

- National strategies must be backed by budgetary commitments. Governments should commit funds from their own resources to these programs, and donors should be prepared to fill remaining gaps where well-designed strategies have been developed. The total cost of providing adequate support for orphans and vulnerable children in Africa has been estimated at $3.5 billion in 2004.
- The five key strategies outlined in the Framework for the Protection, Care, and Support of Orphans and Vulnerable Children (UNICEF and others 2004) should form the basis of national responses.
- The AIDS orphan crisis should be used as a lever to push national governments and the international community to live up to their responsibilities toward all vulnerable children, only a minority of whom are affected by AIDS. The most urgent effort should be directed at areas with very high HIV prevalence, however, because it is here that traditional mechanisms for caring for children are under the greatest strain.
- In general, services should not be targeted specifically to children orphaned or made vulnerable by AIDS. Singling out AIDS orphans is impractical, since the cause of parental death is usually not known; unfair, since children orphaned by other causes are likely to suffer similar deprivations; and unwise, since it could contribute to AIDS stigma. It may make sense to direct some specialized services, including counseling, to children whose parents are dying or have died from AIDS. These services could be linked to home-based care for AIDS patients.
- The primary focus of programs for orphans and vulnerable children should be to assist families, which already care for the great majority of these children, to meet their needs. Institutional care should be available as a last resort for children who would otherwise find themselves on the street or in abusive environments. Governments have the obligation to ensure that orphanages provide adequate care and that children living in institutions have access to education and healthcare.
- Communities should take the lead in most aspects of a comprehensive strategy to assist orphans and vulnerable children. In particular, community-based organizations should be responsible for identifying children at risk, for determining the most urgently needed types of support, and for implementing many programs at the local level. Governments and nongovernmental organizations should support community groups in these roles not only by financing their activities, but by building their capacity to write proposals, manage and account for funds, and monitor their activities.
- School fees should be eliminated for all children as soon as possible, and international support should be available to help the poorest countries bear the additional costs that this will entail. Where elimination of all fees is not immediately feasible, countries should consider waiving fees

Communities should take the lead in most aspects of a compre-hensive strat-egy to assist orphans and vulnerable children

for orphans and other categories of vulnerable children. The poorest families will also need help with the other costs of keeping children in school.

- School lunch programs should be rapidly expanded. These programs can help to feed children from the poorest households and provide a powerful incentive for enrollment. Schools can also serve as a base for other services for vulnerable children.

- National governments must urgently review laws governing inheritance and their enforcement. The inheritance rights of widows and children must be guaranteed, and children should be protected against abuse and exploitative child labor. In addition, birth registration should be made universal as rapidly as possible.

- Programs for orphans and vulnerable children should build strong links with other community-based HIV/AIDS activities, in particular home-based care, adherence support for patients on antiretroviral therapy, and community prevention programs. Together these efforts constitute the kind of comprehensive community response to the epidemic that will be necessary to reverse its course and mitigate its impact.

Finance and implementation

The previous chapters have outlined the major elements of a comprehensive response to the AIDS epidemic: prevention of new infections, treatment and care, and support for orphans and vulnerable children. We have outlined a set of necessary services or interventions in each area and addressed some of the most important issues involved in implementing these measures. In this chapter we turn to topics that cut across the three elements of the response. First we consider the cost of mounting an effective response to the epidemic and review recent data from UNAIDS on current and projected resource availability. We then examine two issues that will have to be resolved if new funds for AIDS programs are to be spent effectively at the country level: poor donor coordination and limited absorptive capacity. Finally, we discuss how the United Nations system could do more to help countries combat the epidemic.

Estimating the cost

Estimating the cost of meeting the Millennium Development Goals is an important part of the UN Millennium Project's mandate. Fortunately, work on resource requirements for AIDS is relatively advanced. As a result, the Working Group on HIV/AIDS has been able to rely on existing work in this area.

UNAIDS estimates

The most comprehensive work on resource needs for HIV/AIDS in the developing world has been done by UNAIDS. Their most recent analysis, which extends and revises earlier work (Schwartlander and others 2001; UNAIDS 2002a), estimates that $11.6 billion will be required in 2005 and $19.9 billion in 2007 (UNAIDS 2004b). Of the 2007 total, prevention accounts for 50 percent, treatment and care for 34 percent, and support for orphans and vulnerable children for 11 percent. About 43 percent of these resources would be

Growth in the number of people requiring treatment will almost certainly cause the annual cost of treatment and care to increase substantially

needed in Sub-Saharan Africa, 28 percent in Asia, 17 percent in Latin America and the Caribbean, 9 percent in Eastern Europe, and 1 percent in North Africa and the Middle East. These estimates result from gathering country-specific data on the unit costs of a set of essential services, estimating the number of people needing each service, and setting feasible targets for coverage of each service. A number of considerations should be kept in mind in interpreting the resulting estimates.

First, this method calculates average costs rather than marginal costs. In some cases, where large fixed costs have already been incurred or where there are increasing returns to scale, the incremental cost of expanding coverage from its current levels may be lower. In other cases, actual costs may rise, as capacity constraints become more binding (see below) or where people who do not have access to a service are more difficult and more expensive to reach. An alternative costing methodology, Marginal Budgeting for Bottlenecks, has been developed to shed light on marginal costs of expanding services and on the costs and benefits of addressing particular constraints to service delivery (Knippenberg and others n.d.). This tool may be a more useful guide to incremental costs over the short run than the average cost approach. The UNAIDS approach is probably the most appropriate for evaluating resource requirements over the longer term.

Second, costs in the UNAIDS model depend on the choice of coverage targets, which in turn reflect estimates of system capacity to deliver services. Thus, in a certain sense these are estimates of the total cost of reaching as many people as system capacity will permit, rather than the cost of providing basic services to all who require them. Capacity is assumed to grow between 2003 and 2007, at a rate that depends on a country's GDP and past performance, but remains a constraint on coverage in many cases. This consideration is particularly relevant to antiretroviral therapy, which places relatively high demands on health systems. The coverage targets for antiretroviral therapy in the costing analysis were revised to make them consistent with the 3 by 5 target (see below); by 2007 coverage corresponds to 52 percent of those in need (Hankins and others 2004). Coverage targets for this and other services cannot be directly compared with the targets set by the working group, which are for 2015, but since the UNAIDS targets are quite high this is not a major obstacle to our use of their estimates.

Third, while the model considers system capacity as a constraint on coverage levels, it does not explicitly consider the costs of expanding capacity, such as the cost of building new clinics, hospitals, or laboratories. Moreover, while the human resource costs of delivering particular interventions are included in the estimates whenever possible, the potentially large costs of relieving the shortage of skilled staff that currently limits coverage (by raising salaries, improving working conditions, or expanding nursing and medical schools) are not considered and would be difficult to assign to particular AIDS services.

**Rapidly
scaling
up both
prevention
and treatment
could cut
costs in
later years**

This is probably the largest category of costs that are not included in these otherwise comprehensive estimates.

Finally, the UNAIDS estimates extend only to 2007 and can thus serve only as a rough guide to costs between 2007 and 2015. Growth in the number of people requiring treatment will almost certainly cause the annual cost of treatment and care to increase substantially, although the extent of the increase will depend critically on the success of prevention in the intervening years, and some of the costs may be offset by further reductions in the price of antiretroviral drugs. Rapidly scaling up both prevention and treatment could also cut costs in later years by reducing the number of orphans and vulnerable children requiring support.

Other estimates

The only other major attempt to estimate the cost of providing a comprehensive set of prevention and treatment services in the developing world was that of WHO's Commission on Macroeconomics and Health (CMH). The CMH, using the same basic methodology as UNAIDS, calculated that expenditures on AIDS in a smaller number of mostly low-income countries would have to rise to $14 billion per year over 2001 levels by 2007, and to $22 billion annually by 2015 (Commission on Macroeconomics and Health 2001). This analysis did not include services for orphans and vulnerable children, but did attempt to incorporate the cost of expanding health system capacity. Given the enormous uncertainties involved in this kind of calculation, the degree of agreement between the CMH and UNAIDS estimates is remarkable and provides some assurance that these figures are at least in the right range.

Some other recent studies have used the UNAIDS analysis or its methodology to shed light on the costs of specific components of the response. WHO and UNAIDS estimated in early 2004 that achieving the target of treating 3 million people by 2005 would cost between $4.9 and $5.4 billion over 2004–05, depending on the path by which the target was reached and the price of drugs (Gutierrez and others 2004). This figure assumes a delivery model consistent with the WHO operational guidelines and includes not only antiretroviral therapy itself, but the recommended set of accompanying services (WHO/UNAIDS 2004b). This estimate reaches $5.4 billion–6.4 billion in the recent UNAIDS costing report. In 2003 the Global HIV Prevention Working Group analyzed the funding gap for prevention, drawing on UNAIDS' work for estimates of resource needs (Global HIV Prevention Working Group 2003).

The UNAIDS costing may have to be significantly revised in the area of programs for orphans and vulnerable children, in large part because there is much less consensus on a set of essential services and on how (and to whom) they should be delivered. A UNICEF survey concluded that the cost of delivering basic services to children at the community level was considerably higher than anticipated and that providing this support to orphans and vulnerable

Providing a set of basic HIV/AIDS services to all those who need them would cost well over $10 billion and as much as $20 billion a year

children in households below the poverty line could cost as much as $6 billion by 2010 in Sub-Saharan Africa alone (see chapter 4). This is considerably more than the $2.2 billion estimated for 2007 by UNAIDS, even though the UNAIDS study included all countries with HIV prevalence above 1 percent. In another respect the UNAIDS study may have overestimated the cost of orphan support, since it assumes a large role for orphanages. Institutional care is considerably more expensive than care in families and communities (Desmond and Gow 2001; Prywes and others 2004).

The working group has not conducted its own costing analysis. The UN Millennium Project Secretariat, however, led an effort to estimate the cost of meeting the health Millennium Development Goals in a small number of case study countries, using a variety of approaches, including a modified version of the UNAIDS methodology (UN Millennium Project 2004). Coverage targets were set at or close to 100 percent for all services in 2015, with gradual scale-up from current coverage in intervening years. An important feature of this study was that it attempted to incorporate the costs of building health system capacity by including allocations for strengthened management, physical infrastructure, substantial increases in health workers' salaries, and other systemwide costs. The cost of salary increases alone constituted a substantial share of the estimated total cost of meeting the health Millennium Development Goals (encompassing AIDS, malaria, tuberculosis, and maternal and child health). Although these estimates should be considered very preliminary, they suggest that a serious attempt to resolve the crisis in human resources for health might add very substantially to the cost of a comprehensive response to HIV/AIDS.

In summary, there is substantial agreement that providing a set of basic HIV/AIDS services to all those who need them would cost well over $10 billion and as much as $20 billion a year. The most important gap in the existing estimates concerns health systems: lack of health system capacity currently limits expansion of some services, especially antiretroviral treatment, but relatively little is know about what it would cost to relieve this constraint. Filling this gap is an important priority, but good cost estimates will depend on better understanding of how to build stronger health systems in various settings.

Current and projected resources

Global resources for AIDS in the developing world have grown enormously in recent years, but they remain insufficient. According to UNAIDS, institutional spending on HIV/AIDS (including funding by bilateral donors, multilateral organizations, and developing country governments) rose as much as ninefold between 1996 and 2002 to about $2.7 billion (UNAIDS 2003b). Spending from these sources has continued to increase rapidly, and when contributions from households and the private sector are included, resources for AIDS are expected to exceed $6 billion in 2004 (UNAIDS 2004b). Almost 40 percent of this total comes from domestic sources (national governments

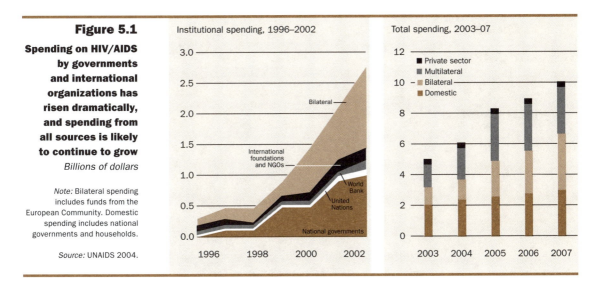

Figure 5.1

Spending on HIV/AIDS by governments and international organizations has risen dramatically, and spending from all sources is likely to continue to grow
Billions of dollars

Note: Bilateral spending includes funds from the European Community. Domestic spending includes national governments and households.

Source: UNAIDS 2004.

Institutional spending, 1996–2002

Bilateral

International foundations and NGOs

World Bank

United Nations

National governments

Total spending, 2003–07

■ Private sector
■ Multilateral
■ Bilateral
■ Domestic

and households), while 21 percent comes from bilateral sources and 34 percent from multilateral channels, including the Global Fund, the World Bank, and the UN system. UNAIDS projects that available resources will rise to more than $10 billion by 2007, with most of the increase coming from international sources (figure 5.1).

Among bilateral donors, the United States and the United Kingdom are by far the largest contributors to AIDS programs, accounting for 35.2 percent and 27.6 percent of bilateral aid, respectively, and the U.S. share is expected to grow as its AIDS initiative gets under way. It should be noted, however, that the United States currently ranks only sixth in its contribution relative to GDP, and last among OECD countries in development assistance overall as a share of national income (UNAIDS 2004b).

Despite these very substantial increases, resources available for AIDS in the developing world are still well below what will be required to bring the epidemic under control and to bring essential prevention, treatment, and support services to those who need them. In 2007, for example, the projected $10 billion would constitute only a little more than half of UNAIDS' estimate of need in that year. Moreover, measurements and projections of expenditure refer to disbursements by donors or governments. Since there is often a considerable delay before these funds reach the project or grassroots level, the real funding gap is larger than these numbers suggest.

The adequacy of AIDS funding depends on many factors beyond the total quantity of funds from all sources. First, it matters a great deal where the money comes from: while some developing country governments have increased funding on AIDS substantially, a disturbingly large share of domestic expenditure comes from households themselves, especially in the poorest countries. Data on AIDS-specific spending are scarce, but so-called out-of-pocket expenditures (formal or informal user fees to public health services or payments to

Quality of donor financing matters as much as its quantity

private providers) are estimated to account for almost three quarters of health spending in low-income countries (World Development Indicators 2004, cited in UNAIDS 2004b). Although it makes sense for people who can afford to contribute to the cost of their care to do so, in the absence of public or private insurance or free public health services for those who need them, the burden of paying for AIDS treatment and care can be catastrophic and contribute in an important way to the impoverishment of families and communities. In addition, little is known about the quality of services purchased from private providers.

Second, the quality of donor financing matters as much as its quantity. Development assistance for AIDS will be more effective if it responds to recipient rather than donor priorities, if fewer conditions are attached to its use, if it is longer-term and predictable, and if the burden of paperwork and reporting imposed on recipients is kept to a minimum. These issues, which apply to all sectors, are considered at greater length in the UN Millennium Project's synthesis report (UN Millennium Project 2005a); see also the discussion of donor coordination below.

Finally, of course, the money must be spent well. Funds must go the right programs—misplaced priorities or inequitable allocation will diminish the impact of AIDS spending—and these programs must be implemented effectively. To the extent that AIDS programs are not well designed or monitored or that the funds allocated to them never reach the clinics, hospitals, or community organizations where they are to be used, more spending will not translate into fewer infections or more people in treatment. Thus, while reaching the goal of bringing the epidemic under control by 2015 will require further increases in resources, and these funds will have to come mostly from the donor nations, equal effort must be devoted to overcoming the barriers to spending these new resources as effectively as possible (see below).

The Global Fund

While all financing channels have a role to play, the working group believes that it is vital to strengthen and ensure the survival of the Global Fund to Fight AIDS, Tuberculosis and Malaria, while continuing to improve its performance. The Global Fund is a multilateral institution designed to rapidly channel money to country-owned and country-implemented initiatives against these three diseases. In its first three years, it has established an innovative grant evaluation and funding process, approved 297 proposals from 128 countries requesting over $3 billion, and disbursed more than $633 million (as of October 2004).

The Global Fund differs from more traditional channels for development assistance in several ways (Radelet 2004). First, it does not implement or oversee funded programs; it is by design a financing mechanism only. In theory, this gives it the potential to be an unusually agile financing vehicle, well suited

It is vital to strengthen and ensure the survival of the Global Fund to Fight AIDS, Tuberculosis and Malaria

to funding rapid scaling up of the AIDS response, although this feature introduces problems of its own (see below). Second, it funds country-initiated and country-designed programs and thus responds to country rather than donor priorities. Moreover, as a multilateral funding mechanism, it pools the contributions of donors in these program areas, in theory reducing the multiplicity of donor projects and administrative demands on recipients. Finally, the Global Fund works at the country level through a novel institution, the Country Coordinating Mechanism (CCM), that brings together donors, civil society, and government. The CCMs endorse and harmonize all grant proposals and are responsible for overseeing implementation by recipients and ensuring transparency and accountability. Although both the performance and inclusiveness of CCMs have varied considerably, in many countries they seem to have opened new channels of communication and enabled broader participation in setting priorities and designing programs.

Ultimately, of course, the Global Fund must be judged by results: by how rapidly it can channel funds to programs against the three diseases and by whether these programs meet their objectives. It is too early to reach definitive conclusions, but early results are promising. The Global Fund's own evaluation of 25 grants that were at least a year old by April 2004 found that 12 had met or exceeded targets, 8 had made good progress but fallen somewhat short of targets, while 5 were doing poorly (GFATM 2004b). Across the set of 25 grants recipients reached an average of 80 percent of one-year performance targets; 6 of 9 HIV/AIDS grants were judged to be on track. Nonetheless, the early experience of the Global Fund suggests several challenges and areas for improvement.

First, disbursement of funds for approved proposals has been disappointingly slow and a source of frustration for some recipients. The main delays have been at the start: on average, it takes six months before a grant is signed, and one or two more months for a first disbursement to be received (GFATM 2004a). While these delays have been decreasing, the process could be accelerated by increasing the fund's unusually small staff of portfolio managers, by reinforcing the role of private recipients for civil society grants, and by offering centralized options for pooled product procurement.

Second, and more seriously, the current proposal process neither requires countries to consider implementation challenges seriously enough nor does it enable the Global Fund itself to adequately evaluate implementation capacity during the approval process. The interests of neither the Global Fund nor recipient countries are served by approving proposals, including those for ambitious AIDS treatment programs, that do not include realistic consideration of human resources or other health system challenges and do not lay out a plausible plan of implementation. This is not to suggest that the Global Fund should reject all proposals from countries where health personnel or critical infrastructure are in short supply—these are just the countries it was designed to serve. But the pro-

The potential harm to health systems can be minimized by interpreting the Global Fund's mandate broadly

cess must be designed to encourage systematic planning by countries themselves for overcoming these obstacles. Three changes or shifts in emphasis might help:

- The proposal form itself should explicitly require applicants to explain how human resource needs will be met. How many health workers of which kinds will be needed to deliver the planned services, and how will they be recruited and trained? Is there a national human resources strategy for the health sector, and how does the proposal fit within it?
- Applicants should be required to review performance on past Global Fund grants, as well as related grants from other international donors. They should be asked explain how they will address any shortcomings that emerged, including those highlighted by the fund's own two-year evaluations, if available. Countries that have not done well in the past should not be automatically denied new grants, but should present a coherent plan for overcoming previous problems. A recent analysis of the fund went a step further and recommended that past performance become an explicit criterion in evaluating proposals (Radelet 2004).
- Although the Fund does not assist countries with implementation, it should encourage countries to request funds for technical assistance where necessary. Moreover, it should help recipients to find qualified partners: difficulty in identifying appropriate partners has slowed the use of funds allocated for this purpose to date.

Third, the Global Fund's basic design might inadvertently promote vertical, disease-specific programs. Thus, it could endanger other disease priorities— and health systems—by underwriting the diversion of staff and other limited resources and the establishment of separate management and logistical systems (Bennett and Fairbank 2003). To some extent this is unavoidable, given the focus on the three diseases and the need to show rapid results in combating them. But the potential harm to health systems can be minimized (and the collateral benefits maximized) by interpreting the Global Fund's mandate broadly to include strengthening of health systems required for delivery of AIDS, tuberculosis, and malaria interventions and by considering the likely impact of proposed programs on health systems.

Thus, an AIDS treatment proposal that would set up a stand-alone network of treatment sites with its own drug distribution, laboratory, and management systems should be viewed less favorably than one that would work through and strengthen existing systems. Precedents for such broad programs exist within the current grant portfolio of the Global Fund—for example, the AIDS grant to Haiti includes funds for building and refurbishing healthcare centers, stocking centers with essential medicines, and staff training—but this approach should be more vigorously encouraged. Moreover, the Global Fund has shown considerable flexibility in harmonizing with other donors: financing from the fund has contributed to sectorwide approaches in Ghana, Mozambique, and Zambia.

Current donor initiatives too often result in a patchwork of poorly coordinated programs

The "integrated" proposal option that the Global Fund introduced in the fourth round of proposals offers a promising way for the fund to support health systems. This option allows countries to propose programs that develop cross-cutting health system capacity, including human resources and infrastructure, and thereby relieve some of the bottlenecks constraining implementation of AIDS, tuberculosis, and malaria programs. However, the Global Fund needs to promote this option more vigorously and provide more specific guidelines for integrated proposals. The lack of clarity and awareness among countries resulted in only six integrated proposals being submitted. None were accepted.

Although the Global Fund can improve its procedures and performance (and has demonstrated a strong commitment to continued innovation), the greatest challenge it faces is a looming shortage of funds. Already it has had to put off a fifth proposal round until 2005. The Global Fund estimates that it will require $2.3 billion in 2005, but has received only $1.0 billion in pledges. In 2006, it will require $2.7 billion simply to renew existing grants, with another $1 billion needed for a new round of grants. The United States is currently the largest donor to the Global Fund, and Secretary of Health and Human Services Tommy Thompson chairs its board. But the majority of U.S. AIDS funding is now channeled through its new bilateral initiative, the President's Emergency Plan for AIDS Relief, with only a maximum of $547 million out of $2.4 billion going to the Global Fund in the 2004 AIDS budget. Other donors share the blame, however, and the United States is currently threatening to reduce its contribution unless others do more. The Global Fund is too important, as a funding channel and as a promising new approach to development assistance, to be allowed to fail for lack of funds. The working group strongly urges that all donor nations increase their contributions to permit the Global Fund to meet its existing commitments and launch new rounds of proposals that correspond to country demand.

Donor coordination

The growth in donor interest and funding for AIDS programs in developing countries, while welcome and long overdue, has in some places exacerbated confusion and inefficiency on the ground, as a growing number of donors, international agencies, and nongovernmental organizations pursue separate agendas. Current donor initiatives too often result in a patchwork of poorly coordinated programs, burdening health personnel and managers with multiple reporting requirements, discouraging integration of services, and impeding rational planning. Better coordination among donors and between donors and national governments will be critical to making good use of new resources for AIDS. The problem of donor coordination is closely linked to the challenge of building national ownership of and control over the AIDS response while ensuring efficiency and accountability.

Figure 5.2

As the case of Tanzania shows, developing a coherent response to AIDS at the country level requires coordinating the activities of many players

Note: Lines represent important institutional links.
Source: Molin 2004.

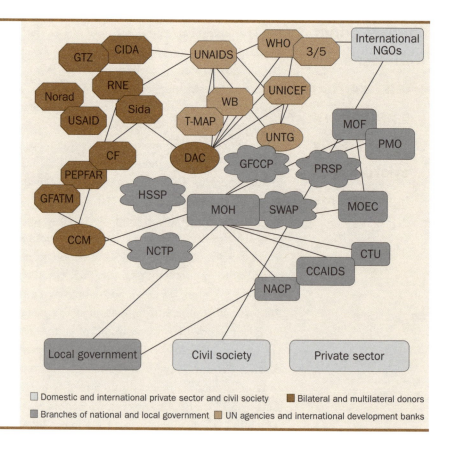

In some countries, the number of international entities—donor agencies and their contractors, UN agencies and international development banks, the Global Fund, international nongovernmental organizations and foundations—involved in funding, implementing, or overseeing AIDS programs or advising national governments can reach into the dozens. Organizations, initiatives, and the relationships among them form a bewildering tangle, as illustrated in considerably simplified form for Tanzania in figure 5.2.

Lack of coordination can harm the AIDS response in a number of ways:

- Uneven distribution of services. In the absence of a rational division of effort, donors, government, and nongovernmental organizations often provide overlapping services, leaving other needs unmet or other populations unserved.

- Destructive competition. Donors, under pressure to disperse funds and achieve results quickly, compete for scarce personnel, government support, and infrastructure.

- Multiple systems and standards. Separate programs establish wasteful separate systems for supply, monitoring and evaluation, and training rather than working together to strengthen existing systems. Clinical guidelines, training requirements, and so on are not harmonized.

Multisectoral national AIDS coordinating authorities should be responsible for setting national priorities

- Excessive demands on government capacity. Multiple donor requirements place unnecessary demands on limited government administrative capacity.
- Lack of national ownership. Dependence on donors with their own agendas makes it difficult for governments to formulate and implement a coherent national vision.

Besides the inevitable challenges of ensuring that so many entities work together efficiently, the problem of donor coordination has at its heart a basic diversion of interests. National governments understandably want to maintain authority over the national response and control the activities of donors and other international entities on their soil, while donors have a legitimate interest in ensuring that the programs they fund achieve results and remain consistent with their own priorities. Even with good will on all sides, any solution will require compromise on these basic objectives.

Existing mechanisms for coordination

A number of institutions already exist to address issues of donor coordination. Within the UN system, UNAIDS theme groups bring together the different agencies working on AIDS, and in some cases, representatives of government, donors, and civil society. While theme groups are useful forums for sharing information, they lack the authority to impose solutions on the separate agencies, whose budgets they do not control, let alone on donors, and thus have limited impact (UNAIDS 2002b). The agencies also prepare Integrated UN Work Plans at the country level, but these documents have been criticized as mere repackaging of agency programs. More broadly, UN country programs are meant to adhere to jointly developed United Nations Development Assistance Frameworks.

Poverty reduction strategies, which in theory result from broad participatory processes, should provide a unified framework for considering the full spectrum of development priorities and for rational allocation of resources. But the treatment of the health sector in these strategies has often been cursory, with little budgetary detail and insufficient assignment of roles and responsibilities (Dodd and others 2004; Soucat and Yazbeck n.d.; Walford 2002).

In principle, multisectoral national AIDS coordinating authorities should be responsible for setting national priorities and for overseeing the activities of the various arms of government, as well as development partners working on AIDS (see below). But in practice, many national AIDS coordinating authorities lack the capacity to remain well informed on donor activities, let alone to impose order on them. In some countries, AIDS coordination within government has been hampered by an unclear division of responsibilities between coordinating authorities and AIDS units within Ministries of Health (SARA 2002).

In addition, donors have often tried to minimize duplication through informal agreements among themselves, sometimes by taking responsibilities for different geographic regions. Although this approach may reduce overlap,

Sectorwide approaches reduce or eliminate the problem of uncoordinated donor programs

it does nothing to enhance government ownership or uniformity of standards and practices. At the global level, the Development Assistance Committee of the OECD has published a set of guidelines on donor coordination, reflecting growing appreciation of the importance of this issue (OECD 2003).

The sectorwide approach

The most comprehensive approach to donor coordination in health is the so-called sectorwide approach, under which donors agree to provide some or all of their funding in a particular sector as direct budgetary support to the relevant government ministry in return for a greater voice in the development and implementation of government strategy (Moore 2003). In principle, sectorwide approaches reduce or eliminate the problem of uncoordinated donor programs, while requiring donors and governments to work together to achieve common aims, embodied in mutually agreed strategies and plans. This arrangement also counters the tendency of donors to avoid funding salaries or other recurrent expenditures. An additional advantage of sectorwide approaches is that they give donors a strong incentive to work to improve government systems rather than bypassing them (Ssengooba and others 2004). In exchange for these benefits, national governments accept a greater degree of donor oversight. Sectorwide approaches in health cannot resolve all coordination issues around AIDS, of course, since a comprehensive response must involve other sectors.

The UN Millennium Project as a whole strongly favors sectorwide approaches and "basket funding" over program funding as a vehicle for donor assistance in meeting the Millennium Development Goals, as outlined in the project's synthesis report (UN Millennium Project 2005a). Sectorwide approaches will not make sense, however, nor will donors agree to them, unless national governments and ministries of health are perceived to meet minimum standards of effectiveness and transparency. If donors believe their money cannot be well spent by national governments or if they cannot come to agreement on priorities and strategies, they will continue to fund their own programs and establish parallel systems to implement them. Conversely, governments will not welcome sectorwide approaches if they are required to cede too much autonomy to a cabal of donors. In general, the working group believes that the long-term aim of combating AIDS while building national capacity is best served by moving toward sectorwide approaches wherever possible. Donors should be willing to sacrifice short-term performance in some cases in return for the benefits of sustainability and national ownership of AIDS programs.

The Three Ones

On April 25 2004, donors, under the leadership of UNAIDS, the United Kingdom, and the United States, agreed to three core principles—the Three Ones—with which to coordinate national AIDS responses.

Box 5.1

HIV/AIDS indicators for monitoring the UN General Assembly Special Session targets

Source: UNAIDS 2002c.

Global commitment and action

1. Amount of funds spent by international donors on HIV/AIDS in developing countries and countries in transition.
2. Amount of public funds available for research and development of vaccines and microbicides.
3. Percentage of transnational companies that are present in developing countries and that have HIV/AIDS workplace policies and programs.
4. Percentage of international organizations that have HIV/AIDS workplace policies and programs.
5. Assessment of HIV/AIDS advocacy efforts.

National commitment and action

1. Amount of national funds spent by governments on HIV/AIDS.
2. National Composite Policy Index.

National program and behavior

1. Percentage of schools with teachers who have been trained in life skills–based HIV/AIDS education and who taught it during the last academic year.
2. Percentage of large enterprises or companies that have HIV/AIDS workplace policies and programs.
3. Percentage of patients with sexually transmitted infections at healthcare facilities who are appropriately diagnosed, treated, and counseled.
4. Percentage of HIV-infected pregnant women receiving a complete course of antiretroviral prophylaxis to reduce the risk of mother-to-child transmission.
5. Percentage of people with advanced HIV infection receiving antiretroviral combination therapy.
6. Percentage of injecting drug users who have adopted behaviors that reduce transmission of HIV.
7. Percentage of young people ages 15–24 who both correctly identify ways of preventing the sexual transmission of HIV and who reject major misconceptions about HIV transmission.
8. Percentage of young people ages 15–24 reporting the use of a condom during sexual intercourse with a nonregular sexual partner.
9. Ratio of current school attendance among orphans to that among nonorphans ages 10–14.

Impact

1. Percentage of young people ages 15–24 who are HIV-infected.
2. Percentage of HIV-infected infants born to HIV-infected mothers.

The Three Ones are:

- **One** agreed HIV/AIDS action framework that provides the basis for coordinating the work of all partners.
- **One** national AIDS coordinating authority, with a broad-based multisectoral mandate.
- **One** agreed country-level monitoring and evaluation system.

The agreed action framework would set out clear priorities for resource allocation, establish systems for joint review and consultation, and outline the

The Three Ones are: one agreed HIV/AIDS action framework, one national AIDS coordinating authority, and one agreed monitoring and evaluation system

links to poverty reduction strategies and other development agreements. The national authority would be responsible for developing and coordinating implementation of the action framework in a participatory manner, while leaving actual implementation to line ministries and other partners. These ideas are not new, but the attention that the Three Ones has attracted may help to reinvigorate efforts to make these institutions function more effectively.

The "Third One" offers the most concrete suggestion for practical progress, since multiple monitoring and evaluation frameworks have imposed unnecessary reporting burdens on managers at all levels and hampered the use of monitoring and evaluation to develop and improve policies. Donors should commit to aligning their monitoring and evaluation requirements at the global level and agree on core elements of country-level systems. Development partners should also invest in developing national capacity to implement these systems.

Country-level monitoring and evaluation and information systems should be linked to, but not limited by the 18 indicators developed by UNAIDS to monitor the UNGASS Declaration of Commitment (UNAIDS 2002c). The core UNGASS indicators fall into several classes, illustrating the basic types of data required for comprehensive monitoring (box 5.1). Some are epidemiological measures (for example, the percentage of young people who are HIV-infected). Other indicators attempt to measure aspects of behavior relevant to disease transmission (for example, the use of condoms). A third set, such as the fraction of people with advanced infection receiving antiretroviral treatment, address how many people are reached by particular services. Finally, the list includes measures of national or international commitment and action, including estimates of spending on HIV/AIDS and indexes of policy or advocacy. The UNGASS monitoring plan calls for information on these variables to be assembled by national governments using standard procedures and submitted to UNAIDS, and for all countries to begin reporting by 2004. The first progress report based on these data was published in September 2003 (UNAIDS 2003b).

These 18 UNGASS indicators are, of course, only a small subset of the kinds of information that would be useful to AIDS planning, which could include more specific behavioral and epidemiological data and better information on service delivery and expenditures. A particularly important innovation in epidemiological surveillance involves linking behavioral and demographic data to HIV serostatus in large, representative samples, such as the Demographic and Health Surveys already conducted in many countries. Surveys of this kind have been carried out in the Dominican Republic and at least seven countries in Africa (Ghana Statistical Service and others 2004; MAP 2002; Shisana and others 2002). Surveys of this kind are expensive and thus cannot replace regular sentinel surveillance for monitoring epidemic trends. Moreover, general population surveys are not useful where epidemics are concentrated in particular populations.

It is likely that continued support for the Global Fund will depend on obtaining concrete results quite soon

The acceptance by the donors of the Three Ones represents an important manifestation of commitment to better donor coordination. This first step will have to be followed, however, by concrete action on the ground in these three areas and by progress toward the "Fourth One" of unified funding mechanisms.

Overcoming capacity constraints

Although there is substantial agreement that providing AIDS services to all those who urgently need them would cost well in excess of $10 billion a year, well more than is currently available, there will be no point in raising these additional resources if they cannot be spent effectively. It is often asserted that many developing countries lack the capacity to "absorb" such large infusions of new money and that some countries are having trouble spending the funds they have already received from the Global Fund, the World Bank, or other sources. These concerns cannot be dismissed, and there is no doubt that capacity issues pose a real challenge to successfully scaling up the response to AIDS, especially in the poorest countries.

One way to get a sense of the scale of capacity constraints, at least in the short term, is to consider the rate at which committed funds are actually disbursed or spent. Both the World Bank's Multicountry HIV/AIDS Program (MAP) and the Global Fund initially encountered difficulties disbursing funds. At the country level, the 2003 Kenya Public Expenditure Review reported that the Kenyan Ministry of Health spent only 24–58 percent of its approved development budget in the three financial years from 1999 to 2001, although these figures may not accurately account for donor resources (Government of Kenya 2003). A bigger test will come soon, as the Global Fund and other donors provide large grants for ambitious treatment programs.

Addressing and resolving the most binding capacity constraints in the next few years will be critical for two related reasons. Unless these obstacles are overcome services cannot be scaled up, and prevention and treatment goals will not be met no matter how much funding is available. In addition, however, failure to break down the barriers impeding the productive use of already committed funds will surely make raising additional resources much more difficult. In fact, it is likely that continued support for the Global Fund, as well as for ambitious bilateral programs such as the U.S. AIDS initiative, will depend on obtaining concrete results quite soon with the substantial resources that some countries have recently received.

Before considering possible solutions, it is worth examining more closely the nature of capacity constraints, since the term is often used—and invoked as an argument against greater donor assistance—in a rather vague way that sometimes conflates quite distinct phenomena. At least three broad categories of obstacles to effective and timely use of funds can be distinguished; we focus primarily on two: relatively short-term administrative bottlenecks and longer

The most important first step is a good diagnosis

term shortages of human or physical infrastructure. Although these two types of constraints interact in important ways, both the nature and timescale of the solutions they require are quite different. Another category of constraint, which arises from limited utilization of available services, is mentioned briefly below. We note as well that the term *absorptive capacity* is also sometimes applied in relation to possible macroeconomic consequences of large infusions of foreign aid, especially inflation and exchange-rate appreciation ("Dutch disease"). These issues are beyond the scope of our report.

Short-term administrative bottlenecks. Administrative bottlenecks arise from weakness in management systems, especially systems for handling funds, purchasing commodities, contracting for services, reporting to donors or governments, and ensuring transparency. These deficiencies slow the flow of money, either from donor agencies to developing country governments or from primary recipients in capital cities to implementing partners, and slow the rate at which it can be spent on goods or services. Particularly common types of bottlenecks involve moving funds from ministries of health to the districts (especially when responsibility for health service delivery has been decentralized), contracting with local nongovernmental organizations and community-based organizations for delivery of services at the community level, and drug procurement (Ssengooba and others 2004). It is likely that problems of this kind account for most of the initial disbursement delays encountered by the Global Fund and other donors.

These problems in financial management need not involve corruption or deliberate mismanagement, although the perceived danger of diversion may cause donors or central governments to impose more onerous accounting and reporting procedures and thus exacerbate delays. Where corruption is pervasive and political will to tackle it lacking, donors may be obliged to bypass government systems altogether. This should be a last resort, however, since the long-term goal must be to strengthen public administration.

How can these constraints be alleviated? The most important first step, of course, is a good diagnosis identifying the most binding bottlenecks to financial flows and disbursement, which can take the form a "tracking" study following the flow of funds. Once the problems are identified, solutions are likely to take four forms.

- *Simplification and harmonization of donor requirements and procedures.* Where management capacity is limited, bottlenecks can be expected to arise in proportion to the complexity of the required procedures. Donors should strive to simplify their requirements to the greatest extent consistent with effective monitoring and should harmonize their procedures with those of other donors and, where possible, with those of recipient governments. In this way the problems of donor coordination and absorptive capacity are linked.

- *Policy changes at the country level.* More efficient management will often require reforms to improve accountability, simplify procedures, and

Many bottlenecks can be reduced by investing in information systems

introduce incentives for better performance. Policies restricting flexibility in the deployment of health personnel should also be reviewed (see below). Many of these necessary reforms can be thought of as part of broader civil service reform. Implementing these changes will require political will.

- *Technical assistance focused on management.* Technical assistance, especially when it is relatively long term, can help ministries of health, national AIDS commissions, district health teams, and other entities involved in running AIDS programs at the country level to improve management systems and train staff. Donors should be ready to fund this kind of assistance, as well as assistance with technical aspects of service delivery. Lack of capacity among local nongovernmental and community organizations—to write proposals, to manage and account for funds, to monitor programs—can also slow implementation of AIDS programs, and assistance should be made available to these organizations as well.

- *Investments in management infrastructure.* In many cases, bottlenecks can be reduced by investing in information systems, especially computerization. In some cases it may also make sense to hire additional administrative staff or to redeploy staff to the most overwhelmed parts of the system.

Thus, relieving management bottlenecks will require both policy changes and further investment to build capacity. Although improving public administration is a long-term process, there is reason to believe that targeted measures based on good diagnoses can improve the flow of funds quite rapidly.

Long-term shortages of infrastructure. The second class of capacity constraints involves deeper problems in the systems required for delivering AIDS services. Although prevention programs in other sectors also encounter capacity constraints, the most serious difficulties are likely to arise in delivering relatively complex interventions, especially antiretroviral therapy, in the health system. As discussed in chapter 3, insufficient or decrepit clinics and hospitals, lack of laboratory facilities, unreliable drug supply systems, and, most important, lack of skilled healthcare workers will pose formidable challenges to expanding treatment in some countries. These deficiencies, which will also hinder delivery of voluntary counseling and testing, treatment of sexually transmitted infections, and services to prevent mother-to-child transmission of HIV, can be considered capacity constraints in that they will limit the expansion of services—and the disbursement of committed funds—even when money is available to buy drugs, train existing staff, and cover other program-specific expenses. Over the longer term, however, many of these constraints can be "bought out" through investments in health systems. Physical infrastructure can be built and refurbished, and equipment can be purchased. The shortage of doctors, nurses, pharmacists, and other health personnel can also be relieved, through a combination of the following strategies.

- *Reassignment of staff roles.* Healthcare workers should be given new roles to make the most of existing staff, for example, by allowing nurses to prescribe antiretroviral drugs in some circumstances and giving community health workers responsibility for supporting adherence. This may require revising regulations. Incentives can also be introduced to encourage staff to move to where they are most needed. This strategy will be particularly important in the short run, when the overall number of healthcare workers cannot easily be increased.

- *Improvements in salaries and working conditions.* In many developing countries higher salaries, along with better working conditions and more supportive management, will be essential for retaining staff and slowing brain drain. In some settings, where there are substantial numbers of already trained healthcare workers who have left the public sector, higher salaries may attract personnel back into the system. There seem to be few studies, however, that explore how much "spare capacity" of this kind really exists in particular countries or how much salaries would have to be increased to have a significant effect on retention or recruitment. It is important that salaries be increased as part of a comprehensive health sector plan, not as a way of luring scarce staff into AIDS programs from other parts of the health system. Donors should be prepared to contribute to salary increases; this is best done through sectorwide approaches. In some countries, expenditure ceilings or public sector hiring freezes may have to be lifted.

- *Expansion of preservice training.* In some cases, it may be necessary to increase the capacity of universities and other institutions to train new doctors, nurses, and other cadres of healthcare workers. This will only make sense where steps have been taken to limit the loss of trained staff to other countries and other professions. Moreover, building new or larger medical and nursing schools in every country may not be the best way to scale up training: regional solutions may be more efficient. These types of investment will take many years to have an impact on service delivery, illustrating the importance of a long-term human resources strategy and longer-term and more predictable donor commitments.

This section has emphasized factors that constrain the delivery of prevention and treatment services. Factors that prevent or discourage people from making use of services ("demand-side constraints") can also be important in limiting the effective reach and impact of AIDS programs. Stigma, lack of awareness, and misinformation are some of the most important factors that might decrease the use of services even when they are available and affordable. (Obviously, user fees can be another critical barrier to uptake.) Community outreach, education, and involvement, exemplified by the concept of community "treatment preparedness," along with campaigns to reduce stigma, are thus essential elements

The United Nations should be bolder in holding to account member nations

of AIDS programs (*International HIV Treatment Preparedness Summit, Final Report* 2003).

As this brief overview shows, while capacity constraints can limit the amount of money that can be spent effectively in the short run, overcoming them will require additional investments in management systems and in health systems. Building capacity while scaling up service delivery will also require good diagnosis, long-range planning, and policy reform. Capacity constraints and strategies for overcoming them are also discussed in the UN Millennium Project's synthesis report.

Roles for the United Nations

The UN system has played a critical role in shaping a global AIDS agenda in the first two decades of the pandemic. Through UNAIDS and the programs of its cosponsors, much progress has been made in formulating standards for care, treatment, and prevention. Furthermore, the United Nations has pushed hard—and successfully—to place AIDS at the top of the international agenda and has contributed in important ways to the mobilization of additional international resources for HIV/AIDS. Yet, the United Nations could do more at the international level. Most important, the working group believes that the United Nations should be bolder in holding to account member nations, in the rich and developing worlds alike, which have failed to honor their commitments to fighting AIDS. Particularly in the nations threatened by the next wave of the pandemic, the United Nations can play a critical role in drawing attention to failures in leadership and gaps in financing that continue to stymie a comprehensive response.

The UN's response to the epidemic, however, has been weaker at the country level. The United Nations must begin to focus on providing far more useful and appropriate technical and management assistance. This may represent a departure from its traditional role. But the United Nations, with its established presence on the ground, its neutrality, its broad legitimacy, and its ties to civil society, is uniquely placed to assist national governments to plan and implement comprehensive responses to the epidemic, as well as to raise funds and coordinate donors and other partners. The United Nations should increase its efforts in the following areas:

- Aiding in the development of strategic plans, new initiatives, and funding proposals.
- Advising on the most effective approaches to prevention and treatment.
- Assisting ministries of health and other line ministries to prepare detailed budgets that more accurately reflect country needs.
- Facilitating the mobilization of additional resources from international and national sources.
- Helping national governments to coordinate donors, nongovernmental organizations, and other partners.

The United Nations is well positioned to offer technical support

- Providing technical and management assistance in implementing funded programs.

The United Nations has already accepted many of these roles, but its record in fulfilling them has been mixed. The fundamental problem has been a shortage of personnel on the ground with the necessary skills to support countries in these areas.

One of the most important challenges facing many of the most affected countries is insufficient management capacity, particularly a lack of skilled staff at the central and regional level to design and implement new programs. While nongovernmental organizations and donor partners have filled in here and there, a more comprehensive effort must begin to build capacity to meet this increasing demand. The United Nations is well positioned to offer technical support to ministries of health, planning, and finance in coordinating country plans. In many cases, however, the UN presence is simply too small to help governments take even these initial steps. WHO, UNICEF, UNDP, and the UNAIDS secretariat should rapidly expand the workforce available for technical assistance in the strategic management of AIDS activities. As countries are called on to scale up their initiatives, the United Nations must follow suit and scale up its own presence at the national level, by mobilizing additional resources or reallocating personnel. WHO has taken significant steps in this direction as part of its 3 by 5 strategy and expects to do more now that more resources are available. But the need for technical assistance is not limited to treatment scale-up: WHO or other parts of the UN system must be ready to help governments develop and implement programs in other areas, including prevention and orphan support. WHO in particular must not abandon its commitment to a comprehensive response to the epidemic and must back this commitment with resources and personnel.

Many of these broad findings were also the main conclusions of an extensive external evaluation of UNAIDS conducted in 2002 (UNAIDS 2002b). According to this report, UNAIDS has met many of its objectives at the global level, including collecting and disseminating technical expertise, monitoring the epidemic, and building international consensus for an expanded response. The evaluation found, however, that UNAIDS has been much less successful in strengthening the UN work on HIV/AIDS at the country level. In part, this is the result of remaining problems in UNAIDS' structure: although the UNAIDS cosponsors have a unified budget for international work, each agency retains control of its budget at the country level. Thus, the UNAIDS Secretariat has little leverage to impose greater coordination, although the recent change in the status of the UNAIDS Country Coordinator is a move in the right direction.

The more prominent issues are probably quantity and quality of staff on the ground. Remedying this shortcoming will require more resources and perhaps also changes in the categories of personnel provided at the country

Donor funding should be guided by a long-term use perspective

level. UNAIDS, as part of its response to the external evaluation, is working to enhance country support and address many of these issues. For example, monitoring and evaluation support officers have recently been placed in priority countries.

Recommendations

- Donors and developing country governments must continue to increase their financial commitments to the health sector as well as to AIDS programs in order to bring essential services to those who need them and to relieve the burden on impoverished households. UNAIDS estimates that more than $11 billion will be required for AIDS in 2005 and more than $19 billion by 2007. Donor funding must be more predictable and less encumbered by restrictions on its use.

- Donor funding should be guided by a long-term perspective, with a substantial share of resources going to building health system capacity, including human resources and management. These investments will in turn enable recipient countries to spend aid money more effectively.

- Donors and recipients should put greater emphasis on measurable results and on monitoring progress toward well defined targets.

- The working group urges donors and national governments to move toward basket funding and sector-wide approaches in the health sector whenever possible to ensure coordinated support for nationally owned AIDS and health strategies. The Three Ones initiative is an important first step toward improved donor coordination.

- The Global Fund to Fight AIDS, Tuberculosis and Malaria must receive the support it needs to survive, evolve, and grow. The donor nations, led by the United States, must provide at least $2.3 billion in 2005 to allow the Global Fund to meet its obligations and plan for future rounds of grants. The Global Fund in turn should confront implementation challenges more directly, by requiring applicants to address problems encountered with earlier grants and by more strongly encouraging investments in health systems.

Notes

Chapter 2

1. Cambodia appears to have sharply reduced HIV incidence, and prevalence is apparently beginning to fall in several countries in East Africa (MAP 2004; UNAIDS 2004a; UNAIDS/WHO 2003). Other countries have apparently stabilized prevalence at low levels: Senegal and Brazil are among the best-known examples (Levi and Vitoria 2002; Pisani, 1999).

2. In India, for example, twice as many urban men as rural women recognized the protective value of condoms (UNAIDS 2002d).

3. It is often assumed that it is women who are primarily at risk in marriage despite monogamy, but this may not be the case where rates of infection are substantially higher in adolescent girls than in boys, as is the case in much of Sub-Saharan Africa.

4. A recent study in Mombasa, Kenya, obtained far less promising results, casting doubt on how effective this intervention may be in actual field settings (Quaghebeur and others 2004).

5. C. Wilfert, personal communication to Paul Wilson. These numbers are derived from the experience of mother-to-child preventive programs supported by the Elizabeth Glaser Pediatric AIDS Foundation's Call to Action Project.

6. According to recently revised UNAIDS data for 2001, this category would include 10 countries, all but one of which, the Central African Republic, are in Southern Africa (UNAIDS 2004a). None shows significant indications of falling prevalence.

7. A fall in adult prevalence from the very high levels seen in parts of southern Africa to 5 percent would not be possible by 2015. But prevalence can drop much more rapidly in young people, since the population in this category is renewed entirely in 10 years.

8. The behavioral implications of treatment are the subject of a background paper for the working group (Moatti and Spire 2003).

9. The 1997 and 2003 figures are not exactly comparable, since methods of estimating prevalence have been revised.

10. Globally, the greater number of women with HIV in Africa is balanced by male majorities in regions where injecting drug use and sex among men play larger roles in transmission.

Chapter 3

1. This number, provided by the Botswana government to WHO, represents the number of people actually on antiretrovirals. A total of 28,000 people are enrolled in the national program.

2. These numbers were provided by the joint WHO/UNAIDS Surveillance Working Group to the UN Millennium Project in November 2004.

3. Ernest Darkoh, Botswana ART program manager, personal communication to Paul Wilson, April 2003.

4. Although it is widely believed that these freezes are imposed by the International Monetary Fund (IMF) or other international financial institutions, the IMF denies that it places restrictions on social spending. The reality is probably in part a question of interpretation. In many countries these restrictions are imposed by ministries of finance, which may in turn be acting in part to ensure compliance with more general agreements with the IMF on fiscal policy.

Chapter 4

1. Concepts of orphanhood in southern Africa were explored by Skinner and others 2004.

2. This is also the definition of children according to the Convention on the Rights of the Child (UN 1989). The previous definition used by UNAIDS included only maternal and double orphans up to the age of 15.

3. Many people now oppose the use of the term AIDS orphan on the grounds that it is potentially stigmatizing and can be misinterpreted to mean "children with AIDS." We will avoid using it as much as possible.

4. Neff Walker, UNICEF, personal communication to Paul Wilson, September 2004.

5. Sara Sievers, Association Francois-Xavier Bagnoud, personal communication to Paul Wilson, September 2004.

6. Roeland Monasch, UNICEF, personal communication to Paul Wilson, September 2004. This study received technical assistance from USAID.

7. A few studies have even predicted a net economic benefit from AIDS, resulting from increased demand for AIDS services (Bureau for Economic Research 2001; Quattek 2000).

8. Neff Walker, UNICEF, personal communication to Paul Wilson, December 2004.

References

AHF Global Immunity. 2003a. *Ithembalabantu "People's Hope" Clinic Kwazulu-Natal, South Africa: First Year Progress Report July 2003*. [Retrieved December 8, 2003, from www.who.int/hiv/pub/prev_care/en/Ithembalabantu.pdf].

———. 2003b. *Uganda Cares First Year Progress Report July 2003*. [Retrieved December 8, 2003, from www.who.int/hiv/pub/prev_care/en/UgandaCares.pdf].

AIDS Healthcare Foundation. 2004. "Bush Global AIDS Plan Results Called Failure." Media release. September 13.

Ainsworth, M. 2000. "Breaking the Silence: Setting Realistic Priorities for AIDS Control in Less-Developed Countries." *The Lancet* 356 (9223): 55–60.

Ainsworth, M., and D. Filmer. 2002. "Poverty, AIDS and Children's Schooling: A Targeting Dilemma." Policy Research Paper 2885. World Bank, Operations Evaluation Department and Development Research Group, Washington, D.C.

Ainsworth, M., and J. Semali. 2000. "The Impact of Adult Deaths on Children's Health in Northwestern Tanzania." Policy Research Paper 2266. World Bank, Washington, D.C.

Altman, L. 2003. "Clinton Group Gets Discount for AIDS Drugs." *New York Times*, October 24.

Attawell, K., and J. Mundy. 2003. "Provision of Antiretroviral Therapy in Resource-Limited Settings: A Review of Experience up to August 2003." Health Systems Resource Centre and World Health Organization. [www.who.int/3by5/publications/documents/dfid/en/].

AVEGA (Association des veuves du génocide Agahozo). n.d. HIV/AIDS, 2003. [Retrieved from www.avega.org.rw/englishhome.htm].

Ball, A. L. 1998. "Overview: Policies and Interventions to Stem HIV-1 Epidemics Associated with Injecting Drug Use." In G. V. Stimson, ed., *Drug Injecting and HIV Injection: Global Dimensions and Local Responses.* London: UCL Press Limited.

Bangsberg, D. R., F. M. Hecht, E. D. Charlebois, and others. 2000. "Adherence to Protease Inhibitors, HIV-1 Viral Load, and Development of Drug Resistance in an Indigent Population." *AIDS* 14 (4): 357–66.

Barnett, T., and P. Blaikie. 1992. *AIDS in Africa: Its Present and Future Impact.* London: Bellhaven Press.

Barnett, T., and A. Whiteside. 2002a. *AIDS in the Twenty-First Century.* London: Pargrave-Macmillan.

———. 2002b. *Poverty and HIV/AIDS: Impact, Coping and Mitigation.* New York: United Nations Children's Fund.

Barnett, T., A. Whiteside, and J. Decosas. 2000. "The Jaipur Paradigm--a Conceptual Framework for Understanding Social Susceptibility and Vulnerability to HIV." *South African Medical Journal* 90 (11): 1098–1101.

Barron, P. 2003. "Scaling Up the Use of Antiretrovirals in the Public Sector: What Are the Challenges?" [Retrieved September 19, 2004, from http://csa.za.org/article/articleprint/237/-1/1/].

Bayer, R. 1991. "Public Health Policy and the AIDS Epidemic: An End to HIV Exceptionalism?" *New England Journal of Medicine* 324 (21): 1500–04.

Bearman, P. S., and H. Bruckner. 2001. "Promising the Future: Virginity Pledges and First Intercourse." *American Journal of Sociology* 106 (4): 859–912.

Beck, E. J., S. Mandalia, I. Williams, and others. 1999. "Decreased Morbidity and Use of Hospital Services in English HIV-Infected Individuals with Increased Uptake of Anti-Retroviral Therapy 1996–1997. National Prospective Monitoring System Steering Group." *AIDS* 13 (15): 2157–64.

Behforouz, H. L., P. E. Farmer, and J. S. Mukherjee. 2004. "From Directly Observed Therapy to Accompagnateurs: Enhancing AIDS Treatment Outcomes in Haiti and in Boston." *Clinical Infectious Diseases* 38 (Suppl. 5): S429–36.

Bell, C., S. Devarajan, and H. Gersbach. 2003. *The Long-Run Economic Costs of AIDS: Theory and an Application to South Africa.* Washington, D.C.: World Bank.

Bennett, S., and A. Fairbank. 2003. *The System-Wide Effects of the Global Fund to Fight AIDS, Tuberculosis and Malaria: A Conceptual Framework.* Bethesda: USAID.

Bessinger, R., and P. Akwara. 2002. "Sexual Behavior, HIV and Fertility Trends: A Comparative Analysis of Six Countries. Phase I of the ABC

Study." University of North Carolina at Chapel Hill, Carolina Population Center, Measure Evaluation Project.

Bicego, G., S. Rutstein, and K. Johnson. 2003. "Dimensions of the Emerging Orphan Crisis in Sub-Saharan Africa." *Social Science and Medicine* 56 (6): 1235–47.

Blower, S., E. Bodine, J. Kahn, and W. McFarland. 2005. "The Impact of the Antiretroviral Rollout on Drug Resistant HIV in Africa: Insights from Empirical Data and Theoretical Models." *AIDS* 19. In press.

Blower, S., L. Ma, P. Farmer, and S. Koenig. 2003. "Predicting the Impact of Antiretrovirals in Resource-Poor Settings: Preventing HIV Infections whilst Controlling Drug Resistance." *Current Drug Targets—Infectious Disorders* 3 (4): 345–53.

Boerma, J. T., C. Nyamukapa, M. Urassa, and S. Gregson. 2002. "Understanding the Uneven Spread of HIV within Africa: Comparative Study of Biological, Behavioral and Contextual Factors in Rural Populations in Tanzania and Zimbabwe." University of North Carolina at Chapel Hill, Carolina Population Center, Measure Evaluation Project.

Boily, M.-C., C. Lowndes, and M. Alary. 2002. "The Impact of HIV Epidemic Phases on the Effectiveness of Core Group Interventions: Insights from Mathematical Models." *Sexually Transmitted Infections* 78 (Suppl. I): i78–i90.

Boulle, A., D. Michaels, and K. Hildebrand. 2004. "Gender Aspects of Access to ART and Treatment Outcomes in a South African Township." Paper presented at the 15th International AIDS Conference, July 11–16, Bangkok.

Brady, M. 1999. "Female Genital Mutilation: Complications and Risk of HIV Transmission." *AIDS Patient Care and STDs* 13 (12): 709–16.

Bray, R. 2003. "Predicting the Social Consequences of Orphanhood in South Africa." Working Paper 29. University of Cape Town, Center for Social Science Research.

Brewer, D. D., S. Brody, E. Drucker, and others. 2003. "Mounting Anomalies in the Epidemiology of HIV in Africa: Cry the Beloved Paradigm." *International Journal of STD and AIDS* 14 (3): 144–47.

Brooks, H., O. Shisana, and L. Richter. 2004. *The National Household HIV Prevalence and Risk Survey of South African Children.* Human Sciences Research Council.

Brugha, R. 2003. "Antiretroviral Treatment in Developing Countries: The Peril of Neglecting Private Providers." *British Medical Journal* 326 (7403): 1382–84.

Bucher, H. C., L. E. Griffith, G. H. Guyatt, P. Sudre, M. Naef, P. Sendi, and M. Battegay 1999. "Isoniazid Prophylaxis for Tuberculosis in HIV Infection: A Meta-Analysis of Randomized Controlled Trials." *AIDS* 13 (4): 501–07.

Bureau for Economic Research. 2001. *The Macro-Economic Impact of HIV/AIDS in South Africa*. Economic Research Note 10.

Buve, A. 2002. "HIV Epidemics in Africa: What Explains Variations in HIV Prevalence." *IUBMB Life* 53 (4-5): 193–5.

Buve, A., S. Kalibala, and J. McIntyre. 2003. "Stronger Health Systems for More Effective HIV/AIDS Prevention and Care." *International Journal of Health Planning and Management* 18 (Suppl. 1): S41–S51.

Buve, A., S. D. Foaster, C. Mbwili, E. Mungo, N. Tollenare, and M. Zeko. 1994. "Mortality among Female Nurses in the Face of the AIDS Epidemic: A Pilot Study in Zambia." *AIDS* 8 (3): 396.

Buve, A., M. Carael, R. J. Hayes, and others 2001. "The Multicentre Study on Factors Determining the Differential Spread of HIV in Four African Cities: Summary and Conclusions." *AIDS* 15 (Suppl. 4): S127–31.

Campbell, C. 2003. *Letting Them Die: Why HIV/AIDS Prevention Programmes Fail*. Bloomington, Ind.: Indiana University Press.

CDC (U.S. Centers for Disease Control and Prevention). 1998. "Prevention and Treatment of Tuberculosis among Patients Infected with Human Immunodeficiency." *Morbidity and Mortality Weekly Report Recommendations and Reports* 47 (RR20): 1.

———. 1999. *Preventing Occupational HIV Transmission to Health Care Workers*. Atlanta.

———. 2003a. *Advancing HIV Prevention: New Strategies for a Changing Epidemic*. Atlanta.

———. 2003b. *Advancing HIV Prevention: The Science Behind the New Initiative*. Atlanta.

Center for Communications Programs. 2003. "Stop AIDS Love Life in Ghana 'Shatters the Silence.'" Communications Impact 15. Johns Hopkins University, Bloomberg School of Public Health, Baltimore, Md..

Chang, H. 2003. "Treating 3 Million People in the Developing World by 2005: Consensus Recommendations from the International Workshop on Strategies for Scaling-Up Treatment in Resource Poor Settings." Paper presented at the International Workshop on Strategies for Scaling-Up Treatment in Resource Poor Settings, July 9–11. Amsterdam.

Chen, S. Y., S. Gibson, M. H. Katz, and others. 2002. "Continuing Increases in Sexual Risk Behavior and Sexually Transmitted Diseases among Men Who Have Sex with Men: San Francisco, California, 1999–2001." *American Journal of Public Health* 929 (9): 1387–88.

Clark, S. 2004. "Early Marriage and HIV Risks in Sub-Saharan Africa." *Studies in Family Planning* 35 (3): 149–60.

Coetzee, D., A. Boulle, K. Hildebrand, V. Asselman, G. Van Cutsem, and E. Goemaere. 2004. "Promoting Adherence to Antiretroviral Therapy: The Experience from a Primary Care Setting in Khayelitsha, South Africa." *AIDS* 18 (Suppl. 3): S27–S31.

Coetzee, D., K. Hildebrand, A. Boulle, and others. 2004. "Outcomes After Two Years of Providing Antiretroviral Treatment in Khayelitsha, South Africa." *AIDS* 18 (6): 887–95.

Cohen, D. n.d. *Poverty and HIV/AIDS in Sub-Saharan Africa*. SEPED Conference Paper Series 2. New York: United Nations Development Programme.

———. 2002. *Human Capital and the HIV Epidemic in Sub-Saharan Africa*. Working Paper 2. Geneva: International Labour Organization.

Cohen, J. 2003. "Can a Drug Provide Some Protection?" *Science* 301 (5640): 1660–61.

———. 2004a. "HIV/AIDS in China. Changing Course to Break the HIV-Heroin Connection." *Science* 304 (5676): 1434–35.

———. 2004b. "HIV/AIDS in India. Sonagachi Sex Workers Stymie HIV." Science 304 (5670): 506.

Commission on Macroeconomics and Health. 2001. *Macroeconomics and Health: Investing in Health for Economic Development*. Geneva: World Health Organization.

Corbett, E. L., C. J. Watt, N. Walker, D. Maher, B. G. Williams, M. C. Raviglione, and C. Dye. 2003. "The Growing Burden of Tuberculosis: Global Trends and Interactions with the HIV Epidemic." *Archives of Internal Medicine* 163 (9): 1009–21.

Coutsoudis, A., K. Pillay, E. Spooner, L. Kuhn, and H. Coovadia. 1999. "Influence of Infant Feeding Patterns on Early Mother-to-Child Transmission of HIV-1 in Durban, South Africa: A Prospective Cohort Study." *The Lancet* 354 (9177): 471–76.

Creese, A., K. Floyd, A. Alban, and L. Guinness. 2002. "Cost-Effectiveness of HIV/AIDS Interventions in Africa: A Systematic Review of the Evidence." *The Lancet* 359 (9318): 1635–43.

Dasgupta, A., and P. C. Okhuysen. 2001. "Pharmacokinetic and Other Drug Interactions in Patients with AIDS." *Therapeutic Drug Monitoring* 23 (6): 591–605.

De Cock, K. M., D. Mbori-Ngacha, and E. Marum. 2002. "Shadow on the Continent: Public Health and HIV/AIDS in Africa in the 21st Century." *The Lancet* 360 (9326): 67–72.

de Waal, A., and A. Whiteside. 2003. "New Variant Famine: AIDS and Food Crisis in Southern Africa." *The Lancet* 362 (9391): 1234–47.

Deany, P. 2000. *HIV and Injecting Drug Use: A New Challenge to Sustainable Human Development*. New York: United Nations Development Programme, HIV and Development Programme.

Desmond, C., and J. Gow. 2001. *The Cost-Effectiveness of Six Models of Care for Orphan and Vulnerable Children in South Africa*. Durban: United Nations Children's Fund.

Dodd, R., E. Hinshelwood, and C. Harvey. 2004. *PRSPs: Their Significance for Health: Second Synthesis Report.* Geneva: World Health Organization.

Dodds, J. P., A. Nardone, D. E. Mercey, and A. M. Johnson. 2000. "Increase in High Risk Sexual Behaviour among Homosexual Men, London 1996–8: Cross Sectional, Questionnaire Study." *British Medical Journal* 320 (7248): 1510–11.

Donahue, J., and J. Williamson. 1999. *Community Mobilization to Mitigate the Impacts of HIV/AIDS.* Washington: U.S. Agency for International Development, Displaced Children and Orphans Fund.

Donovan, P. 2002. "Rape and HIV/AIDS in Rwanda." *The Lancet* 360 (Suppl.): S17–S18.

Dore, G. J., Y. Li, A. McDonald, H. Ree, J. M. Kaldor, and J. M. Kaldo. 2002. "Impact of Highly Active Antiretroviral Therapy on Individual AIDS-Defining Illness Incidence and Survival in Australia." *Journal of Acquired Immune Deficiency Syndromes* 29 (4): 388–95.

Dorrucci, M., M. Balducci, P. Pezzotti, A. Sinicco, F. Alberici, and G. Rezza. 1999. "Temporal Changes in the Rate of Progression to Death among Italians with Known Date of HIV Seroconversion: Estimates of the Population Effect of Treatment. Italian HIV Seroconversion Study ISS." *Journal of Acquired Immune Deficiency Syndromes* 22 (1): 65–70.

Dukers, N. H., J. Spaargaren, R. B. Geskus, J. Beijnen, R. A. Coutinho, and H. S. Fennema. 2002. "HIV Incidence on the Increase among Homosexual Men Attending an Amsterdam Sexually Transmitted Disease Clinic: Using a Novel Approach for Detecting Recent Infections." *AIDS* 16 (10): F19–24.

Dye, C., S. Scheele, P. Dolin, V. Pathania, and M. C. Raviglione. 1999. *Consensus Statement. Global Burden of Tuberculosis: Estimated Incidence, Prevalence, and Mortality by Country.* WHO Global Surveillance and Monitoring Project. JAMA 282 (7) 677–86.

Egger, M., M. May, G. Chene, and others. 2002. "Prognosis of HIV-1-Infected Patients Starting Highly Active Antiretroviral Therapy: A Collaborative Analysis of Prospective Studies." *The Lancet* 360 (9327): 119–29.

Epstein, H. 2003. "AIDS in South Africa: The Invisible Cure." *New York Review of Books* 50.

———. 2004. "The Fidelity Fix." *New York Times Magazine*, June 13.

Esu-Williams, E., S. Geibel, J. Motsepe, and K. Schenk. 2003. *Involving Youth in the Care and Support of People Affected by HIV and AIDS.* Horizons Research Summary. Washington, D.C.: Population Council.

Family Health International. 2002. *Behavior Change Communication BCC for HIV/AIDS: A Strategic Framework.*

Fang, C. T., H. M. Hsu, S. J. Twu, and others. 2004. "Decreased HIV Transmission after a Policy of Providing Free Access to Highly Active

Antiretroviral Therapy in Taiwan." *Journal of Infectious Diseases* 190 (5): 879–85.

Farmer, P. 1999. *Infections and Inequalities*. Berkeley: University of California Press.

Farmer, P., F. Leandre, J. S. Mukherjee, and others. 2001. "Community-Based Approaches to HIV Treatment in Resource-Poor Settings." *The Lancet* 358 (9279): 404–09.

FHI (Family Health International) and SCOPE OVC. 2002. *Psychosocial Baseline Survey Data Highlights*. Lusaka: Family Health International.

Fleishman, J. 2002. *Suffering in Silence: The Links between Human Rights Abuses and HIV Transmission to Girls in Zambia*. Human Rights Watch. [www.hrw.org/reports/2003/zambia/].

Fowler, M. G., and M. L. Newell. 2002. "Breast-Feeding and HIV-1 Transmission in Resource-Limited Settings." *Journal of Acquired Immune Deficiency Syndromes* 30 (2): 230–39.

Gadelha, A., Náurea Accacio, Regina L. B. Costa, and others. 2002. "Morbidity and Survival in Advanced AIDS in Rio de Janeiro, Brazil." *Revista do Instituto de Medicina Tropical de Sao Paulo* 44 (4): 179–86.

Garnett, G. P., and R. M. Anderson. 1995. "Strategies for Limiting the Spread of HIV in Developing Countries: Conclusions based on Studies of the Transmission Dynamics of the Virus." *Journal of Acquired Immune Deficiency Syndromes and Human Retrovirology* 9 (5): 500–513.

GFATM (Global Fund to Fight AIDS, Tuberculosis and Malaria). 2004a. "Current Grant Commitments and Disbursements Summary Report." [www.fundthefund.org/gfatm.html].

———. 2004b. *A Force for Change: The Global Fund at 30 Months*.

Ghana Statistical Service, Noguchi Memorial Institute for Medical Research, and ORC Macro. 2004. "HIV Prevalence and Associated Factors." In *Ghana Demographic and Health Survey 2003*. Calverton, Md.

Ghys, P. D., M. O. Diallo, V. Ettiegne-Traore, and others. 2002. "Increase in Condom Use and Decline in HIV and Sexually Transmitted Diseases among Female Sex Workers in Abidjan, Côte d'Ivoire, 1991–1998." *AIDS* 16 (2): 251–58.

Global Coalition on Women and AIDS. 2004. *AIDS and Female Property/Inheritance Rights*. Media backgrounder: Joint United Nations Programme on HIV/AIDS.

Global HIV Prevention Working Group. 2002. *Global Mobilization for HIV Prevention: A Blueprint for Action*. [www.kff.org/hivaids/200207-index.cfm].

———. 2003. *Access to HIV Prevention: Closing the Gap*. [www.kff.org/hivaids/200207-index.cfm].

————. 2004. *HIV Prevention in the Era of Expanded Treatment Access.* [www.kff.org/hivaids/200207-index.cfm].

Glynn, J. R., M. Carael, B. Auvert, and others. 2001. "Why Do Young Women Have a Much Higher Prevalence of HIV than Young Men? A Study in Kisumu, Kenya and Ndola, Zambia." *AIDS* 15 (Suppl. 4): S51–S60.

Gordon, P., and K. Crehan, 2000. *Dying of Sadness: Gender, Sexual Violence and the HIV Epidemic.* SEPED Conference Paper 1. United Nations Development Programme. New York.

Grant, A. D., G. Djomand, and K. M. De Cock. 1997. "Natural History and Spectrum of Disease in Adults with HIV/AIDS in Africa." *AIDS* 11 (Suppl. B): S43–S54.

Gray, L., M. L. Newell, C. Thorne, C. Peckham, and J. Levy. 2001. "Fluctuations in Symptoms in Human Immunodeficiency Virus-Infected Children: The First 10 Years of Life." *Pediatrics* 108 (1): 116–22.

Gregson, S., C. Nyamukapa, G. P. Garnett, and others. 2002. "Sexual Mixing Patterns and Sex-Differentials in Teenage Exposure to HIV Infection in Rural Zimbabwe." *The Lancet* 359 (9321): 1901.

Grimwade, K., and C. Gilks. 2001. "Cotrimoxazole Prophylaxis in Adults Infected with HIV in Low-Income Countries. [Review]." *Current Opinion in Infectious Diseases* 14 (5): 507–12.

Grosskurth, H., F. Mosha, J. Todd, and others. 1995. "Impact of Improved Treatment of Sexually Transmitted Diseases on HIV Infection in Rural Tanzania: Randomised Controlled Trial." *The Lancet* 346 (8974): 530–36.

Guay, L. A., P. Musoke, T. Fleming, and others. 1999. "Intrapartum and Neonatal Single-Dose Nevirapine Compared with Zidovudine for Prevention of Mother-to-Child Transmission of HIV-1 in Kampala, Uganda: HIVNET 012 Randomized Trial." *The Lancet* 354 (9181): 795–802.

Gutierrez, J. P., B. Johns, T. Adam, and others. 2004. "Achieving the WHO/UNAIDS Antiretroviral Treatment 3 by 5 Goal: What Will It Cost?" *The Lancet* 364(9428): 63–64.

Haacker, M. 2002. "The Economic Consequences of HIV/AIDS in Southern Africa." Working Paper. International Monetary Fund, Washington, D.C.

Hallman, K. 2004. "Socioeconomic Disadvantage and Unsafe Sexual Behaviors among Young Women and Men in South Africa." Working paper 190. Population Council, New York.

Hankins, C., J. P. Guttierrez, S. Bertozzi, and others. 2004. "Resource Needs for an expanded Response to AIDS in Low and Middle Income Countries." UNAIDS. Available on request.

Health Outcomes International. 2002. *Return on Investment in Needle and Syringe Programs in Australia.* Canberra: Commonwealth Department of Health and Aging.

Heise, L., M. Ellsberg, and M. Gottemoeller. 1999. "Ending Violence against Women." *Populations Reports* Series L (11): 4.

Hersh, B., F. Popovici, R. Apetrei, and others. 1991. "Acquired Immunodeficiency Syndrome in Romania." *The Lancet* 338 (8768): 645–99.

Herz, B., and G. B. Sperling. 2004. *What Works in Girl's Education.* Council on Foreign Relations. Washington, D.C.

Hira, S. K., K. Panchal, P. A. Parmar, and V. P. Bhatia. 2004. "High Resistance to Antiretroviral Drugs: The Indian Experience." *International Journal of STD and AIDS* 15 (3): 173–77.

Hirschhorn, L. 2004. "Working Paper on Human Resource Requirements for Providing Antiretroviral Therapy in Resource-Poor Settings." Background Paper for the UN Millennium Project Working Group on HIV/AIDS. UN Millennium Project, New York. Available on request.

Human Rights Watch. 2002. *Epidemic of Abuse: Police Harassment of HIV/AIDS Outreach Workers in India.* New York.

———. 2003. "Fanning the Flames: How Human Rights Abuses Are Fueling the AIDS Epidemic in Kazakhstan." New York.

———. 2004a. *Hated to Death: Homophobia, Violence, and Jamaica's HIV/AIDS Epidemic.* 16: 6B. New York.

———. 2004b. *Lessons Not Learned: Human Rights Abuses and HIV/AIDS in the Russian Federation.* New York.

———. 2004c. "Russia: Drug Law Reforms Help Combat AIDS, Curb Abuses." *Human Rights News*, May 21. [Retrieved November 19, 2004, from http://hrw.org/english/docs/2004/05/21/russia8607.htm].

Hunter, S. S. 2002. "Supporting and Expanding Community-Based HIV/AIDS Prevention and Care Responses: A Report on Save the Children (US) Malawi COPE Project." World Bank, Washington, D.C.

Hurley, S. F., D. J. Jolley, and J. M. Kaldor. 1997. "Effectiveness of Needle-Exchange Programmes for Prevention of HIV Infection." *The Lancet* 349 (9068): 1797–1800.

Hutin, Y. J., A. M. Hauri, and G. L. Armstrong. 2003. "Use of Injections in Healthcare Settings Worldwide, 2000: Literature Review and Regional Estimates." *British Medical Journal* 327 (7423): 1075.

ICRW (International Center for Research on Women). 2003. *Understanding HIV-Related Stigma and Resulting Discrimination in Sub-Saharan Africa: Emerging Themes from Early Data Collection in Ethiopia, Tanzania and Zambia.* Research update. [www.icrw.org/].

INCB (International Narcotics Control Board). 2003. *Report of the International Narcotics Control Board for 2003.* Vienna.

———. 2004. "INCB Cautions on 'Harm Reduction' Measures in Drug Control." Press release. [www.incb.org/].

International AIDS Vaccine Initiative. 2003. "Preventative AIDS Vaccine Approaches Currently in Human Testing." [Retrieved November 22, 2003, from www.iavi.org/science/trials.htm].

International HIV Treatment Preparedness Summit. 2003. *Final Report.* March 13–16, Cape Town, South Africa.

International HIV/AIDS Alliance. 2003a. *Building Blocks—Africa-wide Briefing Note: Resources for Communities Working with Orphans and Vulnerable Children.* [www.aidsalliance.org/].

———. 2003b. *Positive Prevention: Prevention Strategies for People with HIV/AIDS.* Draft Background Paper. [www.aidsalliance.org/].

International Save the Children Alliance. 2003. *A Last Resort: The Growing Concern about Children in Residential Care.* Save the Children UK. [www.savethechildren.net/alliance/index.html].

IRIN (Integrated Regional Information Networks). 2004. "Swaziland: Government to Pay School Fees for 60,000 Orphans." January 30. [www.irinnews.org/].

Jemmott, J. B., III, L. S. Jemmott, and G. T. Fong. 1998. "Abstinence and Safer Sex HIV Risk-Reduction Interventions for African American Adolescents: A Randomized Controlled Trial." *JAMA* 279 (19): 1529–36.

Jha, P., L. M. E. Vaz, F. Plummer, and others. 2001. "The Evidence Base of Interventions to Prevent HIV Infection in Low and Middle-Income Countries." Working Paper. Commission on Macroeconomics and Health, Working Group 5. [www.cmhealth.org/].

Jochem, K., and J. Walley. 1999. "Tuberculosis in High Prevalence Settings. Current Control Strategies and Their Technical and Operational Limitations." In J. D. Porter and J. M. Grange, eds., *Tuberculosis: An Interdisciplinary Perspective.* London: Imperial College Press.

Joint Learning Initiative. 2004. *Human Resources for Health: Overcoming the Crisis.* Cambridge: Harvard University Press.

Jones, J. L., D. L. Hanson, M. S. Dworkin, D. L. Alderton, P. L. Fleming, J. E. Kaplan, and J. Ward. 1999. "Surveillance for AIDS-Defining Opportunistic Illnesses, 1992–1997." *MMWR CDC Surveillance Summaries* 48 (2): 1–22.

Jourdain, G., N. Ngo-Giang-Huong, S. Le Coeur, and others. 2004. "Intrapartum Exposure to Nevirapine and Subsequent Maternal Responses to Nevirapine-Based Antiretroviral." *New England Journal of Medicine* 351 (3): 229–40.

Juma, C. Forthcoming. "The New Age of Biodiplomacy." *Georgetown Journal of International Affairs.*

KaiserNetwork.org. 2003a. "Lack of Funds Only One Problem in Fight against HIV/AIDS, Experts Say ahead of U.N. General Assembly Session on AIDS." Daily HIV/AIDS Report. [Retrieved September 22, 2003, from www.kaisernetwork.org/dailyreports/hiv].

———. 2004b. "Routine HIV Testing Initiative in Botswana Aims to Get More People into Treatment Program." Daily HIV/AIDS Report. [Retrieved November 10, 2003, from www.kaisernetwork.org/dailyreports/hiv].

———. 2004a. "China Begins Legalizing Methadone as Part of Effort to Prevent HIV Transmission among Injecting Drug Users." Kaiser Daily HIV/AIDS Report. [www.kaisernetwork.org/dailyreports/hiv].

———. 2004b. "Clinton Foundation, Global Fund, World Bank, UNICEF Extend Low-Cost Generic AIDS Drug Prices to More than 100 Countries." Kaiser Daily HIV/AIDS Report. [Retrieved June 6, 2004, www.kaisernetwork.org/dailyreports/hiv].

———. 2004c. "New York Times Profiles Botswana's Mandatory HIV Testing Policy." Kaiser Daily HIV/AIDS Report. [Retrieved June 14, 2004, www.kaisernetwork.org/dailyreports/hiv].

Kamali, A., M. Quigley, J. Nakiyingi, and others. 2003. "Syndromic Management of Sexually-Transmitted Infections and Behaviour Change Interventions on Transmission of HIV-1 in Rural Uganda: A Community Randomised Trial." *The Lancet* 361 (9358): 645–52.

Karanja, L. 2003. *Just Die Quietly: Domestic Violence and Women's Vulnerability to HIV in Uganda*. Human Rights Watch. [www.hrw.org/].

Kaufman, J., and J. Jing. 2002. "China and AIDS—The Time to Act is Now." Science 296 (5577): 2339–40.

Kelly, M. J. 2002. "Children in Distress: the AIDS Legacy of Orphans and Vulnerable Children." Paper presented at the Ireland AID Education Forum, October 4, Dublin.

Kelly, R. J., R. H. Gray, N. K. Sewankambo, and others. 2003. "Age Differences in Sexual Partners and Risk of HIV-1 Infection in Rural Uganda." *Journal of Acquired Immune Deficiency Syndromes* 32 (4): 446–51.

Kenya. 2003. "Public Expenditure Review 2003." Nairobi.

Knippenberg, R., A. Soucat, and W. Vanlerberghe. *Marginal Budgeting for Bottlenecks: A Tool for Performance Based Planning of Health and Nutrition Services for Achieving Millennium Development Goals*. United Nations Children's Fund, World Bank, World Health Organization. [http://mdgr.undp.sk/].

Konde-Lule, J. K. 1995. "The Declining HIV Seroprevalence in Uganda: What Evidence?" *Health Transition Review* 5 (Suppl.) 27–33.

Kumaranayake, L. 2002. "Cost-Effectiveness and Economic Evaluation of HIV/AIDS-Related Interventions: The State of the Art." International AIDS Economics Network. [www.iaen.org/].

Kurowski, C., K. Wyss, S. Abdulla, N. D. Yemadji, and A. Mills. 2003. *Human Resources for Health: Requirements and Availability in the Context of Scaling-Up Priority Interventions in Low-Income Countries. Case studies from Tanzania and Chad.* University of London, London School of Hygiene and Tropical Medicine.

Lallemant, M., G. Jourdain, S. Le Coeur, and others. 2004. "Single-Dose Perinatal Nevirapine Plus Standard Zidovudine to Prevent Mother-to-Child Transmission of HIV-1 in Thailand." *New England Journal of Medicine* 351 (3): 217–28.

Laniece, I., M. Ciss, A. Desclaux, and others. 2003. "Adherence to HAART and Its Principal Determinants in a Cohort of Senegalese Adults." *AIDS* 17 (Suppl. 3) S103–08.

Larson, J. 2002. "Iran's Birth Rate Plummeting at Record Pace." In L. R. Brown, ed., *The Earth Policy Reader.* New York: Norton and Co.

Leandre, F. 2002. "Maximizing Adherence and Prevention of Resistance through Directly Observed Therapy: DOT-HAART." Paper presented at the XIV International AIDS Conference, July 7–12, Barcelona, Spain.

Levi, G. C., and M. A. A. Vitoria. 2002. "Fighting Against AIDS: The Brazilian Experience." *AIDS* 16 (18): 2372–83.

Lewis, J. J., C. Ronsmans, A. Ezeh, and S. Gregson. 2004. "The Population Impact of HIV on Fertility in Sub-Saharan Africa." *AIDS* 18 (Suppl. 2): S35–S43.

Livesley, N., and C. Morris. 2004. "Antiretroviral Therapy in the Private Sector of Resource-Limited Settings." *AIDS* 18 (3): 581–82.

Low-Beer, D., and R. L. Stoneburner. 2003. "Behavior and Communication Change in Reducing HIV: Is Uganda Unique?" *African Journal of AIDS Research* 2 (1): 9–21.

Lugalla, J., M. Emmelin, A. Mutembei, and others. 2004. "Social, Cultural and Sexual Behavioral Determinants of Observed Decline in HIV Infection Trends: Lessons from the Kagera Region, Tanzania." *Social Science and Medicine* 59 (1): 185–98.

Luke, N., and K. M. Kurz. 2002. "Cross-Generational and Transactional Sexual Relations in Sub-Saharan Africa: Prevalence of Behavoir and Implications for Negotiating Safer Sexual Practices." International Center for Research on Women. [www.icrw.org/].

Mailman School of Public Health. 2002. "MTCT-Plus Makes HIV Treatment a Reality for Poor Countries." Press release, July 10. Columbia University, New York.

Maman, S., J. Campbell, M. D. Sweat, and A. C. Gielen. 2000. "The Intersections of HIV and Violence: Directions for Future Research and Interventions." *Social Science and Medicine* 50 (4): 459–78.

MAP (Monitoring the AIDS Pandemic). 2002. *The Status and Trends of the HIV/AIDS Epidemics in the World.*

————. 2004. *AIDS in Asia: Face the Facts.* [www.fhi.org/en/HIVAIDS/pub/survreports/aids_in_asia.htm].

Marins, J. R., L. F. Jamal, S. Y. Chen, and others. 2003. "Dramatic Improvement in Survival among Adult Brazilian AIDS Patients." *AIDS* 17 (11): 1675–82.

Martinson, N., L. Morris, G. Gray, and others. 2004. "HIV Resistance and Transmission Following Single-Dose Nevirapine in a PMTCT Cohort." Paper presented at the 11th Conference on Retroviruses and Opportunistic Infections, February 8–11, San Francisco.

Mason, A., and S. B. Westley. 2002. "Population Change and Economic Development: Success Stories from Asia." In *The Future of Population in Asia.* Honolulu, Hawaii: East-West Center.

Mbori-Ngacha, D., R. Nduati, G. John, and others. 2001. "Morbidity and Mortality in Breastfed and Formula-Fed Infants of HIV-1-Infected Women: A Randomized Clinical Trial." *JAMA* 21 (19): 2413–20.

Mbulaiteye, S. M., C. Mahe, J. A. Whitworth, and others. 2002. "Declining HIV-1 Incidence and Associated Prevalence over 10 Years in a Rural Population in South-West Uganda: A Cohort Study." *The Lancet* 360 (9326): 41–46.

McCoy, D. 2003. *Health Sector Responses to HIV/AIDS and Treatment Access in Southern Africa: Addressing Equity.* Regional Network for Equity in Health in Southern Africa and Oxfam. [ftp://ftp.hst.org.za/pubs/equity/equinet10.pdf].

McNaghten, A. D., D. L. Hanson, J. L. Jones, M. S. Dworkin, and J. W. Ward. 1999. "Effects of Antiretroviral Therapy and Opportunistic Illnesses Primary Chemoprophylaxis after AIDS Diagnosis." *AIDS* 13 (13): 1687–95.

McNeil, D. 2003. "Africans Outdo Americans in Following AIDS Therapy." *New York Times*, September 3.

Médecins Sans Frontières Malawi. 2004. *Antiretroviral Therapy in Primary Care: Experience of the Chiadzulu Program in Malawi.* Case Study. Lilongwe.

Médecins Sans Frontières South Africa, Department of Public Health of the University of Cape Town, and Provincial Administration of the Western Cape. 2003. *Antiretroviral Therapy in Primary Health Care: South African Experience. Perspectives and Practice in Antiretroviral Treatment Case Study.* Geneva: World Health Organization.

Moatti, J.-P., and B. Spire. 2003. "Access to Antiretroviral Treatment in Developing Countries: How It May Impact the Future of HIV Prevention?" Background paper for the UN Millennium Project Working

Group on HIV/AIDS. UN Millennium Project, New York. Available on request.

Molin, A. 2004. "Harmonization, Alignment, and HIV/AIDS: A Case." Presentation at the 5th meeting of the DAC Working Party on Aid Effectiveness, July 6–7, Paris.

Monasch, R., and J. T. Boerma. 2004. "Orphanhood and Childcare Patterns in Sub-Saharan Africa: An Analysis of National Surveys from 40 Countries." *AIDS* 18 (Suppl. 2): S55–S65.

Monasch, R., J. Stover, M. Louden, J. Begala, D. Kabira, and N. Walker. 2004. *National Response to Orphans and Vulnerable Children in Sub-Saharan Africa: The OVC Policy and Planning Effort Index, 2004.* UNICEF. Unpublished draft. Available on request.

Monk, N. 2002. *Orphan Alert 2: Children of the HIV/AIDS Pandemic: The Challenge for India.* Association Francois-Xavier Bagnoud.

Montaner, J. S., P. Reiss, D. Cooper, and others. 1998. "A Randomized, Double-Blind Trial Comparing Combinations of Nevirapine, Didanosine, and Zidovudine for HIV-Infected Patients: The INCAS Trial. Italy, The Netherlands, Canada and Australia Study." *JAMA* 279 (12): 930–37.

Moore, S. 2003. "Aid Coordination in the Health Sector: Examining Country Participation in Sector-Wide Approaches." *Journal of Health and Population in Developing Countries*, July 1.

Morrison, S. J. 2002. *Expanding Antiretroviral Treatment in Developing Countries Creates Critical New Challenges.* Washington, D.C.: Center for Strategic and International Studies, HIV/AIDS Task Force.

MSF (Médecins Sans Frontières). 2003. *ARV Simplification Off the Beaten Track for High Prevalence Countries.* A Workshop Organized by MSF's Campaign for Access to Essential Medicines, Nairobi.

————.2004a. *Children and AIDS: Neglected Patients.* [Retrieved November 16, 2004, from www.msf.org/content/page.cfm?articleid=C35A2DA2-D4E3-425A-879860086416E313].

————. 2004b. "MSF AIDS Treatment Experience: Rapid Expansion, Emerging Challenges." Briefing document. Geneva.

Mukherjee, J., P. Farmer, F. Leandre, and others. 2003. *Access to Treatment and Care: Haiti Experience. Perspectives and Practice in Antiretroviral Treatment Case Study.* Geneva: World Health Organization.

Mundandi, C., G. P. Garnett, H. A. C. Voeten, C. A. Nyamukapa, D. Habbema, and S. Gregson. 2004. "Sexual Behaviour Change, Spatial Mobility and Stabilisation of the HIV Epidemic in Eastern Zimbabwe." Paper presented at the XV International AIDS Conference, Bangkok.

Munemo, N. 2004. *HIV/AIDS and Food Insecurity: Findings from Two Rural Districts in Zimbabwe.* Background Paper for the UN Millennium

Project Working Group on HIV/AIDS. UN Millennium Project, New York.

Musicco, M., A. Lazzarin, A. Nicolosi, and others. 1994. "Antiretroviral Treatment of Men Infected with Human Immunodeficiency Virus Type 1 Reduces the Incidence of Heterosexual Transmission. Italian Study Group on HIV Heterosexual Transmission." *Archives Internationales de Pharmacodynamie et de Therapie* 154 (17): 1971–76.

Nachega, J. 2003. *HIV/AIDS Care in Africa: Achievements and Challenges.* [Retrieved December 15, 2003, from www.md.ucl.ac.be/seminfect/ Nachega-27-02-03/Nachega.pdf].

National Intelligence Council. 2002. *The Next Wave of HIV/AIDS: Nigeria, Ethiopia, Russia, India, and China.* [www.odci.gov/nic/].

Newell, M. L., H. Coovadia, M. Cortina-Borja, N. Rollins, P. Gaillard, and F. Dabis. 2004. "Mortality of Infected and Uninfected Infants Born to HIV-Infected Mothers in Africa: A Pooled Analysis." *The Lancet* 364 (9441): 1236–43.

Nkouika-Dinghani-Nikita, G. 2000. *Les determinants du phenomene des enfants de la rue a Brazzaville* [The Causes of the Phenomenon of Street Children in Brazzaville]. Brazzaville, Congo: UERPOD.

Normand, J., D. Vlahov, and L. Moses, eds. 1995. *Preventing HIV Transmission: The Role of Sterile Needles and Bleach.* National Research Council and Institute of Medicine. [www.nap.edu/catalog/4975.html].

Nyamukapa, C., and S. Gregson. Forthcoming. "Extended Family's and Women's Roles in Safeguarding Orphans' Education in AIDS-Afflicted Rural Zimbabwe." *Social Science and Medicine.*

OECD (Organisation for Economic Co-operation and Development). 2003. *Harmonizing Donor Practices for Effective Aid Delivery.* [www. oecd.org/].

Office of the U.S. Global AIDS Coordinator. 2004. "Update on the President's Emergency Plan for AIDS Relief, September 15, 2004." U.S. Department of State, Washington, D.C.

Ogden, J., S. Esim, and C. Grown. 2004. *Expanding the Care Continuum for HIV/AIDS: Bringing Carers into Focus.* Horizons Report. Washington, D.C.: Population Council and International Center for Research on Women.

Onyango, F. E., S. L. Ramothlwa, and D. Veskov. 2004. "Antiretroviral Treatment in the African Region: The Case of Botswana." *Communicable Diseases Bulletin of the WHO Regional Office for Africa* 2 (3): 1–2.

Open Society Institute. 2001. *Drugs, AIDS, and Harm Reduction: How to Slow the HIV Epidemic in Eastern Europe and the Former Soviet Union.* New York.

Opoku, J., and B. Yamba. 2001. *COPE Malawi Program 2002 Annual Report.* Save the Children U.S. Malawi Field Office.

Opuni, M., S. Bertozzi, J.-A. Izazola, J.-P. Gutierrez, and W. McGreevey. 2002. *Resources for HIV/AIDS Prevention and Care.* Washington, D.C.: Futures Group.

Organization for African Unity. 2001. *Abuja Declaration on HIV/AIDS, Tuberculosis and Other Related Infectious Diseases.* Addis Ababa.

Ostrow, D. E., K. J. Fox, J. S. Chmiel, and others. 2002. "Attitudes towards Highly Active Antiretroviral Therapy Are Associated with Sexual Risk Taking among HIV-Infected and Uninfected Homosexual Men." *AIDS* 16 (5): 775–80.

Over, M., P. Heywood, J. Gold, I. Gupta, S. Hira, and E. Marseille. 2004. "Treatment and Prevention in India: Modeling the Cost and Consequences." Health, Nutrition, and Population Series. World Bank, Washington, D.C.

Palella, F. J., Jr., K. M. Delaney, A. C. Moorman, and others. 1998. "Declining Morbidity and Mortality among Patients with Advanced Human Immunodeficiency Virus Infection. HIV Outpatient Study Investigators." *New England Journal of Medicine* 338 (13): 853–60.

Parker, R. 2002. "The Global HIV/AIDS Pandemic, Structural Inequalities, and the Politics of International Health." *American Journal of Public Health* 92 (3): 343–46.

Perlman, D. C., W. M. el-Sadr, E. T. Nelson, and others. 1997. "Variation of Chest Radiographic Patterns in Pulmonary Tuberculosis by Degree of Human Immunodeficiency Virus-Related Immunosuppression." *Clinical Infectious Diseases* 25 (2): 242–46.

Perronne, C., M. Zahraoui, C. Leport, and others. 1988. "Tuberculosis in Patients Infected with the Human Immunodeficiency Virus. 30 cases." *Presse Medicale* 17 (29): 1479–83.

Pettifor, A., H. V. Rees, A. Steffenson, and others. 2004. "HIV and Sexual Behavior among Young South Africans: A National Survey of 15–24 Year Olds." University of the Witwatersrand, Reproductive Health Research Unit, Johannesburg.

Physicians for Human Rights. 2004. *An Action Plan to Prevent Brain Drain: Building Equitable Health Systems in Africa.* Boston.

Pisani, E. 1999. *Acting Early to Prevent AIDS: The Case of Senegal.* Geneva: UNAIDS.

Plusnews. 2003. "Malawi: Demand for ARVs gives rise to grey market." [Retrieved December 8, 2003, from www.plusnews.org/AIDSreport. asp?ReportID=2412andSelectRegion=Southern_Africa].

Policy Project. 2004. *Coverage of Selected Services for HIV/AIDS Prevention, Care and Support in Low and Middle Income Countries in 2003.* Washington, D.C.: Futures Group.

Population Council. 2001. "Sexually-Transmitted Infections and HIV/ AIDS." Fact sheet. New York.

Poundstone, K. E., S. A. Strathdee, and D. D. Celentano. 2004. "The Social Epidemiology of Human Immunodeficiency Virus/Acquired Immunodeficiency Syndrome." *Epidemiologic Reviews* 26: 22–35.

Prywes, M., D. Coury, G. Fesseha, G. Hounsounou, and A. Kielland. 2004. *Costs of Projects for Orphans and Other Vulnerable Children: Case Studies in Eritrea and Benin.* World Bank, Human Development Network, Washington, D.C.

Quaghebeur, A., L. Mutunga, F. Mwanyumba, K. Mandaliya, C. Verhofstede, and M. Temmerman. 2004. "Low Efficacy of Nevirapine HIVNET012 in Preventing Perinatal HIV-1 Transmission in a Real-Life Situation." *AIDS* 18 (13): 1854–56.

Quattek, K. 2000. *Economic Impact of AIDS in South Africa. A Dark Cloud on the Horizon.* ING Barings South African Research. [www.kas.org.za/Publications/OccasionalPapers/Aids/quattek.pdf].

Quinn, T. C., M. J. Wawer, N. Sewankambo, and others. 2000. "Viral Load and Heterosexual Transmission of Human Immunodeficiency Virus Type 1." Rakai Project Study Group. *New England Journal of Medicine* 342 (13): 921–29.

Radelet, S. 2004. *The Global Fund to Fight AIDS, Tuberculosis and Malaria: Progress, Potential, and Challenges for the Future.* Washington, D.C.: Center for Global Development.

Rana, F. S., M. P. Hawken, C. Mwachari, and others. 2000. "Autopsy Study of HIV-1 Positive and HIV-1-Negative Adult Medical Patients in Nairobi, Kenya." *Journal of Acquired Immune Deficiency Syndromes* 24 (1): 23–29.

Rao Gupta, G. 2000. "Gender, Sexuality, and HIV/AIDS: The What, the Why, and the How." Paper presented at the Speech to the XIII International AIDS Conference, July 9–14, Durban, South Africa.

———. 2002. "Cross-Generational and Transactional Sex: A Public Health Crisis and a Moral Dilemma." Paper presented at the Innovations for Adolescent Girls and HIV/AIDS: Addressing Cross-Generational and Transactional Sexual Relations, Washington, D.C.

Rao Gupta, G., D. Whelan, and K. Allendorf. 2003. "Integrating Gender into HIV/AIDS Programmes." World Health Organization, Geneva.

Raviglione, M. C., D. E. Snider, Jr., and A. Kochi. 1995. "Global Epidemiology of Tuberculosis. Morbidity and Mortality of a Worldwide Epidemic." *JAMA* 273 (3): 220–26.

Reid, G., and G. Costigan. 2002. *Revisiting 'The Hidden Epidemic': A Situation Assessment of Drug Use in Asia in the Context of HIV/AIDS.* Melbourne: The Burnet Institute, Centre for Harm Reduction.

Rowden, R. 2001. *The World Bank and User Fees.* Issues briefing: RESULT Education Fund.

Rwanda. 2003. "Ministerial Instruction Determining the Conditions and Modalities for Health Care Delivery to Persons Living with HIV/AIDS." Kigali.

Salomon J. A., D. R. Hogan, J. Stover, K. A. Stanecki, N. Walker, P. D. Ghys, and B. Schwartländer. 2005. "Integrating HIV Prevention and Treatment: From Slogans to Impact." *PLoS Med* 2(1): e16.

SARA (Support for Analysis and Research in Africa). 2002. "Roles and Functions of National AIDs Councils/Commissions and Ministry of Health AIDS Control Programs." Recommendations to the 36th ECSA Regional Health Ministers' Conference, November 18–22, Entebbe. [Retrieved November 23, 2004, from http://sara.aed.org/sara_hiv_news.htm].

Save the Children. 2004. *Beyond the Targets: Ensuring Children Benefit from Expanding Access to HIV/AIDS Treatment.* London.

Schmid, G. P., A. Buve, P. Mugyenyi, and others. 2004. "Transmission of HIV-1 Infection in Sub-Saharan Africa and Effect of Elimination of Unsafe Injections." *The Lancet* 363 (9407): 482–88.

Schonteich, M. 1999. "AIDS and Age: SA's Crime Time Bomb." *AIDS Analysis Africa* 10 (2): 1–4.

Schwartlander, B., J. Stover, N. Walker, and others. 2001. "Resource Needs for HIV/AIDS." *Science* 292 (5526): 2434–36.

Shah, M. K., N. Osborne, T. Mbilizi, and G. Vilili. 2002. "Impact of HIV/AIDS on Agricultural Productivity and Rural Livelihoods in the Central Region of Malawi." CARE International, Lilongwe, Malawi.

Shelton, J. D., D. T. Halperin, V. Nantulya, M. Potts, H. D. Gayle, and K. K. Holmes. 2004. "Partner Reduction Is Crucial for Balanced "ABC" Approach to HIV Prevention." *British Medical Journal* 328 (7444): 891–93.

Shisana, O., L. Simbayi, and F. Bezuidenhout. 2002. "Nelson Mandela/Human Sciences Research Council Study of HIV/AIDS: South African National HIV Prevalence, Behavioral Risks and Mass Media: Household Survey." Human Science Research Council.

Simms, C., M. Rowson, and S. Peattie. 2001. *The Bitterest Pill of All: The Collapse of Africa's Health Systems.* London: Save the Children UK.

Singh, S., J. E. Darroch, and A. Bankole. 2003a. *A, B and C in Uganda: The Roles of Abstinence, Monogamy and Condom Use in HIV Decline.* New York: Alan Guttmacher Institute.

Singh, S., J. E. Darroch, M. Vlassoff and J. Nadeau. 2003b. *Adding It Up: The Benefits of Investing in Sexual and Reproductive Healthcare.* New York: Alan Guttmacher Institute.

Skinner, D., N. Tsheko, S. Mtero-Munyati, and others. 2004. *Defining Orphaned and Vulnerable Children.* Occasional Paper 2. Human Sciences Research Council.

Smith, E., R. Brugha, and A. Zwi. 2001. *Working with Private Sector Providers for Better Health Care: An Introductory Guide.* London: Options Consultancy Services Limited and London School of Hygiene and Tropical Medicine.

Smith, R. L., K. Yew, K. A. Berkowitz, and C. P. Aranda. 1994. "Factors Affecting the Yield of Acid-Fast Sputum Smears in Patients with HIV and Tuberculosis." *Chest* 106 (3): 684–86.

Soares, M. A., R. M. Brindeiro, and A. Tanuri. 2004. "Primary HIV-1 Drug Resistance in Brazil." *AIDS* 18 (Suppl. 3): S9–S13.

Sonnenberg, P., J. Murray, J. R. Glynn, S. Shearer, B. Kambashi, and P. Godfrey-Faussett. 2001. "HIV-1 and Recurrence, Relapse, and Reinfection of Tuberculosis After Cure: A Cohort Study in South African Mineworkers." *The Lancet* 358 (9294): 1687–93.

Soucat, A., and A. Yazbeck. *Health and the New Poverty Reduction Agenda: Learning from the First Eight PRSPs.* Washington, D.C.: World Bank.

Ssengooba, F., V. O. Cruz, and G. Pariyo. 2004. "Capacity of Ministries of Health and Opportunities to Scale Up Health Interventions in Low Income Countries: A Case Study of Uganda." Working paper for the UN Millennium Project. New York. Available on request.

Stadler, J. 2001. *Looking at LoveLife, the First Year. Preliminary Monitoring and Evaluation Findings of the First Year of LoveLife Activity: September 1999–September 2000.* Chris Hani Baragwanath Hospital, Reproductive Health Unit, Soweto, South Africa.

Steinberg, M., S. Johnson, G. Schierhout, and D. Ndegwa. 2002. *Hitting Home: How Households Cope with the Impact of the HIV/AIDS Epidemic. A Survey of Households Affected by HIV/AIDS in South Africa.* Menlo Park, Calif.: Henry Kaiser Family Foundation.

Stillwagon, E. 2000. "HIV Transmission in Latin America: Comparison with Africa and Policy Implications." *South African Journal of Economics* 68 (5): 985–1011.

Stolte, I. G., and R. A. Coutinho. 2002. "Risk Behavior and Sexually Transmitted Diseases Are on the Rise in Gay Men, but What Is Happening with HIV?" *Current Opinion in Infectious Diseases* 15 (1): 37–41.

Stover, J., N. Fuchs, D. Halperin, A. Gibbons, and D. Gillespie. 2003. "Costs and Benefits of Adding Family Planning to Services to Prevent Mother-to-Child Transmission of HIV PMTCT." Washington, D.C.: U.S. Agency for International Development.

Stover, J., N. Walker, G. P. Garnett, and others. 2002. "Can We Reverse the HIV/AIDS Pandemic with an Expanded Response?" *The Lancet* 360 (9326): 73–77.

Strickland, R. S. 2004. "To Have and to Hold: Women's Property and Inheritance Rights in the Context of HIV/AIDS in Sub-Saharan

Africa." Working Paper. International Center for Research on Women, Washington, D.C.

Tolfrey, D. K. 2003. *Community-Based Care for Separated Children*. Stockholm: Save the Children.

United Nations. 1989. "Convention on the Rights of the Child." New York.

UN General Assembly. 2000. "United Nations Millennium Declaration." [www.un.org/].

———. 2001. "Declaration of Commitment on HIV/AIDS." New York.

UN Millennium Project. 2004. "Millennium Development Goals Need Assessments: Country Case Studies." New York.

———. 2005a. *Investing in Development: A Practical Plan to Achieve the Millennium Development Goals*. New York.

———. 2005b. *Who's Got the Power? Transforming Health Systems for Women and Children*. New York.

———. 2005c. *Halving Hunger: It Can Be Done*. New York.

———. 2005d. *Taking Action: Achieving Gender Equality and Empowering Women*. New York.

UN Statistics Division. 2003. "Millennium Indicators Database." [Retrieved December 16, 2003, from http://millenniumindicators. un.org/unsd/mi/mi_goals.asp].

UNAIDS (Joint United Nations Programme on HIV/AIDS). 2002. "Gender and AIDS Fact Sheet: Patterns of HIV/AIDS." Geneva.

———. 2000. "Key Elements in HIV/AIDS Care and Support. Geneva.

———. 2001a. *HIV Prevention Needs and Successes: A Tale of Three Countries. An Update on HIV Prevention Success in Senegal, Thailand and Uganda*. Geneva.

———. 2001b. *Investing in Our Future: Psychosocial Support for Children Affected by HIV/AIDS: A Case Study in Zimbabwe and the United Republic of Tanzania*. Geneva.

———. 2002a. *Financial Resources for HIV/AIDS Programmes in Low- and Middle-Income Countries over the Next Five Years*. Geneva.

———. 2002b. *Five-year evaluation of UNAIDS, Final report*. Geneva.

———. 2002c. *Monitoring the Declaration of Commitment on AIDS: Guidelines on the Construction Core Indicators*. Geneva.

———. 2002d. *Report on the Global HIV/AIDS Epidemic*. Geneva.

———. 2003a. *The Global Coalition on Women and AIDS*. Geneva.

———. 2003b. *Progress Report on the Global Response to the HIV/AIDS Epidemic*. Geneva.

———. 2004a. *2004 Report on the Global HIV/AIDS Epidemic*. Geneva.

———. 2004b. *Financing the Expanded Response to AIDS*. Geneva.

UNAIDS (Joint United Nations Programme on HIV/AIDS)/WHO (World Health Organization). 2002. "AIDS Epidemic Update December 2002."

———. 2003. "AIDS Epidemic Update December 2003." Geneva.

———. 2004a. "UNAIDS/WHO Policy Statement on HIV Testing." Geneva.

———. 2004b. "AIDS Epidemic Update December 2004." Geneva.

UNAIDS (Joint United Nations Programme on HIV/AIDS)/UNFPA (United Nations Population Fund)/UNIFEM (United Nations Development Fund for Women). 2004. *Women and HIV/AIDS: Confronting the Crisis.* Geneva.

UNAIDS (Joint United Nations Programme on HIV/AIDS)/UNICEF (United Nations Children's Fund)/USAID (U.S. Agency for International Development). 2004. *Children on the Brink 2004: A Joint Report on New Orphan Estimates and a Framework for Action.* New York.

UNAIDS (Joint United Nations Programme on HIV/AIDS)/WHO (World Health Organization)/International HIV/AIDS Alliance. 2003. *Handbook on Access to HIV/AIDS-Related Treatment.* Geneva.

UNDG (United Nations Development Group). 2003. *Indicators for Monitoring the Millennium Development Goals.* New York.

UNDP (United Nations Development Programme). 2004. *Thailand's Response to HIV/AIDS: Progress and Challenges.* Bangkok.

UNFPA (United Nations Population Fund). 2000. *The State of World Population.* New York.

———. 2004. *Glion Call to Action on Family Planning and HIV/AIDS in Women and Children.* New York.

UNFPA (United Nations Population Fund)/UNAIDS (Joint United Nations Programme on HIV/AIDS). 2004. *The New York Call to Commitment: Linking HIV/AIDS and Sexual and Reproductive Health.* New York.

UNICEF (United Nations Children's Fund). 2003. *Africa's Orphaned Generations.* New York.

UNICEF (United Nations Children's Fund) and others. 2004. *The Framework for the Protection, Care and Support of Orphans and Vulnerable Children Living in a World with HIV and AIDS.* New York.

UNICEF (United Nations Children's Fund), UNAIDS (Joint United Nations Programme on HIV/AIDS), and WHO (World Health Organization). 2002. *Young People and HIV/AIDS: Opportunity in Crisis.* New York.

University of Wisconsin. 2002. *Availability of Opioid Analgesics in Africa and the World.* Pain and Policies Study Group. Gaborone, Botswana.

U.S. Department of State. 2004. "The President's Emergency Plan for AIDS Relief Five-Year Strategy." Fact sheet. Washington, D.C.

USAID (U.S. Agency for International Development)/SARA (Support for Analysis and Research in Africa). 2003. *The Health Sector Human Resource Crisis in Africa: An Issues Paper.* Washington, D.C.

USAID (U.S. Agency for International Development)/UNICEF (United Nations Children's Fund)/UNAIDS (Joint United Nations Programme on HIV/AIDS). 2002. *Children on the Brink 2002: A Joint Report on Orphan Estimates and Program Strategies.* Washington, D.C.

van der Staten, A. 2002. *Early Age of Coital Debut and Intergenerational Sex Are Risk Factors for HIV among Zimbabwean Women.* Barcelona.

van Rie, A., R. Warren, M. Richardson, and others. 1999. "Exogenous Reinfection as a Cause of Recurrent Tuberculosis after Curative Treatment." *New England Journal of Medicine* 341 (16): 1174–79.

Van Vliet, C., K. K. Holmes, B. Singer, and D. F. Habbema. 1998. "The Effectiveness of HIV Prevention Strategies under Alternative Scenarios: Evaluation with the STDSIM Model." In M. Ainsworth, L. Fransen, and M. Over, eds., *Confronting AIDS: Evidence from the Developing World.* Brussels: European Commission.

Voluntary HIV-1 Counseling and Testing Efficacy Study Group. "Efficacy of Voluntary HIV-1 Counselling and Testing in Individuals and Couples in Kenya, Tanzania, and Trinidad: A Randomised Trial." 2000. *The Lancet* 356 (9224): 103–12.

Walford, V. 2002. *Health in Poverty Reduction Strategy Papers PRSPs: An Introduction and Early Experience.* London: DFID Health Systems Resource Center.

Walker, D. 2003. "Cost and Cost-Effectiveness of HIV/AIDS Prevention Strategies in Developing Countries: Is There an Evidence Base?" *Health Policy and Planning* 18: 4–7.

Walton, D. A., P. E. Farmer, W. Lambert, F. Leandre, S. P. Koenig, and J. S. Mukherjee. 2004. "Integrated HIV Prevention and Care Strengthens Primary Health Care: Lessons from Rural Haiti." *Journal of Public Health Policy* 25 (2): 137–58.

Wambe, M., S. Gregson, C. A. Nyamukapa, and others. 2004. "HIV Infection and Reproductive Health in Teenage Women Orphaned and Made Vulnerable by AIDS in Eastern Zimbabwe." Paper presented at the XV International AIDS Conference, July 11–16, Bangkok.

Watts, C., L. Kumaranayake, P. Vickerman, and F. Terris-Prestholt. 2002. The Public Health Benefits of Microbicides in Lower-Income Countries: Model Projections. Working Paper for the Microbicide Initiative. New York: Rockefeller Foundation.

Wawer, M. J., N. K. Sewankambo, D. Serwadda, and others. 1999. "Control of Sexually Transmitted Diseases for AIDS Prevention in Uganda: A Randomised Community Trial." Rakai Project Study Group. *The Lancet* 353 (9152): 525–35.

Weiser, S. 2002. "Barriers to ART Adherence in Botswana." Paper presented at the XIV International AIDS Conference, July 7–12, Barcelona, Spain.

Weiss, E., and G. Rao Gupta. 1998. *Bridging the Gap: Addressing Gender and Sexuality in HIV Prevention.* International Center for Research on Women. [www.icrw.org/].

WFP (UN World Food Programme). 2001. *School Feeding Works for Girls' Education.* Rome.

WHO (World Health Organization). 1997. "Integrated Management of Childhood Illness." *Bulletin of the World Health Organization Supplement* 75 (Suppl. 1).

———. 2000. "Female Genital Mutilation." Fact Sheet. Geneva.

———. 2002a. *Coverage of Selected Health Services for HIV/AIDS Prevention and Care in Less Developed Countries in 2001.* Geneva.

———. 2002b. *Strategic Framework to Decrease the Burden of TB/HIV.* Geneva.

———. 2002c. "WHO Takes Major Steps to Make Treatment Accessible." [Retrieved December 15, 2003, from www.who.int/mediacentre/releases/release28/en/].

———. 2003a. "The '3x5' Initiative as a Response to the Development Threat of HIV/AIDS." World Health Organization.

———. 2003b. *Adherence to Long-Term Therapies: Evidence for Action.* Geneva.

———. 2003c. *Guidelines for the Implementation of Collaborative TB and HIV Program Activities.* Geneva.

———. 2003d. *Human Capacity-Building Plan.* [Retrieved December 15, 2003, from www.who.int/3by5/publications/documents/capacity_building/en/].

———. 2003e. *A Public Health Approach to Antiretroviral Treatment: Overcoming Constraints.* [Retrieved December 7, 2003, from www.who.int/hiv/pub/prev_care/en/PublicHealthApproach_E.pdf].

———. 2003f. "Report on the WHO/UNAIDS Workshop on Strategic Information for Anti-Retroviral Therapy Programmes." Paper presented at the WHO/UNAIDS Workshop on Strategic Information for Anti-Retroviral Therapy Programmes, June 30–July 2, Geneva.

———. 2003g. *Scaling up Anitretroviral Therapy: Experience in Uganda.* [Retrieved December 8, 2003, from www.who.int/hiv/pub/prev_care/pub41/en/].

———. 2003h. *Treating 3 Million by 2005: Making It Happen—The WHO Strategy.* Geneva.

———. 2003i. "Workshop on Human Resources and Service Delivery Aspects of Scaling Up ARV Treatment in Resource-Limited Settings

Preliminary Discussion Paper." World Health Organization, Department of Health Services Provision, Geneva.

———. 2003j. *The World Health Report 2003: Shaping the Future.* Geneva.

———. 2003k. *Scaling up Antiretroviral Therapy in Resource-Limited Settings: Treatment Guidelines for a Public Health Approach.* Geneva.

———. 2004a. *3 by 5 Progress Report December 2003 through June 2004.* Geneva.

———. 2004b. *Coverage of Adults in Developing Countries on Antiretroviral Treatment by WHO Region, Situation as of June 2004.* [Retrieved November 22, 2004, from www.who.int/3by5/coverage/en/].

———. 2004c. *Global Tuberculosis Control: Surveillance, Planning, Financing.* Geneva.

———. 2004d. *Interim Policy on Collaborative TB/HIV Activities.* Geneva.

———. 2004e. "Tuberculosis." Fact Sheet 104. Geneva.

———. 2004f. "XV International AIDS Conference—'3 by 5' in the spotlight." *"3 by 5" Newsletter.* July/August.

———. 2004g. *Best practice in HIV/AIDS Prevention and Care for Injecting Drug Abusers: The Triangular Clinic in Kermanshah, Islamic Republic of Iran.* Cairo: WHO Regional Office for the Eastern Mediterranean.

WHO (World Health Organization), Department of Gender and Women's Health. 2003. *Gender and HIV/AIDS.* Geneva.

WHO (World Health Organization)/UNAIDS (Joint United Nations Programme on HIV/AIDS). 1998. "Policy Statement on Preventive Therapy against Tuberculosis in People Living with HIV." Geneva.

———. 2004a. "Combining TB Treatment with HIV Testing and Treatment Could Save Lives of Up to 500,000 HIV-Positive Africans Every Year." Press release. Geneva.

———. 2004b. *Emergency Scale-Up of Antiretroviral Therapy in Resource-Limited Settings: Technical and Operational Recommendations to Achieve 3 by 5.* Geneva.

WHO (World Health Organization)/UNAIDS (Joint United Nations Programme on HIV/AIDS)/UNICEF (United Nations Children s Fund)/ MSF (Médecins Sans Frontières). 2003. *Sources and Prices of Selected Medicines and Diagnostics for People Living with HIV/AIDS.* Geneva.

WHO (World Health Organization), UNAIDS (Joint United Nations Programme on HIV/AIDS), and International Council of Nurses. 2000. *HIV and Workplace and Universal Precautions.* Geneva.

WHO (World Health Organization)/UNODC (United Nations Office Drugs and Crime)/UNAIDS (Joint United Nations Programme on HIV/AIDS). 2004a. "Provision of Sterile Injecting Equipment to Reduce HIV Transmission." Policy brief. Geneva.

———. 2004b. "Reduction of HIV Transmission through Drug-Dependence Treatment." Policy brief. Geneva.

———. 2004c. "Reduction of HIV Transmission through Outreach." Policy brief. Geneva.

———. 2004d. "Substitution Maintenance Therapy in the Management of Opioid Dependence and HIV/AIDS Prevention." Position paper. Geneva.

Williamson, J. Forthcoming. "Finding a Way Forward: Reducing the Impacts of HIV/AIDS on Vulnerable Children and Families." In G. Foster, C. Levine, and J. Williamson, eds., *A Generation at Risk: The Global Impact of HIV/AIDS on Orphans and Vulnerable Children.* Cambridge: Cambridge University Press.

Williamson, J., M. Lorey, and G. Foster. 2001. "Mechanisms for Channeling Resources to Grassroots Groups Protecting and Assisting Orphans and Other Vulnerable Children." Unpublished draft. Available on request.

Witter, S., G. Calder, and T. Ahimbisibwe. 2004. *Taking Better Care? Review of a Decade of Work with Orphans and Vulnerable Children in Rakai, Uganda.* London: Save the Children.

Wolfe, D., and K. Malinowska-Sempruch. 2003. "Illicit Drug Policies and the Global HIV Epidemic: Effects of UN and National Government Approaches" Background Paper. UN Millennium Project Task Force on HIV/AIDS and the Open Society Institute.

World Bank. 1999. *Confronting AIDS: Public Priorities in a Global Epidemic.* Washington, D.C.

Zambia Central Statistical Office and ILO (International Labour Organization). 1999. *Zambia 1999 Child Labor Survey Country Report.* International Programme on the Elimination of Child Labour. Geneva.